Software Engineering:
Planning for Change

Software Engineering: __Planning for Change__

David Alex Lamb

Department of Computing and Information Science
Queen's University
Kingston, Ontario, Canada

Prentice-Hall International, Inc.

Library of Congress Cataloging-in-Publication Data

LAMB, DAVID ALEX, 1954-
   Software engineering.

   Bibliography: p.
   Includes index.
   1. Computer software—Development.   I. Title.
QA76.76.D47L36   1988   005.1   87-14321
ISBN   0-13-823279-2

Editorial/production supervision
and interior design: *Mary Jo Stanley*
Manufacturing buyer: *Gordon Osbourne*

*This edition may be sold only in those countries to which
it is consigned by Prentice-Hall International. It is not to be
re-exported and it is not for sale in the U.S.A., Mexico or Canada.*

 © 1988 by Prentice Hall
A Division of Simon & Schuster
Englewood Cliffs, New Jersey 07632

Printed in the United States of America
10 9 8 7 6 5 4 3 2

ISBN 0-13-823279-2   025

Prentice-Hall International (UK) Limited, *London*
Prentice-Hall of Australia Pty. Limited, *Sydney*
Prentice-Hall Canada Inc., *Toronto*
Prentice-Hall Hispanoamericana, S.A., *Mexico*
Prentice-Hall of India Private Limited, *New Delhi*
Prentice-Hall of Japan, Inc., *Tokyo*
Simon & Schuster Asia Pte. Ltd., *Singapore*
Editora Prentice-Hall do Brasil, Ltda., *Rio de Janeiro*
Prentice-Hall, *Englewood Cliffs, New Jersey*

Contents

16 Scheduling and Budgeting   179

17 Configuration Management   185

18 Quality Assurance   193

List
of Figures

Preface

This book introduces the fundamental ideas of software engineering. As with most terms naming broad categories, "software engineering" describes a field with a solid core of key ideas, along with fuzzy boundaries separating it from other fields. The Introduction (Chapter 1) outlines what I mean by the term; the Retrospective (Chapter 20) reflects further on the key ideas and mentions other topics I have left out.

Most of the book requires only general familiarity with programming. You can understand some of the motivations better if you have written moderate-sized (1,000 to 3,000 line) programs in a higher-level language. Many programming examples presume knowledge of Pascal; some use Ada or C. Chapter 6 requires some familiarity with first-order logic. Part III requires some mathematical sophistication; you should be familiar with discrete mathematics, particularly set theory, functions, and mathematical logic.

Although this textbook should be valuable to anyone who wishes to understand software engineering, I have aimed it primarily at senior-level undergraduates or graduate students who have had little or no experience working with others on a large program. Thus I include some material, such as that of Chapter 15, that should be familiar to those who have already had some form of programming job. Furthermore, I believe the only way to teach software engineering is to have students carry out a moderate-sized group project; this text is geared to a one-semester or one-year group project course.

I could not have written this book without the guidance of David Parnas, who has taught software engineering project courses for many years. I based much of the material of Part II on a collection of papers he put together for his course at the University of Victoria. The bibliography lists other sources I consulted. Other material comes from my experience as a member of the technical staff at Bell-Northern Research, and a staff scientist at Tartan Laboratories. While I was building and maintaining systems as a Research Assistant at Carnegie-Mellon University, I learned much from Ivor Durham, Craig Everhart, Joe Newcomer, Brian Reid, Tom Rodeheffer, and Steve Shafer. Some of the material for Chapter 17 came from discussions with Ed Satterthwaite about system modeling, and with Ellen Borison about her Ph.D. dissertation.

Thanks to (in alphabetical order) Richard Beard, John Nestor, Joe Newcomer, and Sid Penstone for enlightening discussions of what it means to be an engineer. Margaret Lamb proofread two earlier drafts of the book, wrote the program that produced the index, suggested some of the projects in Chapter 4, discovered several embarrassing mistakes in examples, and helped me to improve the trace specifications in Appendix E. Thanks also to the students in CISC422 and CISC838 at Queen's University during 1985 and 1986, who endured my efforts to write this book; Phil Beaudet, Susan Lee, Karen Lefave, and Jim Roche helped by commenting on earlier drafts of the manuscript.

Chapter 1

Introduction

The term "software engineering" means different things to different people. We can look at how the term arose, and what subjects people now cover with the term. We can look at the boundaries of the field, and see how it relates to other disciplines. Instead of defining software engineering, we could ask what it means to be a software engineer. This is not just an exercise in semantics; the view we take determines what a text like this should cover.

In the late 1960s, people began to speak of a "software crisis." For reasons discussed in Section 1.2 and throughout this book, large software systems often

- do not provide the functionality that customers want
- take too long to build
- cost too much money to build
- cost too much time, space, or other resource to run, and
- cannot evolve to meet changing needs

"Software engineering" originally meant the application of principles of existing engineering disciplines to try to overcome these problems. In the intervening years practitioners and researchers have developed many techniques for addressing these problems. These include techniques for

- coping with the complexities of large systems
- managing cooperating groups of programmers, and
- measuring the quality of a software system

These perspectives all suggest reasons why customers and managers of software projects should want the discipline of software engineering: it saves money and produces a better system. Why, on the other hand, should someone want to be a software engineer?

The title of "engineer" carries prestige. In the last few decades the people in a variety of jobs have come to call themselves engineers for just that reason; any day now I expect the person who mows my lawn to demand the title of landscape engineer. Along with prestige often comes higher pay and greater independence.

But calling someone an engineer doesn't make him one. In most jurisdictions you may call yourself an engineer whenever you like, but you may not call yourself a professional engineer (sometimes registered professional engineer) without belonging to a particular professional organization or holding a particular license. To obtain professional standing, you must prove to a particular agency that you have mastered a particular technical discipline, and that you understand (and agree to abide by) a code of ethics designed to protect the public and the profession. Typically you gain such a qualification by a combination of studying in an accredited undergraduate program, working under a registered professional, and passing examinations set by the accrediting agency. Legally, you may not claim to offer professional services without accreditation.

What society gets from this arrangement is assurance of standards of service. Many professions are self-governing; the legislature lets the profession set standards and enforce conformance to those standards. Being able to show that one has met the standards of the profession is usually defense against claims of liability, should something go wrong with the service a professional provides.

We have not yet reached the stage of having a professional field of software engineering. Social and economic pressures are mounting, however. Mass marketing of software and computer systems makes software more important to our society each year. Many products come with an explicit disclaimer that the software vendor is not responsible for any losses to the customer as a result of using the software; the time will come when customers will demand better safeguards, either through the marketplace or through the courts.

1.1 Relation to Other Fields

What distinguishes a software engineer from a programmer or from a computer scientist? Most people do not perceive any clear distinction among these terms, particularly between a programmer and a software engineer. If we want to create useful distinctions, we can understand the differences by analogies with other fields. Generally, engineers apply principles to solve problems, while scientists study problems to accumulate knowledge. The distinction is fuzzy, especially since many people who get computer science degrees really wind up doing software engineering work. While solving a new problem, engineers may study the parts of the problem no one has considered before in the same way that scientists do. While studying some problem, scientists may apply known techniques to solve subsidiary problems in the same way that engineers do. Furthermore, there is a serious overlap in "engineering research," an area sometimes looked down on by engineers as impractical and by scientists as mundane.

Nonengineers sometimes think of engineering as cut-and-dried. That is simply not true. There is an art to applying engineering principles; among many possible solutions, one can often find one that is more elegant than the others. The search for elegant solutions is akin to the mathematician's search for elegant proofs. If one simply wants to prove a particular theorem, one looks for any proof that works — but finding an elegant proof, simpler, more general, more beautiful than the others, is one joy of mathematics.

Some scientists assert that the corresponding branch of engineering is a subset of their own field. This is not true, either. An engineer might use a subset of the ideas of the corresponding science, but augments this with problem-solving techniques different from those a scientist uses. Furthermore, engineers sometimes take the lead over scientists, solving practical problems long before anyone comes up with an appropriate theoretical approach.

I prefer to draw distinctions by analogy with electrical engineering. Each area has hobbyists who build small systems on their own. In my view, a programmer should correspond to a technician, a software engineer to an electrical engineer, and a computer scientist to a physicist. The body of knowledge understood by each group overlaps that of the others; an enthusiastic hobbyist or technician might even know more than a weak engineer or scientist. However, typically a technician has a good grounding in current practice, but needs retraining every five to ten years. An engineer learns fundamental principles, as well as the current embodiment of those principles, and expects to keep up with the field on his or her own.

We can also draw useful analogies with building construction. Many people can build small structures on their own. Larger structures require work from technicians in a variety of fields, such as electricians and plumbers. A civil engineer designs large structures such as large buildings, bridges, and highways, and may oversee their construction. A physicist may investigate new materials, the effects of stress on buildings, and so on. Construction also introduces the architect, who combines some of the expertise of an engineer with that of an artist.

In each of these cases the distinction between those at the "programmer" level and those at the "engineer" level is that the latter take a longer view of their work. One expects an engineer to recognize the essentials of a problem and similarities to other problems, and to learn new techniques. A programmer typically gets a more well-defined task.

1.2 Why the Difficulty?

A well-trained programmer sometimes has trouble seeing what could be so different about what a software engineer does. Perhaps an analogy with civil engineering might help: the techniques for building a doll house do not scale up for building a skyscraper.

Writing large programs is hard for several reasons.

1. Customer needs are hard to discover and record. Customers often may not be aware of what a system could do for them and may have trouble being precise about what they need. Sometimes they may not be aware of what they need.

2. Even if customers initially have a clear idea of what a system should do for them, their needs will change with time. They will develop new needs as they become used to what the system does. Moreover, they may well change their minds during system development about what the system should do.

3. The larger the system, the more potential interactions among components. If there are N components, there are $N(N-1)/2$ possible interactions between pairs of components to check for validity. Thus it may be four times as hard to build a program twice as big.

4. No matter how good a single programmer is, there is a limit to how much he or she can produce in a given amount of time. Thus to build large programs acceptably quickly, several people must cooperate. Communication complexity among people can grow in the same way that component interactions grow in the software; three people may only be twice as productive as one.

Typical industrial productivity figures show the effect of communication among people. On a project with few interactions with other people, the average programmer can produce about 5,000 lines of code per year. With moderate interaction this drops to 2,000–3,000, while with complex interactions it becomes 600–800 lines.

1.3 Using This Book

Previous sections discussed and described software engineering. Although I do not think it is productive to define the term, I do need to specify the view I will take of it in this text. This book introduces the body of knowledge and standards of practice you must understand and apply to build large, long-lived, high-quality programs.

The main method for coping with complexity and ensuring quality is planning. Chapter 2 outlines how to approach software development systematically, and Part II describes the development process in detail. The best way to ensure you have mastered this material is to build a small system in a group with several other people. Most of the chapters end with a "Project" section describing what to do next in carrying out your project.

Part III covers an important part of software planning: how to define precisely what a piece of software must do. Part IV discusses several advanced topics, including some management issues. Finally, the appendices give examples of the documents discussed in Part II.

Software engineers must be able to communicate with each other, with subordinates, with superiors, and with customers. Lack of communication skills is the strongest complaint many industrial managers have about entry-level technical employees. Chapter 3 discusses technical writing. Each of the project activities of Part II results in a document recording the decisions made during that activity.

Some sections of this book require that you understand basic discrete mathematics and mathematical logic. Figure 1–1 shows the notation I use. Programming examples use several different languages, including Ada, Pascal, and C. The language of any particular example should be either obvious or unimportant.

$N \pm M$	N plus or minus M, that is, a number in the range from N-M to N+M.
$[N..M]$	The set of numbers from N to M, inclusive.
$\forall x \in S\ P(x)$	For all elements x in set S, predicate P is true.
$\exists x \in S \mid P(x)$	There exists some element x in set S such that predicate P is true of that element.
$\{\ x \mid P(x)\ \}$	The set of all items x for which predicate P is true.
$f: A \times B \rightarrow C$	f is a function with parameters from sets A and B that returns a result from set C.
$A = \mathbb{P}(B)$	A is the powerset of B, that is, the set of all subsets of B.
$A \Rightarrow B$	A implies B.
$A \Leftrightarrow B$	A implies B and B implies A.
$S \equiv T$	Trace S is equivalent to trace T. This notation is used only in Chapter 13.
$A \wedge B$	A and B.
$A \vee B$	A or B.
$\neg A$	Not A.
λ	The empty string of characters.
ϵ	The empty trace. This notation is used only in Chapter 13 and Appendix E.
'expression'	In the specification of a procedure with side effects, the value of the expression before any of those side effects take place.

Figure 1–1: Notation Used in This Book

Further Reading

Brooks' *The Mythical Man-Month* (1975) is an excellent set of essays on aspects of software engineering by the man who was in charge of the development of OS/360, one of the largest software projects of all time [Brooks 1975]. Parnas (1986) gives a convincing description of why software is unreliable and discusses the limits of software engineering methods.

Glass (1977) tells many anecdotes of large computer projects that failed. He has also written several books about computer people, and what building software is like in many industrial shops [Glass 1978, Glass 1979, Glass 1981].

Chapter 2

The Lifetime
of a
Software System

The period of development and use of a software system contains several distinct activities. Ideally, these activities form distinct stages. Each activity begins and ends with a *milestone*, a clearly defined event. For many phases the defining milestone is delivery of a particular document.

In several activities the development organization needs to interact with a customer. With many large systems, a specific customer asks the development organization to build a product. For others, a developer builds a system for a general market without a specific customer; a marketing division may take the place of a customer. I have phrased most of this book as though the project has a single customer; Section 9.4 briefly considers other situations.

2.1 Typical Activities

Figure 2–1 outlines the typical activities in the life of a software system. Treating each activity as a distinct stage, where each activity finishes before the next begins, gives the *waterfall model* for the major stages in the life of a system, so called because its clean breaks from one stage to the next resemble a series of waterfalls on a river. Some phases end with the delivery of documents; others end with reviews of one kind or another; others end when appropriately authorized people *sign off* a phase as complete.

Stage	Documents
Opportunity Study	Opportunity Study Report
Problem Formulation	
Requirements Analysis	Requirements Specification, User Reference Manual, System Test Plan
Project Design	Methodology, Project Plan, Configuration Management Plan, Schedule, Budget, Training Plan, Security Plan
Product Realization	
Design	
Preliminary Design	Module Decomposition, Module Dependencies, Integration Test Plan
Detailed Design	Module Specifications, Module Implementation Plans, Unit Test Plans
Implementation	
Coding	Code Walkthrough Reports
Unit Testing	
Testing	
Integration	
Alpha Test	
Delivery	
Beta Test	
Acceptance Test	
Installation	
Evolution	Release Notices, Problem Reports
Retirement	

Figure 2–1: Stages in a Software Project

2.1.1 Opportunity Study

A project begins when an organization recognizes there is a problem to solve. A customer may approach a developer with a request; a marketing division may do a customer survey; the development organization may come up with a product idea itself. At this point there is typically only a broad statement of what the problem is. The first stage is an *opportunity study* (sometimes called a *feasibility study*), where the development organization defines the problem more clearly, develops criteria for choosing solutions, looks at possible solutions, and recommends what course of action to take. This stage might have to contain parts of each of the stages that follow — enough for the organization to decide what it must do and what resources it needs. Such a study is often informal; it goes into just enough detail to determine whether solutions are feasible, a rough time frame for developing a solution, and approximate costs and benefits of solving the problem. The milestone ending this stage is delivery of the opportunity study document.

The next milestone is the development organization's management deciding whether to proceed further and what solution to adopt. The decision might be to abandon further work; the opportunity study might discover perfectly adequate existing solutions to the problem, or might show that the costs of developing a new system outweigh the benefits. For example, an organization might shelve plans for new product of marginal profitability because it prefers to spend its resources on more profitable products.

2.1.2   Problem Formulation

After the decision to proceed, a development organization must do two things. First, in *requirements analysis* it must determine precisely what the system must do. Second, in *project planning* it must plan for developing the system.

Requirements analysis (Chapter 4) defines the requirements the product must meet, and develops criteria for choosing solutions. The milestone that ends this stage is the delivery of a *requirements specification*, which precisely defines what the product must do.

Project planning defines how the organization will develop the product. During this stage, managers write several planning-related documents. Other chapters discuss several of them: the *configuration management plan* (Chapter 17), the *budget* (Section 16.2), and the *schedule* (Section 16.1). A *methodology* document describes methods to use in the various stages of the project. A company may have a standard methodology document, but the field changes rapidly enough that new large projects may need to define their own. A *training plan* discusses how to bring in new people to staff the project and train them in the appropriate methods.

Some projects may require a *security plan*, especially if it needs to protect information belonging to a customer. A software contract might require the developer to protect the customer's business plans or trade secrets. The plan may impose severe restrictions on who can see certain documents; employees may need security classifications, or may need to be bonded. They may need to sign non-disclosure agreements. There may also be physical security requirements, such as safes to hold customer information, locked rooms, restricted areas, and employee badges.

Sometimes an organization does project planning in stages. To protect itself against making large commitments too early, it may decide after the opportunity study to proceed only as far as preliminary design. At this point it has more information on which to base budgeting and scheduling decisions; it may decide to abandon the project if costs turn out higher than expected from the opportunity study.

2.1.3 Product Realization

Building a product goes through three major steps: design, implementation, and testing. Design is a technical planning activity that decides the overall structure of the system (preliminary design, Chapter 5) and how individual components will do their job (detailed design, Chapter 6). Implementation builds the components and ensures that they work in isolation from the rest of the system (Chapter 7). Testing (Chapter 8) puts components together (integration) and ensures that the overall system meets its requirements (alpha test).

2.1.4 Delivery and Beyond

After building a product, the developer must deliver it to the customer (Chapter 9). This involves transporting the relevant pieces to the customer, providing user documentation, and perhaps providing extensive training. With a product designed for a wide market, several customers may agree to do preliminary testing of the system (beta test) before the product is ready for the marketplace. Finally, customers may have criteria that the system must satisfy before they agree to purchase it (acceptance testing).

Once a product is in the customer's hands, the customer may find problems or request new features. Thus the development organization needs to upgrade the software it delivers (evolution: maintenance and enhancement, Chapter 10). After many years of use, a system may become obsolete; users and maintenance organizations may then need to plan for retiring the software, possibly by shifting to a newly designed system.

2.2 Project Documents

Most of the activities of Figure 2–1 end with the delivery of some document. Many technical people hate writing documents, and avoid doing so whenever possible. "Document" suggests maintenance documentation or user documentation, which people write only after finishing the software. This guarantees that those writing the documents do not need them, and thus have no interest in doing them. In contrast, all the documents mentioned in Figure 2–1 and throughout this book are working papers. Those working on the project use them to record their decisions, and refer to them later in the project. If you will need to use a document you are writing, you will have much more interest in completing it.

The following anecdote from a software development firm illustrates this point. Each project had its own directory containing all the files for that project. The company had a disk tidying tool for deleting unneeded files in each directory. The person responsible for the project would create an input file for the tool, describing what files were source files, what files were outputs from tools that took the source files as inputs (derived files), and what files of either kind were needed by people outside the project (exported files). The tool typically deleted all the derived files except the exported files. People never had any direct interest in creating or maintaining these files, since the consequence of not using the tool was simply that too many files stayed around. Eventually someone came up with the idea of documenting the purpose of each file in the directory via comments in the input to the tidying tool. Suddenly more people were willing to create the input files for projects they maintained. The comments helped keep track of what each file meant, which project maintainers had previously had to spend much time figuring out once they had been away from the project for a few months.

Project documents are also useful because each delivery is a valuable milestone. It may be hard to tell when you have finished designing your system, but it is easy to tell that the customer has accepted your requirements document. Section 16.1 discusses scheduling and the need for milestones.

2.3   Overlap and Cycles

Few systems follow precisely the lifetime model of Figure 2–1. Some practitioners totally reject the model and propose others. I mention this issue in Section 20.3, after the rest of the book presents the waterfall model of Figure 2–1 in more detail.

Even within the waterfall model, several steps proceed in parallel. For example, testing activities occur throughout the life of the project. The requirements specifications completely determine what the system must do, so you can begin planning system tests immediately after finishing the requirements document. Planning how to integrate modules into the system can begin immediately after delivery of the module dependency document. Unit testing of some modules can proceed in parallel with integration of already tested modules.

Activities in one stage may show flaws in earlier ones. For example, the preliminary design stage subjects the requirements to intensive study, and may show flaws not seen in the reviews. Module implementation may discover the need for a few additional modules back in the preliminary design. System testing may uncover surprising behavior that requires changes as far back as preliminary design (or even requirements analysis). Thus carrying out one stage may force changes to an earlier stage; a maintainer must propagate the effects of changes forward through the intervening stages. Chapter 17 discusses controlling changes of this sort. A major purpose of the module decomposition stage discussed in Chapter 5 is to design the system to limit the damage this type of change causes.

Further complicating the issue is the need to develop a large system as a series of subsets, to guarantee that some portion of the full system is available early. Early stages of one subset may proceed in parallel with late stages of a prior one.

Despite these problems, you are better off to treat your software as though you built it the way Figure 2–1 outlines. The steps follow each other rationally; you do not begin a task until you know what you should accomplish during that task. Starting out with undefined requirements, or changing your mind halfway through, is not rational — though it is often unavoidable. Documenting your project rationally, even though you did not build it that way, is perfectly sensible and honest. A mathematician makes many false starts and follows many blind alleys in developing a proof, but presents the final result in a rational, well-structured manner.

Developing a system rationally requires that you plan each step as well as you can, knowing that you will probably change things later. You therefore structure all your documents and your plans to make change easier. As you discover problems, you go back and fix the original documents, and propagate forward changes to later documents.

2.4 Personnel

The different stages require different talents from the people who do them. Requirements analysis needs the ability to communicate with users, to understand their needs, and to view the system as a whole, in the context of the user's environment. Preliminary design also requires a general view of the system, but usually does not involve interacting with users. It requires considerable understanding of how to organize a large system and break it up into manageable units. Detailed design requires familiarity with algorithm design, data structures, programming methods, and mathematical specification techniques. Testing requires craftiness — and perhaps paranoia — to design test cases for detecting possible defects.

Most commercial organizations have a hierarchy of jobs. System architects do requirements; system analysts do preliminary design; senior programmers do detailed design; junior programmers do coding and testing. This leads people to think that the senior jobs are more fun, or take more creativity, or better talents, or are more important to the success of the system.

All the steps require creativity, although in different areas. Requirements analysis crucially impacts the system's understandability and usability. Preliminary design is crucial for adapting to changes. Detailed design can be crucial for performance — though typically only a few modules are critical. Thus none of these activities is inherently more or less creative than the others, and all are important.

Further Reading

Bell and Thayer (1976) attribute the term "waterfall model" to W. W. Royce. During 1985 and 1986, several issues of *Software Engineering Notes*, the newsletter of the ACM Special Interest Group on Software Engineering, discussed different life-cycle models and attacked the waterfall model. Hester et al. (1981) discuss using documentation as a medium for developing and expressing software designs. Parnas and Clements (1986) go further, and propose that we ought to document software developments as though we followed waterfall-like models, even though we often don't really build them that way.

Technical
Writing

Many technical people are poor communicators; this is the primary complaint about entry-level programmers from many employers. However, software engineering requires much communication. A software engineer needs to communicate via

- Technical writing, aimed at professional colleagues (planning documents, design documents, maintenance documents).
- Expository writing, aimed at less technical audiences (user documentation, executive summaries of planning documents).
- Presentations, aimed at a variety of audiences.

A full discussion of technical communication (and, in particular, making presentations) is beyond the scope of this book. This chapter discusses a few issues about writing in a software project; throughout it "you" means the person writing a particular document.

3.1 Planning a Document

When planning a document, you need to consider the topic, the audience, and the purpose of the document.

Audiences vary in how much common background they share with you. Writing intended for yourself (such as a personal log) may contain your own peculiar notation and terminology. Writing intended for a close group (such as minutes of a meeting) may contain jargon peculiar to the group, and may presume certain background information, but avoids your idiosyncrasies. Writing for a large but homogeneous group (such as design documents or user documentation for a special- ized system) may need to explain more background information, but may at least presume that the group shares goals and interests. Writing for a large, heterogene- ous group (such as user documentation for general-purpose software) is the most difficult, since it needs to appeal to a wide variety of backgrounds and interests. If you are a programmer just beginning to do technical writing, the large first step is to write a document while keeping the needs and interests of your intended audience in mind; far too much technical writing considers only the point of view of the developers.

The purpose of most technical writing is to inform or instruct someone, or to explain something. Some technical writing explains an idea or a technique but goes on to exhort the readers to do something, such as adopting a particular course of action. Individual technical documents have more specific purposes. A document may be a reference, a decision tool, a contract, or a goal.

- A reference describes something. You must organize it so that readers may easily answer questions. Readers typically need to access pieces of the docu- ment without having to read the whole thing; they need cross-references and indices to help them find things quickly. User's guides are reference documents, as are program listings.

- A decision tool is the basis for some decision. Its audience is the person who makes the decision; you must organize it so alternatives are clear. The opportunity study is a decision tool, as is a report on the results of an acceptance test. A budget is primarily a decision tool, since it guides alloca- tion of resources.

- A contract is an agreement between two parties. Only the agreement of the two parties can change it. A requirements specification is often a contract; a legal contract for building a software system might include the require- ments as a supplement defining what the developer must deliver.

- A goal describes a result to achieve. A schedule is a goal; it defines when the organization must meet certain milestones. Design documents are also goals.

A document may serve several of these purposes, but one of them is primary. For example, a requirements specification is primarily a contract between a customer and a developer, though it is a reference for the preliminary design. Each of the documents mentioned in Figure 2–1 on page 8 is the output of some process and the input to certain others. For example, the requirements specification comes from the requirements analysis process and guides preliminary design.

3.2 Organizing a Document

Technical writers develop a document by a process that strongly resembles stepwise refinement (see Section 5.2.2).

1. Start with an abstract statement of the content of the document.
2. Break it into components.
3. Arrange the components in a sensible order.
4. Refine the components until you reach the level of individual paragraphs.

In stepwise refinement, one stops when the components correspond to simple constructs in the implementation language. In writing, one stops when a component is a single, coherent topic; a paragraph should have a topic, and all sentences should be relevant to that topic.

The order mentioned in step 3 depends on the purpose of the document. In a reference manual, for example, one organizes for ease of access, which typically means alphabetical order. In a tutorial manual, one organizes for ease of understanding, which typically means increasing order of complexity.

Once you organize the document and write the major content, you must provide connecting material that guides a reader through the document smoothly. The opening sentences of a subsection should link it with the previous subsection, or the section that contains it. Each major section, such as a chapter, should have an introduction that clarifies the relation of the major section to the rest of the document.

The document as a whole needs an introduction. For technical writing, the introduction should state the purpose of the document, in a single sentence or paragraph, early on the first page. It should state the intended audience: who should read the document. It should state what knowledge a reader must have before reading the document, perhaps pointing to other documents to read first, or to a glossary summarizing technical terms. Finally, it should give an overview of the document — without simply restating the table of contents.

Your document may need appendices to present information that doesn't fit in the main body of the document. Glossaries, lists of exception messages, and summaries of material scattered through the document make good appendices.

Any software document evolves. Your document should have a change log at the front; this lets someone quickly tell how this week's document differs from last week's. This is a particular instance of *configuration control*, which Chapter 17 discusses in more detail. To make it easier to change parts of a document, you should number pages within chapters, for example, 3-1, 3-2, and so forth for the pages of Chapter 3.

3.3   Proofreading

Once you think you've finished your document, you've done about half the work. The other half is proofreading, the extra effort that makes the document easier for your reader to follow without stumbling.

Technical writing suffers from flab. Passive verbs are a primary culprit; users' manuals abound with vague descriptions where unspecified actors perform vague actions. Most readers of users' guides are users; there is no excuse for saying "when the user does thus-and-so, the system responds such-and-such" when you can say "Do thus-and-so, and the system responds such-and-such." Direct prose is shorter, crisper, and easier to read. Much use of the passive voice is a holdover from early training in science lab classes, where you learned to efface yourself to give a greater impression of objectivity.

To proofread, go through your document circling all forms of the verb "to be" (is, are, was, were, has been, will be, might be), all sentences that you had to read twice to understand them, and all nominalizations. Marked sentences are candidates for change. A nominalization is a noun derived from a verb or an adjective; you can often make your prose crisper by rephrasing to use the verb or adjective, instead. Nominalizations often occur near passive verbs. Nominalizations typically end in -ion (documentation), -ment (establishment), -ness (carelessness), -y (discovery), and -is (analysis). Not all nominalizations are bad, but you do need to examine them. For example, you might turn

The establishment of judgment criteria is an important prerequisite to document analysis.

into

Before you analyze a document, establish criteria for judging it.

Style guides can provide you with lists of trite phrases you should eliminate or replace with better ones. "Note that X" is precisely equivalent to "X"; "at the moment when X" is equivalent to "when X." "Through the use of" means "by" or "with"; "due to the fact that" means "because." You can usually eliminate "appropriate," "very," and "in nature" without changing the meaning of a sentence. The auxiliary verb "may" is often ambiguous; replace it with with "might" or "can," depending on which sense you mean.

Use parallel style in lists. Make sure the main verbs of all the elements have the same voice, all active or all passive. Use the same construction for each element, all sentences or all sentence fragments. Repetition of the same word or phrase slows the reader down, but repetition of style aids the reader.

Avoid using technical terminology (or jargon) for nontechnical audiences. If you must use a technical term, even in a document intended for a technical audience, make sure you define it in a glossary.

It would be wonderful if we could do all these things on the first draft of a document. Unfortunately, with a first draft our minds are on organization and content. Trying to get the details of expression right the first time bogs you down and makes the initial writing too much of a chore.

Further Reading

Lustman (1985) describes a somewhat different collection of purposes a document may serve. He uses the term *baseline document* instead of *goal document*, but this use of the word "baseline" conflicts with the use in configuration management (Chapter 17). The latter usage corresponds more closely with common meanings of *baseline*, such as in surveying.

Browning (1984) shows technical writers how to write software documentation; if you want more detail than I give above, you will find it readable and useful. Any good style guide contains helpful instructions on how to write; Strunk and White (1972) wrote the classic reference.

Exercises

3–1   Find the user's manual for some program or system you have used frequently. Take a complete section of two to three pages from this manual. Apply the proofreading techniques mentioned in this chapter to rewrite it.

3–2   Find some program you have written in the last two years. Write a guide to using the program; you might want to read Section 4.4 first. Ideally the program should be small enough that you could write the guide in five to ten pages. Exchange guides with a co-worker or fellow student. Proofread and edit the other person's guide. Exchange edited guides, and compare your original with the one your co-worker edited. Can you see an improvement?

Chapter 4

Requirements Analysis and Specification

During requirements analysis, system developers interact with users to produce a detailed specification of what the system must do. This is the most important stage for ensuring the system does what the customer wants; if the developers neglect it, the system will fail to satisfy its users. Other terms for this stage include *problem analysis* and *requirements definition*.

The industry has several titles for the person who analyzes requirements. A common title in electronic data processing is *systems analyst*. Systems analysts often also do preliminary design, as discussed in Chapter 5. Recently people have begun to use the term *system architect* for the analyst who interacts with users to determine what the system should do for them, especially if such a person supervises several other analysts. Throughout this chapter, "you" means a person acting as a system architect.

Defining requirements is extremely important. Too many projects have started implementing something without determining whether they were building what the customer wanted. A technical person often thinks of a requirements document as a reference; it might be more important to think of it as a contract.

4.1 What Is a Requirement?

A requirement is a specification of what a system must do — the things about the system users can observe. Some people call this the *architecture* of the system.

Good requirements have three primary characteristics.

1. They are precise, with no room for misinterpretation by users or implementors.

2. They specify just *what* the system must do, not *how* to do it. They avoid specifying implementation details.

3. They show *conceptual integrity*, building on a simple set of facilities that interact well with each other.

From the user's point of view, the last property is the most important. Conceptual integrity is the key to making a system users can understand. If it has too many features, or if each facility has its own peculiarities, the user has an enormous task to understand the system. The key to conceptual integrity is to have one architect, or at most a few architects. More than about three people can hardly agree when to meet, let alone what to do.

While defining system requirements, an architect may also define *constraints* and *goals* for the system. Some writers use the term *nonfunctional requirements*, which means the same as constraints. In the past, some writers have lumped these terms with requirements, but it is important to keep them distinct.

A constraint is a limitation on possible implementations of the system. For example, a customer may require a particular implementation language, a particular algorithm for one part of the system, or a particular format for a temporary data file not visible to users. It is often in your best interest to negotiate away constraints, since they limit implementation freedom. However, since the customers are paying for the product, they normally get to impose constraints if they really want them.

A goal is a statement that guides tradeoffs among design decisions. For example, a customer may care a lot about maintainability of the software, but not care much about efficiency. A goal may become a requirement if you find a way to quantify it. For example, "high throughput" is a goal, but "at least 47 transactions per second" is a requirement.

Since requirements are specifications of the observable behavior of the system, an "implementation detail" is any property of the system that should not be visible to users. Some people use "requirement" to mean any property of the system they care about, and "implementation detail" to mean any property they don't care about. This terminology leads to confusion. Using our terminology (see Figure 4–1), an implementation detail the customer cares about is a constraint. A requirement the customer doesn't care about is simply a requirement more likely to change. If you list several alternatives, the customer may choose one, or at least reject a few. If the customer still doesn't care what choice you make, you may discover after delivering the system that users are unhappy with your choice; you should try during system design to minimize the consequences of changing this particular requirement.

In the last decade or so there has been considerable interest in paying careful attention to the *user interface* of software systems. By this people usually mean the

| Customer Doesn't Care | Customer Cares | |
	Measurable	Unmeasurable
Observable to Users — Requirement likely to change	Requirement	Goal
Not Observable to Users — Implementation detail	Constraint	Goal

Figure 4–1: Matrix of Requirements Terminology

portion of the system that presents information to the user and accepts input from the user. Since requirements define all observable behavior of a system, the requirements *are* the user interface.

4.2 Problem Analysis

Analyzing the problem requires interacting with users, understanding what the customer's business currently does, and how the system would fit in to the business. It requires communication skills, especially the ability to see things from the customer's point of view.

4.2.1 Dealing with Customers

You might deal with one of three sorts of customer representatives during requirements analysis. An *initiator* is the person who sees a need that the system should satisfy, and understands the place of the system in the wider context of the organization. An initiator is likely a manager, perhaps even part of upper-level management. An *end user* is a person who will interact with the system. This category consists of *operators*, those who interact directly with the system (operators, data entry clerks, technicians, and so on), and *end-line users*, typically lower-level managers who read the system's reports.

You may deal occasionally with an initiator, but input from end-line users and operators can be crucial to the system's success. Commonly, an initiator might delegate a middle-level manager to interact with you; if this person is an end-line user and is willing to bring in operators, your system is more likely to meet the customer's real needs.

Many customers feel that they lack the technical expertise to deal with a development organization. A customer might hire a consultant to serve as a buffer between the customer's organization and the development organization. If the consultant really understands both technical issues and the customer's needs, this can work out well. Unfortunately such a combination of talents is rare and such people are in high demand. You might have to deal with a less-qualified consultant, who may understand neither you nor your customer.

When dealing with customer representatives, expect the session to proceed according to their general goals, not yours. Few customers think of their needs in a framework such as the one Section 4.3.1 outlines. You and the customer probably will pick one particular topic, go through several iterations of analyzing that part of the problem, then move on to a new topic. Customers will often discuss details of how their organization currently handles some aspect of their problem, many of which are implementation details rather than requirements. You will need to take notes of your sessions, extract requirements from the details, and organize them into a logical framework later. You might find that some of the customers' desires are vague; you must make them more precise. Rather than decide yourself, you should help the customers decide, by pointing out alternatives.

4.2.2 Why Build This System?

People who build software for a living tend to view the creation of programs as an end in itself. When interacting with customers, you need to break out of this way of looking at things and discover why customers want the software you are designing for them. People build software for one of three reasons:

1. To automate an existing manual system, or improve an existing automatic system. Payroll programs, program generators, and some Artificial Intelligence systems fall in this category. This is the only type of system whose value you can measure in economic terms: the reduction of cost in using the new system.

2. To manage large amounts of information. The value of such a system is the value of the information it manages.

3. To do some task that one could never do without computers. Much real-time software falls into this category; for example, modern high-performance aircraft are not dynamically stable, and cannot fly without the rapid adjustments the software makes. It is hard to judge the value of such software, or to decide what it should do.

The three categories overlap somewhat. Many systems that automate manual tasks also enable customers to do new things they could never have done before; such systems are a combination of types 1 and 3. I have heard some people say that automated systems are never cheaper or simpler than the manual ones, and that their only value is in the new facilities or more flexible behavior.

4.2.3 Requirements Considerations

You need to understand the context into which the system will fit. Any system has an environment, separated from the system by a boundary. The boundary can be physical, but it can also be conceptual; rather than trying to solve all the customer's problems, you may need to leave some problems outside the system. The environment may contain other systems with which the new one must interact. For example, the new system may need to accept data from existing sources. An embedded system may need to drive peripheral devices designed by other manufacturers. Furthermore, the environment contains people who will interact directly with the system; you need to understand their background and viewpoint.

During requirements analysis you must also decide what level of quality to provide in the system. Higher quality often means higher cost, so the best level to choose is not necessarily the highest level you can achieve. The customer's hardware may have limits on disk space and computer memory. The customer may require a new system within a limited time, or may have a limited budget. The following paragraphs describe several software qualities you should consider.

Human factors depend on the skills, strengths, and weaknesses of the users. The customer may already have employees who will interact with the new system; you must adapt the system to their needs. Typical human factors to consider include

- *ease of use*. The system should be neither too challenging nor too boring to use.

- *information availability*. When is information available to a user? This is part of ease of use. If a user needs two pieces of information at the same time to do a task, the system should provide the information together. Psychologists have shown that people keep 7 ± 2 "chunks" of information in short-term memory at one time. People cannot remember details for long periods, and will not like a system that makes them do so.

- *ease of learning*. This is not necessarily the same as ease of use. Some systems are hard to learn because they have many capabilities. Once an expert user absorbs them all, he or she can accomplish tasks much more quickly than with a simple system.

- *response time*. How fast must the system respond to typical input? If it responds too slowly, users will be under stress from annoyance; too quickly, and they may get rattled.

- *response to user errors*. What typical mistakes will users make, and how can the system respond to them or avoid them? For example, if two similar indicators confuse a user, you can place them further apart or make them more distinct.

Reliability is a collection of qualities having to do with how much you can trust the system to do what you want. *Correctness* is the primary quality of this sort: a correct system meets its requirements. Unfortunately, "correct" software may still not be particularly reliable. There is little evidence that we are close to being able to define our requirements well enough, or to show that our systems conform to their requirements. Thus you need to consider other aspects of reliability, such as the following.

- *Availability* is the fraction of the time that the system is working. A system might fail frequently but still be highly available, if it recovers from failures in a time much smaller than the mean time between failures.
- *Robustness* is the ability of the system to recover from undesired events without human intervention.
- *Repairability* is the ease with which a human can get the system working again when it fails. For a robust system, repairability may be less important.
- *Safety* is the ability of the system to avoid catastrophic behavior. Thus a temperature control process may be completely incorrect, but it might be safe if it doesn't start fires.
- *Security* is the safety of data. A system is secure if unauthorized personnel cannot get at protected information.
- *Accuracy* measures how close to correct answers the system needs to come. Users may not need exact answers, as long as the answers are within certain limits from the correct ones.

Maintainability is a collection of qualities connected with how easy it is for the system to change.

- *Portability* is the ease of moving the system to new hardware or a new operating system.
- *Adaptability* is the ease of changing the program to correspond with more-or-less predictable changes in the operating environment. For example, a payroll program needs to adapt to yearly changes in the tax laws.

Some of these qualities have well-understood measures; this means you can define a requirement for them. For example, you can say that the system must respond within 2 seconds to 90 percent of all requests. For others, there are no measures, but you can sometimes tell that one approach is better than another. For these, you can state goals so that the developers can judge various possible solutions against each other. For example, you can say that you want it to be easy to port the system to a particular collection of machines you have in mind as possible future acquisitions.

4.2.4 Sketching Initial Requirements

To design a system, you must model some aspects of the user's situation. The user's environment has

- *objects*, such as data, physical devices (sensors, indicators, displays), and agents. An agent might be a person such as an operator, or might be a device such as a monitor that causes an interrupt when certain conditions occur.

- *conditions* or *predicates* (functions that are either true or false at any given moment) and *events* (changes in the values of predicates). For example, the position of some switch is a condition; a change in its position is an event.

- *relationships* among objects and events, especially *actions* that agents take on other objects, or events that agents cause.

As you begin to firm up some notions of the user's requirements, a good way to check your ideas and discover further requirements is to develop *scenarios* of how typical users might interact with your system. A scenario is a sketch that describes what the user wants to do and a hypothetical set of actions they might make and responses they might get from your system. For example, for a database program on borrowing library books, you might hypothesize

A patron brings several books to be checked out. The librarian enters the patron's identification, then records the identification of each of the books.

This leads you to realize you might want to enter several books for the same patron, and would lead you to avoid designing commands where the librarian must reenter the patron's identification for each book. You might reuse some of these scenarios later to review the requirements (Section 18.3.1).

Once you begin to have an idea of what objects the system must model, and what actions agents might perform on those objects, you can begin to be more precise about your requirements by sketching what states each object might be in, and what actions cause transitions among those states. This gives you a finite state

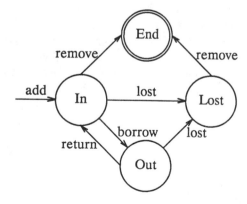

Figure 4–2: State Diagram for Library Books

machine, which gives a visual representation that you may be able to reason about more easily than you can with a textual representation.

For example, Exercise 4–3 describes a small library system. The description says that you can add a book, remove a book, mark it as lost, borrow it, and return it. This gives us states In, Out, and Lost, meaning, respectively, that someone can borrow a book, that someone has borrowed it, and that the book is missing. A "borrow" operation takes us from In to Out; a "return" goes the other way. Figure 4–2 shows the finite state machine you get by drawing the states and adding all the transitions mentioned in the description. It also has state End to represent a removed book; by the usual conventions for finite state machines, concentric circles mean a final state. This diagram says that you can only return a book if it is Out, you can only borrow a book that is In, and you cannot remove a book that is Out.

From the diagram, you can see that the only thing you can do with a Lost book is to remove it; there might seem to be little point to having such a state. You can deduce it would be useful to be able to report that someone has found a Lost book. Also, although the description mentioned books could be overdue, there is no state for this. You could handle this in two ways. You could add a new Late state, or you could split Out into two substates, Out and Late. The former is appropriate if operations going from Late to other states might be different from operations going from Out to those states; it may lead to more complex diagrams. The latter is appropriate if these operations are nearly identical; you can draw a separate diagram showing that Out has two substates. In either case you need some operation that goes from Out to Late. This shows that the original description failed to mention an important operation, the one that marks a book as overdue. There might be a special command to mark books as overdue, or there might be an automatic operation at the start of the library's business day.

State diagrams may not be a good way to represent objects that contain collections of other objects. Suppose you need to represent a collection, and do things differently depending on how many elements there are in the collection. For example, a class grows as students enroll in it; beyond a certain size, you may need to allocate a bigger classroom. Such a collection has at least as many states as elements. If not all size transitions matter, you can group several real states into super-states, as Figure 4–3 shows. This state diagram is nondeterministic; it says that certain adds or drops might force you to change state, while others do not. You would certainly need an auxiliary description that says when to take each of the nondeterministic transitions.

4.3 The Requirements Specification Document

A requirements document has several objectives.

1. It specifies the *external behavior* of the system. It must not specify implementation details, just behavior a user could observe.

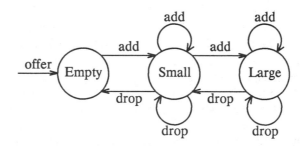

Figure 4–3: Nondeterministic State Diagram for Class

2. It specifies constraints on the implementation. For example, if the system must use certain interfaces, the requirements document should specify them.

3. It records forethought about the lifetime of the system: things that are likely to change, and fundamental assumptions about what will not change.

4. It characterizes acceptable responses to undesired events.

In addition, the document must be easy to change — since the requirements will almost certainly evolve during the life of the system. This means that you must organize the document according to the principle of *separation of concerns*. For example, a section that discusses a particular hardware device must not say anything about how the system should use the device.

The requirements document is a contract between the customer and the development organization about what the latter must deliver. The experienced programmers who will build the system will use it as a reference. For both these reasons,

1. It must be as precise as possible. It should use equations wherever appropriate. If it provides similar information about different aspects of the system, it should use a standard format for both places.

2. It must help readers answer questions quickly.

When organizing the requirements specification, you should consider typical questions readers will ask, then group related questions together in their own section or chapter. You must state the questions before trying to answer them. This helps ensure you answer all the right questions, and helps you organize the chapters according to classes of similar questions.

4.3.1 Document Organization

Figure 4–4 shows a table of contents for a typical requirements document. Not every document would have all these chapters. For example, Chapter 8 on Quantitative Requirements may not be relevant for a data processing program.

The *Environment Characteristics* chapter describes properties of the environment with which the system will interact. For any system, this includes what skills the people who interact with it must have. For some systems (those where the part under construction is mostly software) it will include what hardware the system will run on and what devices the system interacts with. For other systems, you have not yet decided what portions of the system you will implement in hardware and what portions you will implement in software; this chapter discusses only those hardware

---

1. Introduction
2. Environment Characteristics
   2.1 Hardware
   2.2 Peripherals
   2.3 People
3. Fixed Interfaces
   3.1 Devices
   3.2 Operating System
   3.3 Databases
4. Input and Output
5. Modes
6. Software Functions
7. Constraints and Goals
8. Quantitative Requirements
   8.1 Timing
   8.2 Precision
   8.3 *Other Sections as Necessary*
9. Responses to Undesired Events
10. Life-Cycle Considerations
    10.1 Subsets
    10.2 Fundamental Assumptions
    10.3 Potential Changes
11. Glossary
12. Sources
13. Index

Figure 4–4: Requirements Document Table of Contents

---

decisions your customers have already made. Hardware description should include minimum, average, and maximum requirements for physical main memory, address space (on a virtual memory system), and secondary storage. Identify any peripheral devices the system will interact with, but leave details of how the system uses the devices for later chapters.

The *Fixed Interfaces* chapter applies to *embedded systems*, which must deal with interfaces beyond the control of the software developers; they are a special type of constraint on the implementation. The requirements specification must document these interfaces, since they are part of the contract between the developer and the customer. Sometimes the requirements document can point to an existing specification, such as a particular device in a manufacturer's catalog. For many embedded systems, the hardware is as new as the application; the requirements document might contain the only written description. If the system must interact with existing databases, this chapter would describe the databases. As with the Environment Characteristics section, you document only those interfaces that are not under your own control.

The *Input and Output* chapter for an interactive system describes the format of commands and the format of reports. It does not discuss what the system does in response to a command, or how it produces a report; these belong in the *Software Functions* chapter (Section 4.3.3, which also discusses the *Modes* chapter). Section 4.3.2 discusses input and output specifications in more detail.

The *Quantitative Requirements* chapter lists requirements that involve a measure of some quantity, especially measurable system qualities. For example, some outputs from the Software Functions chapter might involve calculations with real numbers. The *Accuracy* section of the Quantitative Requirements chapter would specify how close an approximation to the correct answer to accept.

The *Life-Cycle Considerations* chapter focuses on how the system may change over time, since this greatly affects its design. The section on *Subsets* defines fallback positions if the development organization cannot deliver the full system in the scheduled time. It also allows for phased development; developers might deliver a small subset early to allow the customer to become familiar with the system. The sections on *Changes* and *Fundamental Assumptions* tackle changes from two directions. The first lists expected changes, based on change logs from similar systems, input from the customer, information from manufacturers of equipment with which the system must interact, and so on. The second explicitly records assumptions you would like to make about things that will not change. Both guide the module decomposition, discussed in Chapter 5, to protect the system against changes.

Undesired events are situations where the system cannot behave normally. Figure 4–5 gives a checklist of typical undesired events. For example, running out of memory for new data might be a permanent resource failure; in a system with garbage collection, it might be a temporary resource failure requiring the system to delay responding for a short time while it frees up memory. A checksum failure is

---

1. Resource Failure
   a. Temporary
      for example, out of dynamic storage in a system with garbage collection
   b. Permanent
      for example, insufficient storage immediately after garbage collection
2. Incorrect input data, detected by
   a. examining the input
      for example, syntax errors on commands
   b. comparing input with internal data
      for example, when some key from a command is not in a database
   c. user realizing his mistake
      for example, noticing that the last command is wrong
   d. user seeing incorrect output
      for example, when the user asks for the wrong report
3. Incorrect internal data, detected by
   a. comparing with redundant internal data
      for example, inconsistent forward and backward links
   b. comparing internal data with input
      for example, address cache gets out of date in a distributed system,
      detected by seeing requests for addresses not in cache
   c. user seeing incorrect output
      for example, memory parity error in a buffer gives gibberish on screen

Figure 4–5: Checklist for Undesired Events

---

bad input data detected by examining the input. Attempting to retrieve a key not found in a database is bad input data detected by comparison with internal data.

4.3.2 Input and Output

The input and output chapter describes any user-visible data types, the syntax of commands, and the format of output reports. For example, one command may have the form

    SET variable value

where "variable" is one of a half-dozen names, and "value" is one of "ON" or "OFF." This chapter would describe the command format, and define types "variable" and "value." These types may have an explicit representation in the implementation, but you should not discuss implementation data structures here. These are merely types visible to a user.

A realtime system must deal with interfaces to hardware devices; part of the requirements document must specify these fixed interfaces. Typically a system interacts with hardware by reading and writing device control and status registers.

Typically, manufacturer's hardware descriptions discuss their devices using specific bit patterns. The requirements document should step back from this and describe data types and symbolic values, and define mappings from the types to the bit patterns. For example, a controller for an antenna might rotate the device in fractions of a full revolution (based, perhaps, on mechanical gear ratios). The requirements document should discuss angles in standard units, and give mappings to the specific bit-patterns for a given device.

Several different devices might provide similar data in different formats, defined in slightly different ways. For example, several sensors might report angles. The description of each sensor should use a standard form for defining terms. For example, to define an angle-measuring sensor you might say "measured from line X to line Y in the Z direction." Thus you might measure an aircraft directional antenna angle from the axis of the aircraft to a particular axis of the antenna in the clockwise direction.

Sensors, dials, and switches might report their position as one of a few bit patterns. The Input and Output section should define symbolic values for those bit patterns, and how to check the values for validity. For example, a four-position switch might report its position as one of the bit patterns 1000, 0100, 0010, or 0001, with several bits set (or none set) if the switch is between positions. The rest of the document can speak about $Position_1$, $\cdots$, $Position_4$, and a validity condition IsValid.

Effects on external hardware define output interfaces. For example, setting a particular bit in a device register might invert the state of some physical switch.

The Input and Output section of a requirements document must not specify how the system uses the device; that belongs in the section on software functions. Specifying how to read or write the device registers does not violate this principle; there is usually only one way to do so, and it is a fundamental part of the device interface.

4.3.3   Describing Software Functions

The software functions chapter can be the hardest to write. This chapter says what the software does, but must not say how an implementation does things. Most of us need some image of a possible implementation to understand what is happening, and so find it difficult to do the abstraction involved in writing a good requirements document.

Within this chapter, you should use an organization that groups together related requirements. For example, the requirements related to a particular output device might belong together. Psychological studies have shown that presenting clusters of related requirements to a designer leads to better designs. You should remember the principle of separation of concerns within this chapter (and all the other chapters): each section should deal with one topic. This approach makes your requirements document easier to maintain when your customer adds or changes requirements.

There should typically be one software function for each output the system must produce. Since requirements must not specify implementation details, you should derive values of outputs from inputs whenever possible. Some devices serve multiple purposes. For example, your system might use a numeric display for several different numeric outputs. Here the software function description would pretend each output went to a separate "virtual output," then give rules for choosing the virtual output to display on the device.

4.3.3.1 Modes

When you cannot describe outputs as functions of inputs, you may be able to use *modes*. The *state* of a system is a list of the values held in all the memory of the system. States are an extremely implementation-dependentidea, so they should not appear in a requirements specification. Modes, on the other hand, are sets of states with two important characteristics.

1. Externally visible behavior of the system differs from one mode to the next.

2. The system moves from one mode to another when certain externally visible events happen.

If you are careful, you can talk about these sets of states without ever having to prescribe any particular implementation. The classic example of a system with modes is a text editor. Many such editors have a *command mode*, where it interprets sequences of characters as instructions, and an *input mode*, where it inserts sequences of characters into the file. Figure 4–6 shows the classic text editor mode diagram. The system starts up in command mode when a user enters it via the Edit command, but in insert mode when a user enters it via the Create command. The Append, Insert, and Replace commands take it from command to input mode; the Escape and Interrupt commands (perhaps the ASCII escape character and control-C characters, respectively) take it in the other direction.

4.3.3.2 Concurrent Systems

A nonconcurrent system simply responds to user commands. You can write the requirements for such a system using module specification techniques such as those discussed in Chapter 6 or Part III. Each command corresponds to an interface procedure (see Section 5.3). You can specify the effects of commands with side effects by showing what results they have on commands that produce visible results. For example, the effect of text editor commands might be to change a display screen, or change the contents of a file.

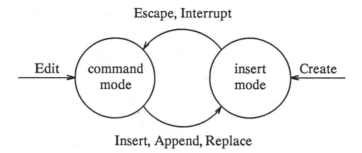

Figure 4–6: Text Editor Modes

With a concurrent or realtime system, multiple things may go on in parallel. For such systems, it can be useful to define software functions as responses to *events*.

All software functions are either *demand* functions or *periodic* functions. For a demand function, the description says what event invokes it. For a periodic function, the description says what events start and stop invoking the function, and how often it repeats. The repetition may vary between minimum and maximum rates.

A *condition* is a boolean expression. For the purposes of requirements specification, a condition will typically mention the values of certain inputs or certain modes. A condition is either true or false. An *event* is the change of state of a condition, from true to false or vice versa. If X is a condition then @T(X) and @F(X) are the events of X becoming true and X becoming false, respectively. An event might also take into account some other condition. Thus

@T(X) when Y

defines the event of condition X becoming true at a time when condition Y is also true — but the state of condition Y need not change.

4.4   User Documentation

A requirements document can be hard for your customer to follow. You may wish to consider writing a user reference manual as an alternative. A reference manual should have some of the same goals as a requirements document: it gives a complete description of the observable behavior of the system. You organize it for ease of access, just like a requirements document. For example, a chapter on commands would list them in alphabetical order. Furthermore, you can use it as a design document in almost the same way that you would use a requirements document.

When you use a reference manual this way, system architects write the first few drafts, then have technical writers turn it into a real manual. When someone wishes to change the observable behavior of the system because of an implementation difficulty, the reference manual can provide a valuable sanity check. If the change results in a manual section that customers have trouble understanding, you should reject it. Brian Reid used this approach while writing the manual for the Scribe[1] document formatter [Reid and Walker 1979]. When he came to a part of the system he had trouble describing, he found a related behavior that was easier to explain, and changed the system to match the documentation. Several nontechnical users have remarked that the resulting system is the easiest-to-learn computer program they have ever seen.

Do not confuse a reference manual with a tutorial or an introductory user's manual. A tutorial manual shows novices how to use the system, and may explain basic ideas such as how to log in and what a file is. It typically covers the minimal subset of commands that lets someone get started using the system. An introductory manual assumes some prior knowledge. It introduces most of the system's facilities in a logical order from basic to complex. It need not describe all the facilities. Both manuals contain examples; the tutorial has many examples (you should take the precaution of executing your examples to make sure they work; far too many don't). If a reference manual has examples, they must be the sort that one can examine in isolation; examples that build on previous examples are good in introductory or tutorial manuals, but deadly for reference manuals. One rarely expects technical people to even draft tutorial and introductory manuals, though they should check that the technical writers who do write them have correctly interpreted the reference manual.

Both should describe a conceptual model of how the system works; users will build up such models anyway, and have an easier time if you start them off right. A reference manual lacks such a model because one expects experienced users to have already built their own model. A requirements document lacks a model because giving one amounts to prescribing a candidate implementation.

A reference manual lacks descriptions of fixed interfaces and lifetime considerations, and probably omits constraints and goals, too. If you use a reference manual to define requirements, you must supply an additional document for these topics.

A reference manual mixes things kept separate in a requirements document. A typical reference manual describes command formats at the same time as it

---

[1]Scribe is a trademark of Unilogic, Inc.

describes the function of the command. A requirements document separates these concerns better, and is thus easier to maintain.

Another form of user documentation is the *functional description*, a brief document that describes the general capabilities of the system. Its main use is to introduce users to what the system can do for them. It avoids detail and may omit some system features. It can be useful to draft the functional description early in requirements analysis. Avoiding detail makes it easier for the developer and the customer to agree. Under no circumstances should you mistake a functional description for a set of requirements; at best it is a basis for beginning to pin down requirements.

4.5 Designing Subsets

When you start designing a large system, it is difficult to judge how long it will take you to build it. However, typically you must commit to delivering a product long before you have enough detailed information to be confident of your estimates. When you get far enough into the project to discover that you can't meet the original schedule, you must usually either extend the schedule or deliver less of the system than you originally promised. If on the original delivery date the customers have a working subset system in hand, they are much more confident that you can keep your promise of delivering a full system a few weeks or months later.

It is much easier to deliver a subset if you have planned for subsets in advance. During preliminary design (Chapter 5), you may be able to design entire modules that you can eliminate in early subsets. You can thus concentrate your efforts on completing the modules that are part of the earliest subsets, and defer those that aren't. Of course, you must take the design of the omitted modules far enough to be sure you will not have to make many changes to early modules when you finally include the later ones.

A key step in deciding on reasonable subsets is to list the commands and facilities the full system must provide, and determine dependencies among them. You can then pick subsets by starting with facilities that depend on nothing else, and gradually build larger subsets by adding facilities that depend on things in earlier subsets. When you have a choice of several things to add, you may bring in other factors, such as what facilities are most important to your customers, or how much code you expect you might need to write for each new facility.

Figure 4–7 shows a sample facilities diagram for the genealogy system of Appendix A. Each ellipse represents a command (such as "Add") or other facility (such as "Input," meaning the ability to read in the database file). Each box represents some data structure, condition, or capability required by some facilities and produced by others. For example, the Change and Delete commands require existing internal data as input, and produce internal data as output. The Who and What commands require internal data and produce output reports. Multiple arrows into an ellipse mean that the facility requires all the inputs. For example, the input

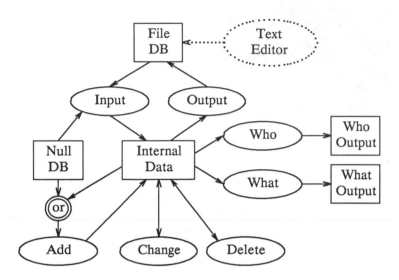

Figure 4–7: Dependencies Among Features of Genealogy Program

capability depends on the existence of an input file ("File DB") and on facilities for constructing an internal database ("Null DB"). Multiple arrows into a box mean that any of the facilities can produce the structure. For example, internal data can come from input or from the Add, Change, or Delete commands.

Ignoring the dotted ellipse labeled "Text Editor" for the moment, it appears that the only way to create internal data from scratch is via the Add command. Thus the smallest subset might consist of modules to manipulate the internal database, the Add command, and one facility for producing output (the Who command, the What command, or "Output" to the file). Later subsets might add the other output capabilities in some order. Once the program can produce an output file, you might add the Input capability. The last subsets might add the Change and Delete commands, since editing facilities like this might be low priority.

Sometimes a system contains loops such as the one from File DB via Input to Internal DB and back via Output. Such loops can be troublesome, because it may not be clear how to get started at any point in the loop. You might be able to start such a loop by creating one structure by some means outside the normal mechanisms of the system you are designing. For example, if the file database is a simple text file, you might create an initial version of it with a text editor. Thus an alternative subsetting path for Figure 4–7 is to create a file database with the text editor, and build a small system containing just input and one output-producing facility. This is the path taken in the sample subset plan of Appendix B.

4.6 Validating Requirements

Once you have written a requirements document, you must validate it to ensure that it meets the customer's needs, and that it is complete and consistent. Some organizations use special requirements languages, which have corresponding analyzers that check for consistency and completeness. By the mid 1980s, this work had not come to the point where any of the current languages had widespread acceptance. The main means of validation was through reviews, as described in Section 18.3.1.

Further Reading

Most of what I have seen about requirements specification is fuzzy. In contrast, Henninger (1980) gives a crisp set of guidelines for how to write a requirements document for realtime systems. The basic ideas of Section 4.5 came from Bastani (1985). Cameron (1986) gives an overview of Jackson System Development. This method uses the idea of modeling sequences of actions on objects as part of requirements definition, and goes on to show how to translate such models into implementations. It uses a slightly different technique from the state diagrams of Section 4.2.4.

Exercises

4–1   Pick one project description from Problems 4–2 to 4–6. Draw a facilities dependency diagram (see Figure 4–7) for it, and list two distinct series of subsets you could derive from the diagram.

Project Exercises

Pick one of the following system sketches and write the requirements document for it. Alternatively, write a user's manual and a separate document summarizing lifecycle considerations (assumptions, changes, and subsets). Appendices A and B give examples of the latter two documents.

4–2   Write a program to keep track of a personal calendar. You need not provide commands with the syntax I use in the examples; you may impose a more restricted format on the way the user must express requests. Your program should provide the following facilities.

     a. Keep track of appointments, such as "meet Smith at 4:30 in Goodwin 553 on Wednesday for an hour about plumbing."

b. Specify repeating appointments, such as "Group meeting every Thursday at 1:30 PM," "Issue paychecks every second Friday," or "Pay rent by 3rd of every month."

c. Cancel any appointment.

d. Cancel a repeating appointment for some particular date without canceling other instances of the appointment.

e. List all appointments for today, the next few days, this week, the next month, and so on.

f. Give advance warning of some appointments; for example, warn two working days before some big meeting that the meeting is about to happen.

g. Take several people's calendars and find a suitable time for a joint meeting. Each person can say that certain times are off limits even if they don't have any specific appointments; for example, a night-owl might want no meetings before 3 PM.

4-3 Write a program to help run a small library. Your program should provide the following facilities.

a. Add a new library patron.

b. Remove a patron. Ensure that the patron has no books borrowed and no unpaid fines.

c. Print a list of all patrons (in some sensible order).

d. Print a list of all patrons with outstanding fines.

e. Add a new book to the catalog.

f. Remove a book from the catalog. Ensure no one has it borrowed.

g. Record a book as lost.

h. Record that a particular patron is borrowing a particular book.

i. Record that someone has returned a particular book. Report any fines owing.

j. Record that a patron has paid some money toward his or her outstanding fines.

k. Print all overdue books, and who has them.

l. Set today's date.

Do not attempt to provide card catalog services for allowing patrons to search for books. You may assume each book has a unique *acquisition number*, and you may use these numbers to refer to books borrowed and returned. For each book, record acquisition number, title, author, and any other information you need to process the above commands.

4–4 . Many hobby and game shops stock *mini-games*: board games that come in small packages (typically 3-by-6 inches), have simple rules, and cost $10.00 or less. Pick one such game and implement a program that permits people to play it. Do not try to have the program play one side of the game; that is likely to be a much harder task. Many of these games should have boards small enough to represent on a typical terminal screen. Beware that the complexity of different games varies by at least a factor of ten; the simplest are simple to implement, the most complex much too difficult. The number of rules and subrules can serve as a rough guide to complexity. Avoid games that have any rules with checks or conditions requiring real-world knowledge or human judgment.

4–5   Write a program to help manage a household budget. Your program should provide the following facilities.

     a.   Add and delete budget categories.

     b.   Handle paychecks. Associate with each category an amount of money to automatically deposit in the category with each paycheck. The difference between the sum of the deposits and the paycheck should go into a special "savings" budget category.

     c.   Keep a log of expenditures, and what category to charge for each expenditure.

     d.   Transfer money between categories.

     e.   Figure the balance in each category.

     f.   Compare the money in all budget categories with the total assets of the household (that is, the contents of all bank accounts and cash held by members of the household). Charge any difference to a "petty cash" budget category. Ignore other assets such as stocks, bonds, and equity in a mortgage.

4–6   Obtain the manual for a modern programmable scientific pocket calculator. Develop a program to simulate the operation of such a calculator. This might be a large program; pay careful attention to subsets.

Chapter 5

Preliminary
Design

Once you know the requirements a system must satisfy, you must begin to design the system. This normally happens in two stages. A preliminary design breaks the system into smaller units, and a detailed design refines the specification of the individual units. This chapter concentrates on the preliminary design; Chapters 6 and 7 discuss detailed design. The two major tasks of preliminary design are decomposing the system into *modules* and determining relations between modules.

Different writers use different definitions of what a module is. The common ground of these definitions is that a module is a collection of related programming-language entities (procedures, types, and so on); Section 7.1 discusses modules in a variety of implementation languages. The purpose of preliminary design is to break the system into modules that are small and coherent enough to understand individually, having relations with other units restricted enough that the system is easy to understand.

I take the view that the right way to break a system into modules is via information hiding, described in Section 5.3. Earlier sections lead up to explaining why this is the right approach.

5.1 System Structure

As outlined in Section 1.2, the number of interactions among the N components of a system can grow as $N(N-1)/2$. Thus you cannot understand a multi-thousand-line program all at once, but must break it into smaller components of a few hundred lines. Furthermore, you must restrict the relations among modules to cut down on the interactions between them.

Mathematically, a relation on modules is a function

R: module × module → boolean

where we say that A is related to B if and only if R(A,B) is true. A relation is not necessarily symmetric; the relations for modules are anti-symmetric (that is, if R(A,B) then ¬R(B,A)). A relation defines a hierarchy if it partitions modules into levels.

Level$_0$:   { a | ¬∃b ∈ Module | R(a,b) }
Level$_i$:   { a | ∃b ∈ Level$_{i-1}$ | R(a,b) and
              ∀c ∈ Module, R(a,c) ⇒ c ∈ Level$_k$, k∈ [0..i−1] }

Level$_0$ is all those modules not related to any others. Level$_i$ is all those modules related to at least one element from level$_{i-1}$ and to no elements at level$_k$ for k≥i. Module A is "higher level" than module B if and only if

$$A ∈ level_j ∧ B ∈ level_k ∧ j > k$$

By these definitions, if there is a circular chain of modules

$$a_i, i∈ [1..n] | (∀j∈ [1..n−1]R(a_j, a_{j+1})) ∧ R(a_n, a_1)$$

the relation does not define a hierarchy.

Many possible relations may define hierarchies. A hierarchy may be useful if

- For each x, the set of elements {b | R(x,b)} to which it relates is small.

- There is more than one level.

- There aren't too many levels.

The next few sections discuss some useful relations. The module decomposition document (Section 5.4) defines the *is composed of* relation (Section 5.1.1); the module dependency document (Section 5.5) defines the *uses* relation.

5.1.1 The *Is Composed Of* Relation

The *is composed of* relation and its inverse, the *is part of* relation, always give a hierarchy. Higher-level modules are groups or classes of lower-level modules that share some common purpose. Lower-level modules have more and more specific purposes the further down they are in the hierarchy. In many systems, higher-level modules may not have any physical existence; the leaves of the hierarchy might be the only ones that correspond to programming language constructs.

A simple example is a Peripherals module containing submodules for record-oriented devices and character-oriented devices. Within each of these submodules, leaf modules might define interfaces to particular devices. The module decomposition document described in Section 5.4 records the *is composed of* relation; that section gives another example.

5.1.2 The *Uses* Relation

X *uses* Y if and only if the system must contain a correct version of Y in order for X to be correct. Usually, only the modules at the leaves of the *is composed of* relation participate in the *uses* relation. *Levels of abstraction* is what some people call the hierarchy that *uses* defines; each level might define an *abstract machine*. The term "higher-level modules," usually means modules in higher-numbered levels of the *uses* hierarchy. If X uses Y, then X is a *client* of Y. A module and its client must each be able to ignore the internal workings of the other. A subset system might contain lower levels without higher levels, but higher levels require the lower ones. The module dependency document (see Section 5.5) documents this relation.

At first glance this seems to be a strange way of describing a relation. A first approximation is to consider that X uses Y if procedures in X call procedures in Y. This certainly fits the definition, since in order for X to call Y, the system must contain Y. Furthermore, if Y is incorrect, callers of X will see unexpected behavior. However, *uses* is not the same as *calls*.

1. Procedure calls are not the only way for modules to interact. In a concurrent system, one module may send messages to another. The *uses* relation should be general enough to handle whatever communication mechanisms new languages might introduce.

2. Not all calls are uses. For example, a numerical integration procedure may have a parameter for the function to integrate. This does not constitute a use of the module that contained the definition of the function; parameterization decouples the two modules. The integration procedure does require that some module call it and provide it with a function parameter, but does not depend on any particular module.

3. Even a direct call may not be a use. For example, a lower-level procedure may call a higher-level procedure of a particular name under certain circumstances, such as for reporting exceptions. Part of the purpose of the procedure is to make this call; the lower-level procedure is correct even if the higher-level procedure fails in some way.

On the surface this relation seems to forbid recursion and pairs of modules that send messages to each other. However,

1. Recursion within a module does not affect this relation.

2. If two modules call each other, both must be present in the running system. You cannot test either without some version of the other. For the purposes of the *uses* relation, you can group them together into one large pseudo-module, and the rest of the modules may well form a hierarchy.

There are several techniques for decoupling modules to avoid recursion.

1. If a procedure in module X passes another procedure of module X to a procedure of module Y, then calling the procedure parameter is not a use of X by Y.

2. If a process in module X sends a message to a port that the operating sys-
    tem connects to some other port that some process in module Y reads, nei-
    ther module uses the other. The module that sets up the connection
    between the ports does use both X and Y.

3. If some procedures in module X call procedures in module Y, which in turn
    call other procedures of module X, then you may be able to eliminate the
    circularity by splitting X into X_1 and X_2, then have X_1 use Y and have Y
    use X_2. In parallel, you would need to record that X *is composed of* X_1 and
    X_2, but no module uses X directly.

It is sometimes useful to refine the *uses* relation into two subrelations. Module X
uses $_V$ module Y (V for visible) if the interface of module X uses objects (usually
types) that module Y exports. Module X uses $_H$ module Y (H for hidden) if it uses
module Y but does not uses $_V$ it. The Ada programming language represents these
two relations via **with** clauses in a package specification (uses $_V$), and **with** clauses in
the corresponding package body (uses $_H$).

The distinction is important because the existence of Y is visible to callers of X
if X uses $_V$ Y, and invisible otherwise. Obviously, if W uses X and X uses $_V$ Y, then
W uses Y. This can arise if W and X use Y only because they pass through data
from yet higher levels; Figure 5–1(a) shows an example where V passes data to W,
which passes it to X, which passes it to Y, which finally uses it. Someone probably
told the designers of this system to avoid using global variables, and pass everything
via parameters. Sometimes it can be simpler to add a procedure to Y for V to pass
it the data directly, so that neither W nor X needs to do so. This results in Figure
5–1(b).

5.2   Desiderata for Modular Systems

There are four major reasons for dividing a system up into modules.

1. *Comprehensibility.* A system with no substructure is hard to understand.
    Years of experience shows that modules with high cohesion and low cou-
    pling result in easier-to-understand systems. High cohesion means that the
    functions and objects within a module are closely related to each other.
    Low coupling means that each module interacts with few others, and
    through a narrow interface.

2. *Division of labor.* To get a large task done in reasonable time, you must
    parcel out pieces of it to different people. Each module should be small
    enough that you could hand it to one person to implement within a
    moderate time period, such as a few days or weeks. If you believe imple-
    menting a module would take more than a couple of months, try to break it
    into smaller pieces.

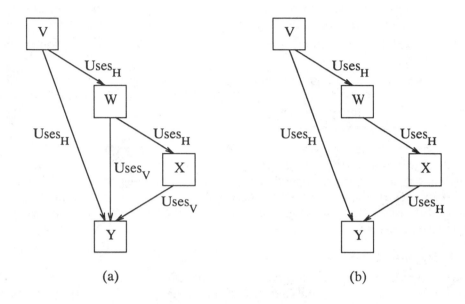

Figure 5–1: Multiple-Level *Uses* Relationship

3. *Response to change.* Change is a fundamental characteristic of software systems. Users ask for new features or changes to old ones; the system moves to new hardware or a new operating system; testing discovers bugs; performance measurements show bottlenecks. The presence of a new system in a customer's organization changes the environment, which changes the customer's needs. Folklore is full of anecdotes of the incredible cost of changing existing software.

4. *Reuse.* When you build a new system, it saves much effort if you can reuse modules of a previous one.

Most current methods of breaking a system into modules address the first two needs; this book contends that the method of *information hiding* outlined below is the best way of addressing the others.

5.2.1 Program Families

An important source of change for a large system is creation of distinct versions. Distinct versions arise because of

- implementing the system on different hardware or different operating systems

- tailoring the system to different environments, with different performance requirements or resource consumption requirements

- evolution of the system to respond to new user requirements or to improve quality

The different versions of a program make up a *family* of related programs. The different members of the family presumably show a strong family resemblance; any design method should try to take advantage of these similarities to reduce the cost of producing multiple versions.

In developing any program, you make a series of design decisions. Different members of a family result from making certain design decisions differently. Typically later design decisions depend on earlier ones; changing an early design decision can require redoing the entire design process over from the point of the changed decision. Thus a design technique should minimize the cost of changing design decisions.

5.2.2 Stepwise Refinement

The classic way to design a program is *stepwise refinement*, sometimes called *top-down design*. The fundamental characteristic of this technique is breaking a problem up into a series of processing steps, then refining each step into greater levels of detail. You write a program in pseudo-code, where some of the steps are "high-level instructions": English statements of what the step should accomplish. You start with a single step, a statement of what the overall program should do. You then refine that single step into several substeps, refine the substeps into sub-substeps, and continue until each step is at the level where you could readily translate it into operations in an implementation language.

Introductory programming classes now teach this method, so it should be familiar to most programmers. Figure 5-2 shows the first two levels of a stepwise refinement intended to solve a small problem, that of finding misspelled words in a document.

Stepwise refinement is a good method for tackling problems up to a certain size. It lets a designer concentrate on a small area (a single step) at a time, thus reducing the complexity of the task. It gives some help to the problem of defining program families. The sequence of design decisions is the sequence of refinements; you can derive new members of the family by choosing different refinements.

However, stepwise refinement has several problems that show up in dealing with larger systems

1. Later design decisions depend on earlier ones. For example, if a user of the program from Figure 5-2 asks for a sorted list of misspelled words, instead of lines with misspellings, the entire original design is irrelevant.

Show misspelled words in a file.

Step	Level 1	Step	Level 2
1. for each line with misspellings		1. /* for each line with misspellings */ 1.1 for each line 1.2 if line has misspelled words	
2. highlight misspelled words		2. /* highlight misspelled words */ 2.1 for each word 2.2 if misspelled 2.3 then highlight 2.4 else leave alone	
3. print line		3. print line	

Figure 5–2: Stepwise Refinement for a Small Problem

2. Some design decisions, such as representations for key data structures, permeate the entire program.

Thus stepwise refinement rapidly leads to a design for a single member of a family, but deriving a new member can be almost as much work as deriving the first member. Furthermore,

3. Some problems are sufficiently large and ill-understood that it is difficult to find a top-level breakdown to start the top-down design.

The only approach people have managed to make work for such poorly understood problems is to carve off and design small portions of the system. Eventually the remainder becomes small enough that you can see how to do it by gluing together the other parts.

5.3 Information Hiding

Stepwise refinement (and other software design methods in general) almost always suffers from the problems Section 5.2.2 outlines. In particular, whenever design decisions change, many of the later design decisions become invalid. *Information hiding* is a software design method that avoids these problems.

The principle of information hiding is that each module *hides* some design decision, called the *secret* of the module. If the design decision changes later, then no clients of the module should need to change. Information hiding is the other side of the coin from abstraction. With both, you hide some information and reveal other information. Information hiding focuses on what to hide; abstraction focuses on what to reveal. Information hiding tries to protect you from change; you ask what design decisions might change, and arrange to hide them so you cannot depend on them.

Procedures provide the oldest form of abstraction, and thus of information hiding. Given the specification of a procedure, you do not care what algorithm the procedure uses to implement that specification. Information hiding generalizes this idea; Section 5.3 gives examples of other decisions you might hide.

In addition to a *primary secret*, a module might hide a *secondary secret*, such as the existence of some other module. For example, one module might hide the primary secret of the representation of words from an input file. It might make use of a symbol table module so that there is only one copy of each word. The existence of the symbol table module is a secondary secret of the word representation module.

The sorts of decisions one might hide include

1. The algorithm for carrying out some operation.

2. The representation of some data structure.

3. The details of an interface to an operating system, or to special-purpose hardware.

4. The policy for allocating some resource or ordering certain operations.

Figure 5–3 gives examples of typical *secrets* (design decisions) one might hide.

5.3.1 Hiding Representations

After algorithms, the easiest design decisions to hide are the representations of data structures. An *abstract data type* is an information hiding module of this sort. Such a module provides a collection of procedures for manipulating the data structure. For example, a module might hide the representation of a stack. It would provide operations for pushing elements onto a stack, popping elements off the stack, and reading the top element of the stack. Figure 5–4 shows a stack implemented as an array; Figure 5–5 shows it implemented as a list. For simplicity, both examples ignore exceptional conditions such as stack overflow and underflow. Both implementations provide Push, Pop, Top, and Init operations with identical headers and identical observable behavior (Part III shows how to specify the behavior and prove that both implementations display the same behavior). These four subprograms are the *interface procedures* of the module.

The two implementations differ in performance. The list implementation takes less space if stacks are short, but the Push operation may be slow because it needs

Module: Sequence
Secret: Representation of sequence
Change: Alternate between linked-list and array implementations

Module: Sort routine
Secret: Algorithm for sorting
Change: Use different algorithm tuned to size of data or
           expected degree of sortedness

Module: Disk request handler
Secret: Policy for picking next disk access
Change: Favor certain kinds of requests to improve overall
           system performance

Module: Panel indicator interface
Secret: How indicator display modes (on, off, blinking) are
           implemented
Change: Replace device that can blink with one that cannot, so
           you must simulate blinking by sequences of on/off

Figure 5–3: Some Typical Secrets

```
stack : record sp:integer; arr:array[1..Max] of element end;
procedure Push(e:element) is
    begin stack.sp := stack.sp + 1; stack.arr[stack.sp] := e; end;
procedure Pop is
    begin stack.sp := stack.sp-1; end;
function Top return element is
    begin return stack.arr[stack.sp]; end;
procedure Init is
    begin stack.sp := 0; end;
```

Figure 5–4: Stack Implemented as an Array

```
type stackptr;
type stackelement is record elem:element; next: stackptr; end record;
type stackptr is access stackelement;
stack : stackptr;
procedure Push(e:element) is
     item : stackptr;
   begin
     item := new stackelement; item.elem := e;
     item.next := stack; stack:=item;
   end;
procedure Pop is
   begin stack := stack.next; end;
function Top return element is
   begin return stack.item; end;
procedure Init is
   begin stack := null; end;
```

Figure 5–5: Stack Implemented as a List

to call a storage allocator. The array implementation requires less space if stacks are moderately full (depending on the relative sizes of elements and stackptrs). Once the system works, measurements may show either a space or speed bottleneck, which would lead a maintainer to switch implementations. Changing implementations is easy if clients of the stack module use only the interface procedures. If clients access the representation directly, the maintainer might need to edit every client to make the change.

A more problematic difference is that the array implementation inherently implies a limit on the size of the stack, while the linked-list implementation appears not to. However, the maximum size of dynamic memory, and the amount of dynamic memory other dynamic structures use, limit the linked list. Thus you should hide this difference by requiring that the linked-list implementation detect and report stack overflows, too — though you might not be able to specify *a priori* what the limit is.

5.3.2 Hiding Policies

Sometimes controlling some facility has two separate aspects: a mechanism for manipulating some data structure or resource, and a policy for how to use the basic mechanisms. The principle of separation of concerns says that one module should implement the mechanism, while a separate module should implement the policy.

Operating system researchers call this *policy/mechanism separation*. Policies are much more likely to change than mechanisms.

For example, one portion of an operating system handles requests for reading and writing the disk. The disk controller provides a mechanism for requesting an operation; a queue manager provides a mechanism for inserting and removing requests, perhaps based on priority; a policy module uses the basic queue mechanism to choose a request to remove and hand over to the disk controller mechanism.

5.3.3   Hiding Time of Operations

Sometimes a designer has a choice about when to do a certain operation. Suppose you must create a sorted list of elements. Two basic strategies are to insert items in sorted order (giving an insertion sort), or to insert elements into some temporary structure that you sort later (at which point you have a choice of many sorting methods).

You can hide the choice by creating a *sorted sequence* module that contains operations to

- Create an empty sequence.
- Insert a new element into the sequence.
- Sort the sequence.
- Fetch elements from the sorted sequence.

A client calls *Create* once, then calls *Insert* several times, then calls *Sort*, then calls *Fetch* several times. The point of this arrangement is that, since you cannot call *Fetch* until you call *Sort*, you really do not care to distinguish between the two cases:

1. *Insert* adds elements in order and *Sort* does nothing, and

2. *Insert* adds in any convenient place and *Sort* does all the work.

5.4   The Module Decomposition Document

The module decomposition document records the division of the system into modules. Its main use is as a baseline document for detailed design. Its intended audience is the senior programmers who would write the specifications for individual modules.

The document's organization is simple. It has an introduction stating its purpose, with an overview of the major divisions of the system. Remaining chapters have the same structure as the system; the module decomposition documents the *is composed of* relation of Section 5.1.1. Top-level modules become chapters, second-from-top-level modules become sections, third-from-top-level modules become subsections, and so on. The portion describing a module simply states what secrets the modules hides, primary secrets first, followed by any secondary secrets. Appendix D shows a sample module decomposition for the genealogy system of Appendix A, combined with a sample module dependency description.

At this stage you should minimize thinking about dependencies between modules; that is a separate design step. The purpose of the module decomposition phase is to decide what secrets your system must hide; deciding on dependencies is part of designing how the modules work.

Some experienced system designers advise making a preliminary *resource budget* for your modules at this stage. A resource budget constrains how large a module can get, how much data it can allocate, and how fast its functions must be. You do not have reliable enough information at this stage to draw up an accurate budget, but most modules should be small enough that most of your estimates are not wildly wrong. Many systems wind up squeezed for some resource, and you need to have early warning to cope with the eventual trouble. A rule of thumb is to ensure your initial budget has a 50 percent safety margin; that is, don't initially budget for more than two-thirds of your maximum code space, data space, file space, or execution time.

A reasonable top-level split for many systems is to have a system-hiding module, a behavior-hiding module, and a software-decision-hiding module; the following sections outline these divisions. The boundaries between these modules are somewhat fuzzy.

5.4.1 System Modules

System modules hide fixed interfaces: those that are not under the control of the designers. Most software will have operating system interface modules. Embedded systems must often hide interfaces to peripheral devices. The *Fixed Interfaces* chapter of the requirements document (Chapter 3 in Figure 4–4) is your starting point for this part of the system. System characteristics to hide include

- character set properties, such as how to convert from uppercase letters to lowercase letters and how to translate a digit into the corresponding integer.
- low-level interactions with hardware devices, including the user's terminal.
- interactions with the file system.

System modules are almost as important to portability as choosing a portable implementation language. They are hard to design unless you have had experience writing software on several different systems. Avoid looking at what facilities your operating system defines, except to learn what is possible. Instead, concentrate on what high-level operations your system requires.

For example, suppose you need to create a temporary file that will disappear when your program terminates. On some operating systems, you create an ordinary file and either delete it yourself or put it in a special directory where an operating system process will delete it if you don't. On others, you call special system operations that create files that go away when you log out. The appropriate common functionality is "create temporary file," which you implement as creating an ordinary file (perhaps with a special name) on systems that do not provide primitives for creating temporary files. Since some systems will not delete these for you automatically, you also need either a "delete temporary file" operation, which clients call when they finish with the temporary file, or a "delete all temporary files" operation, which you call once at the end of your program. For an operating system that takes care of deleting temporary files for you, these routines would do nothing.

5.4.2 Behavior Modules

Behavior modules protect against changes to the requirements. A module goes in this section if it implements a requirement that might change; you need not hide implementations of fundamental assumptions. For example, one module might hide the syntax of several commands (corresponding to part of the *Input and Output* chapter of the requirements); another might hide the functionality of these commands (corresponding to parts of the *System Functions* chapter).

If your system must run on several operating systems, portions of its behavior that depend on the operating system might belong under either behavior hiding or under system hiding. My preference is to put them in system hiding; however, putting them in behavior hiding follows the simple rule that every requirement goes under behavior.

For modules in this section, you must keep track of what requirements each module handles, and what requirements you have assigned to each module. This helps ensure you remember to handle all the requirements. These are the two halves of a two-way mapping between modules and requirements. Technically the relation is many-to-many, because each module might implement several related requirements and several modules might implement parts of the same requirement. There is no harm in the first, provided the requirements really are related. The second is dangerous; if the requirement changes, you ideally want to change only one module.

5.4.3 Software Decision Modules

Software decision modules hide decisions under the control of the designers, such as algorithms, internal data structures, and formats of files not visible to users. This section may also include "common code" modules, containing subroutines used several places in the rest of the system.

Sometimes you discover during detailed design that you need to add more modules. A significant portion of these are software decision modules, because they represent decisions you didn't realize you needed to hide until you began to think about how to implement some other module. System and behavior modules come from the requirements document, so they should be less subject to change unless the requirements themselves change. The right thing to do is go back and add your new modules to an appropriate portion of the module decomposition document (under the appropriate configuration controls; see Chapter 17), then carry forward the implications of the change to later documents such as module dependencies and module specifications.

5.4.4 How to Modularize

In decomposing a system into modules you go through three phases.

1. Identify major groups of design decisions (such as the three mentioned above), subgroups within those groups, and so on. These become the higher levels of the *is composed of* hierarchy, and chapters, sections, and so forth of the decomposition document.

2. Identify all the major design decisions (secrets) in your project, and record modules that hide them in the decomposition document. These become the leaves of the *is composed of* hierarchy.

3. Estimate the size of each module. If it seems too large for one person to handle in a typical work assignment, break it into smaller pieces.

The first place look for guidelines on breaking a system into modules is the requirements specification.

1. Many nouns in the requirements document name objects the system must represent. For example, a library management system must represent books and patrons. Each of these becomes a module; if there are multiple instances of an object, the module would define and export a type representing the object.

2. The system may need to interact with a variety of devices. For example, the library system may include an online catalog accessible from display terminals. Add a module for each type of device.

3. Some modules might represent relationships between objects. For example, a registry system might have modules representing students and courses. Adding a third module to represent the *is enrolled in* relation between students and classes allows us to hide the decision about where to store information about the relation. Relations are in general bidirectional; you might want to know what courses a student takes, and what students take a particular course. You can represent a relation in many ways, either storing information within the objects (such as pointers to related objects), or storing information externally to all the objects (such as a set of ordered pairs). Changing requirements, or measures of performance, may change our ideas of how and where to store the information. A relation representation module may require that each of the modules representing objects involved in the relationship provide a *restricted interface* (see Section 6.5) to let it store information efficiently about the relationship.

4. You may need to implement modules that represent collections of objects from one or more other modules. Normally a collection is a separate module from the one that represents the elements of a collection. The one exception is that a module defining a dynamically allocated data type may also define one particular collection that includes all objects of the type. This is uncommon; you typically need it only if other modules do some form of resource management or exception checking. If the collection has any structuring to it (such as if you need to get at objects in a particular order) you would normally provide a separate module.

5. Data that persists beyond a single execution of the program requires a module to provide file storage. Normally you would have a module whose secret is the format of the information on secondary storage, which provides information to extract information from secondary storage (input) and stores information on secondary storage (output). For pragmatic reasons you might split this module into separate input and output modules, but both are parts of the same file storage module since they share the same secret. Normally such a module does not also "understand" the internal format of the data. The input module would call procedures from the internal representation module to create the internal data structure, or a separate module would call the input module to extract information and the internal representation module to store it.

6. Verbs in the requirements document may correspond to operations on the basic objects. For example, a patron borrows and returns a book. Each such verb may lead to operations in one or more modules. This is part of module interface design, discussed in Chapter 6.

A key part of any design step, including module decomposition, is to explore several different designs and compare them. It can be hard to define even one decomposition, so it may seem like too much work to define several. However, exploring alternatives is the only way to have confidence you have settled on the best design.

Information hiding tries to limit the effect on the rest of the system of any one design decision. There are a few decisions whose consequences seem like they ought to affect a large part of the system. For example, extremely tight space or time constraints may force you to use particular algorithms or data organizations. Placing certain functions in hardware strongly affects related software. You should still try to limit the effects of such decisions to one or a few modules, unless you are certain you will never change these decisions. Anything that permeates your system will be expensive to change.

In common with all other design documents, as you work on later development stages you may discover problems with the decomposition you began with. You should revise the document under your usual configuration control disciplines, and carry forward the implications of the change to later stages.

5.5 Module Dependencies

Decomposing a system into modules begins to constrain the implementation; you add more constraints by deciding dependencies among modules. A module dependency document defines the *uses* relation discussed in Section 5.1.2. Appendix D shows a sample module dependency document for the genealogy system of Appendix A, combined with a sample module decomposition.

It surprises programmers new to information hiding that one could document module dependencies before finishing the detailed design of each module. Detailed design may add or change dependencies, but this is no different from any other occurrence of a later development stage requiring changes to an earlier stage (see Section 2.3). A designer can predict most of the important dependencies long before detailed design. As a simple example, consider a table lookup module that maps between names and some other data type. It must use both the module implementing names and the module implementing the other data type. No one needs to know the design of any of the three modules to detect this dependency.

Some dependencies do not surface until the detailed design stage. For example, preliminary design may define a module to represent words taken from some text file. Detailed design may decide to represent words as indices into a symbol table, so that there is only one copy of each word. Since the preliminary design team did not predict this design detail, they did not plan for the symbol table module, let alone dependencies on the module. On the other hand, this local detail impacts only the word representation module, so this omission during the preliminary design phase is not important. The existence of the new module may become a secondary secret of the original module.

The module dependency document should describe a hierarchy. Separate subgraphs of the hierarchy correspond to subsets of the full system, and may correspond to useful partial systems. If a chain of modules call each other recursively, then all modules in the chain must be present in any release of the system, and thus recursive chains limit the possibilities for subsets.

5.6 Relation to Other Methods

Information hiding solves the three problems of stepwise refinement. You make a special effort to separate design decisions so that you have fewer "later" design decisions that "earlier" ones might invalidate. You isolate the effects of changing key design decisions, so they do not permeate the entire system. You create a module for each design decision you can see how to make, thus carving identifiable pieces off a large (and possibly ill-defined) problem.

People who design mixed hardware and software systems speak of a design step they call *system design*, where they partition a system into software and hardware components. Information hiding decompositions serve this purpose as well. The module decomposition step, and the later module specification step, do not determine anything about how you implement any given module. In particular, during the detailed design phase you might choose to implement most of a module as a hardware device. You would likely keep a minimal software module to provide an interface to the device for the rest of the software.

Some design methods concentrate on how information flows through the system and allocate modules to handle significant transformations of the data during the flow. This approach to design does not give the protection from changes that information hiding does.

Module dependencies have little to do with the flow of information from one module to another. If module X passes information to module Y, you may have one of three situations.

- X depends on Y. A procedure from X may call one from Y and supply it with input parameters.

- Y depends on X. A procedure from Y may call one from X and get a result back.

- Neither depends on the other. A higher-level module Z may call a procedure from one, passing a procedure of the other as a parameter. However, Z depends on both X and Y.

Given that you know information must flow from one module to another, you must still decide which one depends on the other. For example, you may have a module that hides the syntax of the command line. Various modules of your system may have optional behavior that a user can change via command line options. A weaker design has all these modules depend on the option module; a stronger one has the option module depend on them all. The reason is that with the better choice, you can build the lower-level modules to have fixed default behavior and provide procedures for changing that behavior. In a subset, you can eliminate command line option scanning and still have a working system. With the other direction of dependency, none of the modules with optional behavior can work until you build the command line scanner. You could build a stub of the scanner (see Section 8.1), but even this is more work than you need with the other design.

Information flows can be useful as a design verification tool. During requirements analysis you developed scenarios for how your system might handle particular sequences of interactions. To validate your design, you might try to sketch the sequence of information flow through your system in response to several scenarios.

Further Reading

Parnas (1972) wrote the classic paper on information hiding. I based the discussion of program families in Section 5.2.1 on his 1976 paper. Section 5.1 summarizes his discussion of hierarchies [Parnas 1974]. Some textbooks on data structures cover the

basics of abstract data types [Wulf et al. 1981a]. Reid (1980) gives a good example
of system hiding in his description of the Scribe[1] document formatter's "virtual
operating system" interface. Wulf et al. (1981b) describe the idea of
policy/mechanism separation.

Exercises

5–1   Compare the module decomposition of Appendix D with the life-cycle con-
        siderations of Appendix B. For each possible change, identify (if possible)
        which module or modules would need to change in response. What possible
        changes are not reflected in the module decomposition?

5–2   Compare the module decomposition of Appendix D with the possible subsets
        that Appendix B lists. Identify what modules each subset requires. To what
        extent can subsetting this system correspond to taking a subset of the
        modules? What modules would you need to modify in going from each sub-
        set to the next, and in what way?

Project Exercises

5–3   Continue the project you began in Chapter 4 by writing a module decomposi-
        tion and module dependencies document. Appendix D gives a sample docu-
        ment based on the genealogy system of Appendix A.

[1]Scribe is a registered trademark of Unilogic Ltd.

_____ Chapter 6 _____

Module
Interfaces

Before you can write a module or use it, you must decide what functionality it provides and give a clear, precise description of what it does. This chapter discusses
how to design module interfaces, what a specification is, how software developers
use specifications, and what things you should say in a module specification. Section
6.1 shows how to pin down what functions you should provide in your interface.
Section 6.2 discusses several things to think about when you are designing module
interfaces according to the principle of information hiding. Section 6.3 talks about
what a specification is, and Section 6.4 talks about the basics of writing specifications
for interfaces. Part III extends the introductory material of Section 6.4 by describing
several formal specification techniques in detail. Appendix E gives examples of
specifications using several different techniques.

In industry, senior programmers typically design interfaces and write specifications. In this chapter, "you" means a person acting as an interface designer or
module specification writer.

6.1 Deciding on Functionality

Section 5.3 discussed the idea of information hiding. Briefly, each module hides
some secret, a design decision that might change. The specification defines a collection of *interface procedures*, which are the only ways clients may interact with the
module.

According to Figure 2–1 on page 8, you have the module decomposition and module dependency documents when you start on module specifications; a coder begins an implementation only after the specifications are complete. To specify a module, you must first decide what interface procedures it will export. How do you go about deciding what functionality a module must provide, before deciding its implementation or those of its clients?

6.1.1   Abstract Interfaces

The problem of defining interfaces for an embedded system gives a good illustration of what it means to consult potential clients. An embedded system must use interfaces that are outside the control of the system developers. Moreover, the interfaces may change arbitrarily. Here, it is crucial to define interfaces that provide the functions that clients need without regard to any implementation, since the implementation may change enormously.

Consider the problem of reading dates from input files. Any given source of dates might be consistent in format, but different sources may choose completely different formats. Figure 6–1 shows some possible formats for dates. For all these formats, you can make certain assumptions.

1.   It is possible to calculate the month.
2.   It is possible to calculate the day-in-month.
3.   It is possible to calculate the year. A two-digit year implies a particular century.

You can embed these assumptions in an interface like the one shown in Figure 6–2. This is an *abstract interface* because it hides details of several possible interfaces.

6.1.2   Imports and Exports

A first step toward writing a module specification is to list what procedures it should *export* (make available to clients), and what assumptions clients might make about

---

Feb 14, 1989	Month name, day of month, year
14 Feb 89	Day of month, month name, last two digits of year
2/14/89	Numeric month (American style)
14/2/89	Numeric month (Canadian style)
14-II-89	Roman numeral for month
890214	Easily sorted encoding of date
89.45	Two-digit year, day-in-year

Figure 6–1: Possible Date Formats

---

type year = 1900..1999;
month = 1..12;
monthday = 1..31;

GetDay: → monthday
GetMonth: → month
GetYear: → year

Figure 6–2: Abstract Interface for Dates

---

them. Similarly, you might list procedures you expect to *import* (make use of) from modules yours calls.

For modules that implement representations of objects mentioned in the requirements, you can get an initial list of possible interface procedures from verbs and adjectives in the requirements specification. For example, the phrase "borrow a book" might lead you to invent a Borrow procedure in the Book module. References to lit, unlit, and blinking lights might lead you to add a Status function in the Light module; it would return one of three values corresponding to the adjectives.

Deciding what functions to provide in a module often requires some idea of how clients will use the module, which may require some idea of how you will implement clients. This does *not* mean that you write specifications after implementations, but merely that you must give some thought to how clients might use the module. For example, a system might contain a table lookup module. With experience, you would know that something like Figure 6–3 serves the needs of a wide variety of clients, without considering any implementations. However, studying the preliminary design might show that clients would never delete items, so you need not specify a delete procedure. Alternatively, your study might suggest that the pattern

if Lookup(key) then Delete(key); Enter(key,new element)

would be common; you might therefore choose to specify Enter as

Name: Enter
Parameters: Key k, Item i
Effect: Lookup(k) = (true,i)

eliminating the Exceptions clause so that Enter simply replaces an existing element. If some clients need the functionality of the old Enter, they can get it by saying

if Lookup(key) then ErrAlreadyEntered else Enter(key, new element)

You might also choose to provide both forms of Enter.

---

type Table = ...
function Enter(**var** t:Table; k:Key; v:Value):boolean;
{ Add v as value of key k to table t. If the key already exists, return false and leave the table unchanged. Otherwise return true. }

function Lookup(**var** t:Table; k:Key; **var** v:Value):boolean;
{ Returns true if key k exists in table t, and sets v to the corresponding value. Otherwise leaves v untouched and returns false. }

function Delete(**var** t:Table; k:Key):boolean;
{ Delete the item with key k from table t. Returns true if the element was in the table, false if it wasn't. }

procedure Init(**var** t:Table);
{ Initialize t to an empty table. }

Figure 6–3: Sketch of Table Module Interface

If you are responsible for specifying the interface for a particular module, you should not assume you can simply dictate what interface procedures to provide. You must negotiate with those responsible for client modules. Some projects keep an *interface definition book* with specifications (or outlines, in early stages) of the current interfaces. This book must remain stable (that is, under configuration management; see Chapter 17) because many people depend on the information in it. Once you have negotiated approximate functionality with potential clients, you can write a precise specification.

6.2 Information-Hiding Complexities

Section 6.1 talked about how to decide what interface procedures to provide in a module. As you are deciding on the exact signature of each procedure, you need to plan carefully for possible changes to the design decision the module hides. This section shows that this is not easy, and suggests several things you should consider at this stage.

The easiest secrets to describe are representational decisions. Hiding representations of data structures ties in with the modern idea of an abstract data type: a collection of values and operations that manipulate those values. Introductory and intermediate programming courses introduce abstract types such as sequences, and give several representations of the same abstract operations. The remainder of this section illustrates information hiding ideas by showing how to develop an abstract interface for sequences.

A sequence is a variable-length ordered collection of values. The two main representations of sequences are fixed-length arrays and linked lists. There are many operations you might wish to have on sequences, such as

- create an empty sequence

- append an element to a sequence

- determine the number of elements in a sequence

- fetch a particular element of the sequence

- operate on each element of a sequence

- concatenate two sequences

- delete an element from the start, middle, or end of a sequence

If you choose to implement only the first four operations, you might come up with the array implementation of Figure 6–4 or the list implementation of Figure 6–5 (in both cases, ignore undesired events for the moment; see Section 7.2.3). A typical use of one of these two sequence modules might be

```
var X : Seq;
...
while ... do
    begin { gather elements }
    ... Append(X, AnotherElement); ...
    end;
```

This small example survives a change of representation, since it depends only on parts of the interface that do not change if you swap implementations.

6.2.1 Iterators

Any use of a sequence almost certainly requires some way to operate on each element of the sequence in turn. Hiding the representation of the sequence prevents us from indexing into the array directly, or directly following pointers in the linked list. One way to iterate over the sequence without directly manipulating the representation is to use the *Length* and *Fetch* interface procedures in a loop such as

```
var I:LengthType;
...
for I: =1 to Length(S) do
    DoSomething(Fetch(S,I));
```

```
type
IndexType = 1..Max;   LengthType = 0..Max;
Seq = record
  LastUsed : LengthType;
  Arr : array[IndexType] of ElementType
  end;

procedure Init(var S:Seq);
  begin  S.LastUsed := 0  end;

procedure Append(var S:Seq; E:ElementType);
  begin
    if S.LastUsed < Max
      then begin
          S.LastUsed := S.LastUsed + 1
          S.Arr[S.LastUsed] := E
          end
        else EXCEPTION
  end;

function Length(var S:Seq):LengthType;
  begin  Length := S.LastUsed  end;

function Fetch(var S:Seq; I:IndexType):ElementType;
  begin
    if I < =S.LastUsed
        then Fetch := S.Arr[I]
        else EXCEPTION
  end;
```

Figure 6–4: Array Implementation of Sequence

In the array implementation, the *Fetch* is moderately efficient, and some languages can get better efficiency by expanding *Fetch* inline. However, the linked-list implementation must chase down a list of pointers each time, making the loop execution time quadratic in the length of the list.

Modern languages such as Alphard and Clu provided special constructs for iteration that allow efficient loops while hiding the representation of the data type.

```
type
CellP = Cell^;
Cell = record  Next : CellP;  Elem : ElementType  end;
Seq = record  Last : CellP;  First : CellP  end;

procedure Append(var S:Seq; E:ElementType);
    var Item : CellP;
  begin
    new(Item);   Item^.Elem := E;    Item^.Next := nil;
    if S.First = nil
       then S.First := Item
       else S.Last^.Next := Item
    S.Last := Item
  end;

procedure Init(var S:Seq);
  begin  S.First := nil;  S.Last := nil  end;

function Length(var S:Seq):LengthType;
    var Count:LengthType; This : CellP;
  begin
    Count := 0;  This := S.First;
    while This < > nil do begin
       Count := Count + 1;  This := This^.Next;
       end
    Length := Count;
  end;

function Fetch(var S:Seq; I:IndexType):ElementType;
    var Count:LengthType; This : CellP;
  begin
    Count := 0;  This := S.First;
    while (Count < I) and (This < > nil) do
       begin  Count := Count + 1;  This := This^.Next;  end
    if This < >nil
       then Fetch := This^.Elem
       else EXCEPTION
  end;
```

Figure 6–5: List Implementation of Sequence

Figure 6–6 shows how to simulate these constructs in Pascal. An *iterator* is a type that hides control information for the loop. Procedure *Initialize* starts the iterator. Function *Finished* determines whether there are any elements left. Procedure *Advance* goes on to the next element, if any. *Current* returns the current element of the list. Figure 6–7 shows an implementation of these procedures for the linked-list representation.

However, there is a problem trying to implement this collection of procedures for the array representation of Figure 6–4. The basic ideas are simple. The iterator must remember an index for the current element. The *Initialize* procedure sets the index to 1; procedure *Advance* adds one to the index. Function *Finished* compares the index with the length of the array (S.LastUsed). However, function *Current* must subscript the array S.Arr, and has no way to get at it.

In some low-level systems implementation languages, *Initialize* could store a pointer to S in the iterator data structure. However, strongly typed languages like Pascal do not permit this unless you redefine Seq as a pointer type. This would force all sequences onto the heap. In some systems this might be acceptable, but it does force extra complexity onto an application that otherwise does not need it.

```pascal
type
Seq = ...;
Iterator = ...;
procedure Initialize(var G:Iterator; S: Seq); ...
function Finished(G:Iterator):boolean;...
procedure Advance(var G: Iterator); ...
function Current(G:Iterator):ElementType;
...
var S:Seq; G:Iterator;
begin
    ...
    Init(G,S);
    while not Finished(G) do begin
        process(Current(G));
        Advance(G);
    end;
end;
```

Figure 6–6: Using an Iterator

```
type
Iterator = CellP;
procedure Initialize(var G:Iterator; S: Seq);
    begin G : = S.First; end;
function Finished(G:Iterator):boolean;
    begin Finished : = (G = nil) end;
procedure Advance(var G:Iterator);
    begin G : = G^.Next end;
function Current(G:Iterator):ElementType;
    begin Current : = G^.Elem end;
```

Figure 6–7: Linked-List Iterator

This is an example of a *distributed overhead*: the possibility that some clients might use an iterator forces all clients into slightly higher access costs, and potentially much more expensive storage management.

Alternatively, you can simply pass S as an extra parameter to *Current*. Indeed, any iterator procedure might need access to S, depending on the representation. This shows that the original iterator interface, which was perfectly adequate for the linked-list representation, is not enough for the array representation. Thus when deciding what interface procedures to provide, and what parameters they should take, you must consider the needs of several alternative implementations.

6.2.2 Accumulators

In some applications, it is typical to go through a brief period when the program builds up a sequence, followed by a longer interval when the sequence no longer grows or shrinks. The examples of Figures 6–4 and 6–5 both require some additional storage overhead during a growth phase. The array implementation is as large as the most elements one might ever append. The list implementation no longer needs the *Last* field after the growth phase. This may seem like a small overhead. However, if an application has many sequences, while only a few grow at any given time, the space overhead can be significant.

To allow clients to release this storage when they do not need it, you could export another type, called an *accumulator*, to represent the overhead. If you did not care about space overhead, you would have no need to add accumulators to the module interface, and could simply make them part of the representation of sequences. A partial interface to a sequence module with an accumulator is

```
type
VArr(N:integer) = record Arr : array [1..N] of ElementType end;
Seq = VArr^;    CellP = Cell^;
Cell = record Next:CellP; Elem:ElementType end;
Accum = record Len : integer;  Elems : CellP end;

procedure Initialize(var S: Seq; var A: Accum);
   begin A.Len := 0; A.Elems := nil end;

procedure Append(var S: Seq; var A: Accum; E:ElementType);
   { Accumulate items in reverse order }
    var Item : CellP;
   begin
    new(Item);  Item^.Elem := ElementType; Item^.Next := A.Elems;
     A.Elems := Item;  A.Len := A.Len + 1
   end Append;

procedure Finish(var S: Seq; var A: Accum);
   { Fill in array in correct order }
     var Item1, Item2 : CellP;
   begin
    new(S,A.Len); { allocate array of particular length }
    Item1 := A.Elems;   A.Elems := nil;
    for I := A.Len downto 1 do begin
       S.Arr[I] := Item1^.Elem;  Item2 := Item1^.Next;
       Free(Item1);  Item1 := Item2
    end
   end;
```

Figure 6–8: Array Sequence Accumulator

```
type
Seq = ...;
Accum = ...;
...
procedure Initialize(var S:Seq; var A: Accum); ...
procedure Append(var S: Seq; var A: Accum; E:ElementType); ...
procedure Finish(var S:Seq; A: Accum); ...
```

A typical use is

```
var S:Seq; A:Accum;
begin
   Initialize(S,A);
   for ... do begin { some loop that gets elements }
      ... Append(S,A, OneMoreElement); ...
   end;
   Finish(S,A)
end;
```

Clients use the accumulator only during a short period of the lifetime of the sequence. Figure 6–8 shows a possible implementation for the sequence module, in a Pascal-like language that allows dynamic determination of the size of an array. Using arrays here avoids the overhead of links. The accumulator is a reverse-order linked list that holds elements until the client finishes building the sequence, thus determining its final length. *Finish* allocates an array of precisely the right size and fills in its elements from the temporary list. Figure 6–9 shows an alternative implementation where *Finish* does no real work. It represents the sequence as a linked list; the accumulator points to the last element of the list.

```
type
CellP = Cell^;   Seq = CellP;   Accum = Seq;
Cell = record Next : CellP; Elem : ElementType end;

procedure Initialize(var S: Seq; var A: Accum);
   begin S := nil; A := nil end;

procedure Append(var S: Seq; var A: Accum; E:ElementType);
   { Build list in correct order }
      var Item : CellP;
   begin
      new(Item);   Item^.Elem := E;   Item^.Next := nil;
      if S = nil
         then S := Item   { Initialize sequence }
         else A^.Next := Item;   { Append to end }
      A := Item   { new end of sequence }
   end;

procedure Finish(var S: Seq; var A: Accum);
   begin { nothing to do } end;
```

Figure 6–9: List Sequence Accumulator

6.2.3 Path Expressions

The previous section showed that in general an accumulator needs a "finish accumulating" procedure like *Finish*. Some iterator implementations need such procedures also. For example, a long sequence of large elements might not fit in core. An iterator implementation might keep the sequence in a temporary file, and need to open the sequence file on a call to *Initialize*. It would need to close the file when finished.

At first it might seem that the iterator's *Advance* procedure could hide closing the file. However, this stops a client from quitting an iterator loop early. The iterator needs an explicit *Finish* procedure. Figure 6–10 shows an example of a client procedure that tests whether a particular value is a member of a sequence; it quits early when it finds a matching element.

This is a particular example of a general pattern: one often has to call a particular procedure or group of procedures several times, and must bracket the sequence of calls with a beginning procedure and an ending procedure. One technique for specifying the order in which clients must call a group of procedures is *path expressions*. For example,

Initialize { Append }* Finish

says that one must first call *Initialize*, then call *Append* several times, then call *Finish*. Saying

{ Initialize { Append }* Finish }*

instead means that a client could restart an accumulator, rather than having to declare a new one. A trace specification could give similar constraints on calling order (see Chapter 13).

```
function IsMember(S:Seq; E:ElementType):boolean;
     var G:Iterator; label 999;
   begin
     IsMember := false;  InitIterator(S,G);
     while not Finished(S,G) do begin
        if Current(S,G) = E then begin IsMember := true; goto 999 end;
        Advance(S,A);
        end;
 999:  Finish(S,A);
   end;
```

Figure 6–10: Iterator with Early Exit

   Most languages lack facilities for declaring and enforcing path expressions. If
the language allows procedural parameters, the module designer might choose to
enforce the order of calls to iterator procedures by defining a *cover procedure* (often
called a "cover function") for the iterator procedures. A caller must define a procedure containing the body of the loop and pass the procedure to the cover function.
The module would export the cover function instead of the iterator type and the *Initialize, Finished,* and *Advance* procedures. Figure 6–11 shows a use of a cover procedure for the iterator of Figure 6–7; the *process* procedure passed as a parameter
to *AllSeq* is the same as the *process* procedure of Figure 6–6. If you need to allow
the loop body the freedom to end the loop early, then the procedural parameter
must return a boolean value (via a **var** parameter) to the cover procedure.

6.2.4   Editors

Iterators and accumulators are both straightforward, in that you cannot modify a
sequence while iterating over it, nor iterate over a sequence while accumulating it.
You sometimes need more complex interactions between an iterator or accumulator
and the body of the loop that uses it.

   Editors are more general iterators that allow modifications to a structure. For
example, a sequence editor might allow you to insert elements either before or after

---

```
type
Seq = ...;
procedure AllSeq(S: Seq; procedure Each(e:ElementType));
      var G:CellP;
   begin
   G := S.First;
   while G < > nil do begin
      Each(G^.Elem); G := G^.Next
      end
   end
...
var S:Seq;
begin
   ...
   AllSeq(S, process);
end;
```

Figure 6–11: Using an Iterator Cover Procedure

---

the current one, or delete the current element. The editor would take care of any interactions between the code that iterates over the sequence and the code that modifies the sequence; both are part of the same module, and so both understand the underlying data structure.

6.3   What Is a Specification?

Once you know the signature of all the interface procedures of a module, you must specify the precise meaning of each interface procedure. Agreeing on what "specification" means is surprisingly difficult. In the common speech a specification of a thing is a description of the thing that pins down what it does, what it looks like, how one builds it, and so on. For an engineer, a specification is a precise description of the requirements a thing must meet. One characterization is that a specification says *what* to do, while an implementation says *how* to do it. For example, a particular electrical circuit may require a capacitor; the specification will say "one capacitor, so many microfarads capacitance." The specification may also say how big the capacitor may be, to fit into the rest of the circuit. It will not usually say anything about how to build the capacitor, or what shape it must be.

For software, a specification is typically non-procedural. However, proponents of some specification techniques and some "very high-level languages" say that in their techniques one writes "executable specifications." Program transformation systems, which turn specifications into implementations, further blur the distinction.

It ought to be easier to understand a specification than an implementation, because the specification has less information to master. An implementation must have all the information of the specification, plus details peculiar to the implementation technique and the implementation language. However, most people find specifications much harder to understand than implementations. Part of the problem is that we have strong biases toward thinking about how things get done; it is hard to back away and think in more abstract terms. When confronted with an abstract specification, most people claim not to be able to understand it until they see how an implementation would work.

6.3.1   Using Specifications

People use specifications for five purposes.

1. To aid in understanding the system. Large systems are too big for people to understand as a whole. However, if you understand the specification of the modules used by the module you are studying, you need not know how they work.

2. For communicating a division of labor among programmers. Large systems require cooperation among several people. If one person uses a module written by another, both must have the same understanding of what the module does.

3. To describe the problem a programmer must solve. Just as you must understand a large system one piece at a time, you must build it that way. A programmer needs to have a precise description of what his or her module must do before he or she can build it.

4. To describe how to test a module. If you do not know what problem you are solving, you cannot tell whether you have solved it.

5. To support changing software. There may be several versions of a program. For example, you may have several possible algorithms for one module that differ in resource consumption (usually, time and space). Different customers may require different tradeoffs. A specification says what is common to these different versions, allowing the rest of the system to remain unchanged between versions.

All these purposes require precision, so that there is no ambiguity about what a specification means. For example, one programmer may interpret the specification of the module she is writing one way, while her colleague who uses it in another module interprets the specification another way. The two modules are not compatible; at least one must be rewritten for the system to work.

A software specification must be abstract, as well as precise. An abstract specification is one from which you have abstracted away all implementation-specific details. The only sure way to do this is to write the specification using things a user of the module could verify without reference to what is going on inside any implementation of the module. For example, one procedure may modify some data structure (such as the Enter procedure of Figure 6–16 on page 78). Since the details of the data structure are implementation-specific, you cannot explain what Enter does by describing its changes to the data structure. Instead, you explain it by its effect on the values that the Lookup procedure returns.

6.3.2 Abstract Programs

A reflection of our bias toward thinking about implementations is that many people write *abstract programs* and call them specifications. An abstract program is a pseudo-code sketch. Many statements in such an abstract program are brief English descriptions of what to do next; some of the constructs may be much higher-level than the typical implementation language. However, at best such a program is a partial implementation of some unspecified set of requirements. There may well be many better implementations. Unfortunately, if you come up with an alternative program that you wish to claim implements the "specification" given by the abstract program, you get into severe trouble. No algorithm can exist for proving two programs equivalent; the problem is undecidable (that is, equivalent to the halting problem). An abstract program may well be an important part of the design of a module implementation (see Chapter 7), but it is not a specification.

The following example shows some of the things wrong with giving an abstract program as a specification. I asked an undergraduate class to build a program for examining family trees. I gave a precise specification of a module to represent a person (shown in detail in Section E.6), then gave the sketch in Figure 6–12 for finding all the relationships between two people. This algorithm takes persons P_1 and P_2 and finds all persons P and integers K_1 and K_2 such that P is a "nearest common

---

Declare sets P1Ancestor, P2Ancestor, P1Add, P2Add, CommonAncestor;
integer Depth.

CommonAncestor := P1Ancestor := P2Ancestor := nullset;
Depth := 0;
P1Add := { P1 }; P2Add := { P2 };
forall Persons P do InitWaysRelated(P);
repeat
   P1Ancestor := P1Ancestor union P1Add;
   P2Ancestor := P2Ancestor union P2Add;
   Depth := Depth + 1;
   P1Add := AddGeneration(P1Add,Depth,1);
   P2Add := AddGeneration(P2Add,Depth,2);
   CheckAncestor(P1Add,P2Ancestor);
   CheckAncestor(P2Add,P1Ancestor);
until IsEmpty(P1Add) and IsEmpty(P2Add);
foreach P in CommonAncestor
   for I:=1 to NUMWAYSRELATED(P,1)
      for J:=1 to NUMWAYSRELATED(P,2)
         P is DISTANCE(P,I,1) generations from P1 and
         DISTANCE(P,J,2) generations from P2.

AddGeneration
Parameters: set P1, integer Depth, I

Returns a set consisting of the parents of each person in S1. For each such parent P, call AddRelation(P,Depth,I) to record that P is at distance Depth from person Pi.

CheckAncestor
Parameters: sets S1, Ancestor

Add (S1 intersect Ancestor) to CommonAncestor, and remove the same set from S1. The latter step prevents finding parents of common ancestors as additional common ancestors.

Figure 6–12: Incorrect Abstract Program

---

ancestor" of P_1 and P_2, and the two are K_1^{th} cousins K_2 times removed. Consider a tree rooted at P with arcs from each person to all his or her children. If the distance (number of arcs) from P to P_1 is D_1, and to P_2 is D_2, then the two are $\min(D_1, D_2) - 1$ cousins $abs(D_1 - D_2)$ times removed. The sign of $D_1 - D_2$ tells which one is closer to the common ancestor. A -1th cousin is a direct ancestor or descendant; a 0th cousin is a sibling; a 0th cousin once removed is an aunt, uncle, nephew, or niece. You cannot simply look at all ancestors of the two, since a parent of a common ancestor does not necessarily define any new relationships.

The algorithm of Figure 6–12 tries to search through the set of ancestors to find all nearest common ancestors. It searches through increasingly distant ancestors of P_1 and P_2. Since there are finitely many persons, and a person cannot be his or her own ancestor, this process will always end. Each time the procedure adds someone to the set of ancestors, it records their distance from P_1 or P_2 via the AddRelation function of the Person module.

Unlike some abstract programs, this one is precise — at least, for an implementor. Unfortunately, for a user, it does not give a precise specification of what information it returns. It claims to return triples of the form (person, integer, integer) with certain relationships between triples and the parameters, but does not pin down what it means by a nearest common ancestor.

The information returned by this program corresponds only loosely with what most of us would assume a nearest common ancestor would mean. The algorithm works in simple cases, but fails miserably in an inbred family, such as the British royal family. It does not find all possible relationships, because it excludes ancestors of common ancestors from consideration. If person X has children X_1 and X_2, and persons P_1 and P_2 have nearest common ancestor X_1, but one of them also has ancestor X_2, then the algorithm of Figure 6–12 fails to find X as another nearest common ancestor. When I discovered this during testing, I came up with an even more complicated algorithm, which worked in a few more cases but failed in yet others. Finally, I decided I needed a precise definition of what it meant to be a nearest common ancestor, and came up with the specification of Figure 6–13. In this specification, the assertion

$$\exists X_j, j \in [a..b] \mid P(X_j)$$

means there exists a sequence of elements $X_a, X_{a+1}, \cdots, X_b$ such that predicate P holds for each X_j. This specification may be as hard to read as the abstract program, but precisely characterizes the behavior I wanted without prescribing a particular algorithm. Given this definition, I quickly arrived at a working solution.

6.4   Defining Interface Procedures

The module specification should list all the assumptions the module makes about clients, and all the assumptions clients may make about the module. How can you specify the meaning of an interface?

Find: Person$\times$Person $\rightarrow$ Powerset(Person$\times$integer$\times$integer)
Find(p_1,p_2) =
$\quad$ {(p_3,d_1,d_2) |
$\qquad$ $\exists a_{1,i},a_{2,j},i \in \{1..d_1\},j \in \{1..d_2\}$ |
$\qquad$ $a_{1,1}{=}p_1 \wedge a_{2,1}{=}p_2 \wedge a_{1,d_1}{=}a_{2,d_2}{=}p_3 \wedge$
$\qquad$ $\forall k \in [1,2] \forall m \in [2..d_k]\ a_{k,m} \in$ Parents($a_{k,m-1}$)$\wedge$
$\qquad$ ((not IsAncestor(a_{1,d_1-1},p_2))$\vee$(not IsAncestor(a_{2,d_2-1},p_1))) }
where IsAncestor(x,y) =
$\quad$ $\exists n{\geq}0$ | $\exists b_i,i \in \{1..n\}$ | $b_1{=}x \wedge b_n{=}y \wedge b_i \in$ Parents(b_{i-1})
where Parents(x) =
$\quad$ { y | y$=$Mother(x) or y$=$Father(x) }

Figure 6–13: Specification of Find Procedure

Name:	The name of the interface procedure.
Parameters:	Parameter types, possibly with parameter names used in other sections of the specification.
Results:	Type of values returned by the interface procedure.
Initial Value:	If the value of the interface procedure is changed by some other interface procedures, this specifies the value before any of the others are called.
Value:	An expression involving the parameters, if the value of the interface procedure can be defined this way.
Effects:	Side effects of the interface procedure, expressed in terms of other, value-returning interface procedures.
Exceptions:	Boolean expressions indicating circumstances under which the interface procedure cannot proceed normally, and must report an undesired event to its callers.

Figure 6–14: Information in a Specification

6.4.1 Specification Content

Figure 6–14 lists the information a specification might contain. Not every procedure needs all this information. For example, a procedure with an initial value will likely have neither a value nor an effect. Instead, the effect of some other procedure defines its value. Figure 6–15 shows a pair of procedures that illustrate some of these ideas. These are part of some module that defines a type, Item; its secret is the representation of type Item. FetchSubitem and StoreSubitem fetch and store some particular component of the information contained in an Item. The specification shows the effect of StoreSubitem as changing the value FetchSubitem reports.

Each specification technique has its own way of expressing this information. Part III discusses several techniques. Some of them cannot deal with side effects, and so will not have anything corresponding to initial value or effects. Many techniques combine the name, parameter types, and possible values into a *signature* such as

$$\text{FetchSubitem: Item} \rightarrow \text{SubItem}$$

which says that FetchSubitem takes an Item as a parameter and returns a SubItem.

Figure 6–16 shows a specification of a table lookup module. It illustrates several points about such specifications.

1. It defines the value of Lookup implicitly through the side effects of Init-Table, Enter, and Delete.

2. Specifications with side effects need some way of distinguishing between expressions evaluated before any side effects take place, and those evaluated afterward. A typical convention is normally to evaluate expressions after side effects take place, while evaluating expressions in single quotes before side effects take place. Thus the Effect clause for the Enter procedure says that the value of Lookup(k) after side effects take place is (true, i); the Exceptions clause says it is an undesired event if Lookup returns (true, anything) before side effects take place.

3. An interface procedure may return several results, as well as taking several parameters. Section 7.2.1 shows how to implement returning multiple results in typical programming languages.

Name:	FetchSubitem	**Name:**	StoreSubitem
Parameters:	Item I	**Parameters:**	Item I, subitem J
Results:	Subitem	**Results:**	None
Initially:	Undefined	**Effect:**	FetchSubitem(I) = J

Figure 6–15: Fetch/Store Pair of Interface Procedures

Name: Lookup
Parameters: Key
Results: Boolean, Item + {undefined}
Initially: $\forall$ k, Lookup(k) = (false,undefined)

Name: Enter
Parameters: Key k, Item i
Effect: Lookup(k) = (true,i)
Exceptions: if $\exists$ i$\in$Item | 'Lookup(k)' = (true,i) then
                    ErrAlreadyEntered

Name: Delete
Parameters: Key k
Effect: Lookup(k) = (false,undefined)
Exceptions: if $\neg \exists$i$\in$Item | 'Lookup(k)' = (true,i) then ErrNotPresent

Name: InitTable
Effect: $\forall$ k, Lookup(k) = (false,undefined)

Figure 6–16: Sample Specification: Table Module

Name: FetchVal   **Name:**   SetVal
Results: Element + {undefined} **Parameters:** Element e
Initially: Undefined   **Effect:**   FetchVal = e
Exceptions: if FetchVal = undefined then
                 ErrUndefinedVal

Figure 6–17: Fetch/Store Pair with Undefined

6.4.2 Undefined Values

A specification often uses some notion of the undefined values for a function. Figure 6–17 shows an example; clients may not call FetchVal until some client calls SetVal. Figure 6–18 shows how to obtain a similar effect without using undefined values. The interface provides the procedure HasVal to detect whether some client

Name:	FetchVal	**Name:**	SetVal
Results:	Element	**Parameters:**	Element e
Exceptions:	if not HasVal then	**Effect:**	FetchVal = e and
	ErrUndefinedVal		HasVal = true

Name:	HasVal
Results:	Boolean
Initially:	False

Figure 6–18: Fetch/Store Pair without Undefined

Name:	FetchVal	**Name:**	SetVal
Results:	Element + {undefined}	**Parameters:**	Element e
Exceptions:	if FetchVal = undefinedthen	**Effect:**	FetchVal = e
	ErrUndefinedVal		

Name:	HasVal
Results:	Boolean
Value:	FetchVal = undefined

Figure 6–19: Fetch/Store Pair with HasVal and Undefined

has called SetVal. The major difference between the two is that clients of the second may ask whether someone has called SetVal. Figure 6–19 shows a third possibility that shares characteristics of both.

6.4.3 Implementation Languages

The specification outline of Figure 6–14 avoided syntactic details of the implementation language, as do the specification techniques of Part III. This lets you use the same specification for different implementations in different languages. However, many implementors find the gap between such specifications and their implementation languages too large for comfort.

Section 7.2 discusses how to recast a specification into particular implementation language. This process involves deciding what language construct (procedure, function, macro, and so forth) to use to implement each interface procedure, and how to report undesired events to clients. Specifying a module and recasting that specification are separate tasks. However, the specification most useful to an implementor, as opposed to a designer, is the one that results from recasting. A project pressed for time might consider merging these into one step, and write the "recast" specifications without an original, language-independent specification.

Figure 6–20 shows a Pascal recasting of the specification of Figure 6–16. It uses Pascal function and procedure definitions to define each interface procedure's name, parameters, and results. The Enter procedure reports exception ErrAlreadyEntered via a status result; Delete reports ErrNotPresent via a boolean return value. I phrased the Effect and Exceptions clauses slightly differently from the ones of Figure 6–16 on page 78, but they convey similar information.

6.4.4 Specifying Input/Output Operations

For modules that maintain some internal data structure, it is easy to imagine how a specification supplying the information outlined in Figure 6–14 might tell the implementor and users of the module enough to know what it does. It is harder to see

---

function Lookup(k:key; **var** i:Item):boolean;
Initially: ∀ k, Lookup(k,i) = false
                  Lookup never reads i, just sets it. Whenever Lookup
                  returns false, i remains untouched.

procedure Enter(k:Key, i:Item, **var** s:Status);
Effect: Lookup(k,i1) = true; i1 = i; s = EnterOK
Exceptions: if 'Lookup(k,i)' = true then sets s to ErrAlreadyEntered
                  and does not change the effect of Lookup.

function Delete(k:key):boolean;
Effect: Lookup(k,i) = false
Result: Returns true iff 'Lookup(k,i)'. The specification
                  considered this to be an undesired event.

procedure InitTable;
Effect: ∀ k, Lookup(k,i) = false

Figure 6–20: Sample Pascal-Level Specification: Table Module

---

how to specify a module that hides the format of an input or output file without revealing too many implementation details. For example, if a module hides the format of an input file, it is hard to see how to say much besides

Name: GetInput
Effect: Read contents of input file

To give any further information the specification must say something about the information contained in the input file, which was part of the secret of the module. The Command module of Appendix E.2 is an example of a weak input specification of this sort.

A slightly better approach is to use equations showing conditions that must be true of internal data structures after reading a correct input file. The GetFile procedure of the GenFile module in Appendix E.4 shows an example of this approach. It gives a weak description of the overall effect of GetFile, then follows with an explanatory paragraph that reveals the format of the input file, then gives equations describing the correspondence between information in the input file and information in the internal database.

The fundamental problem is that the naive description of the module's purpose (reading the input file) contains two secrets: the format of the input file, and the processing required to translate the information from the input file into an internal representation. Similarly, a command module of this sort hides the syntax of the command line (or the sequence of menus that collect information from the user) as well as the semantics of individual commands.

An alternative is to split input modules in two: one that retrieves information from the input file, and another that translates information from the input file into internal representations. The first is amenable to normal methods of specification. The second is a sequence of calls on operations provided by the modules implementing the internal representation. Information hiding has no good way of specifying sequencing; the best way to "specify" a sequencing module may simply be to write a pseudo-code sketch.

For example, the genealogical input file of Section E.4 contains a sequence of lines of the form

XName$_1$*Name$_2$*Name$_3$*

Each line defines one person in the family tree. Name$_1$ is the person's name; Name$_2$ and Name$_3$ are the names of that person's father and mother, respectively. X is a letter (M or F, in either upper or lower case) saying whether the person is male or female. The module of Figure 6–21 reflects the information content of this file. OpenFile, HasInput, GetLine, and CloseFile are the Initialize, Finished, Advance, and Finish operations of an iterator. You can then capture the semantics of the input file with a pseudo-code sketch like that of Figure 6–22. Notice the similarity and the differences between this and the sketch of Figure G–3 on page 261.

---

procedure OpenFile(f:file);
{ Open an input file. Must be called before HasInput or
  CloseFile. }

function HasInput:boolean;
{ Returns true iff the current input file contains more data. }

procedure NextLine(**var** Sex:boolean;
    var ThisName,Fathername,MotherName:Name);
{ Retreive the information from the current input line. Call
  this procedure only after HasInput returns true. }

procedure CloseFile;
{ Close current input file. }

Figure 6–21: Information-Hiding Input Interface

---

procedure HandleInputLine(sex:boolean;name1,name2,name3:name);
    if name1 already in table
        then
            if already defined (that is, has parents)
                then report duplicate definition
            endif
        else make new person P1; enter in table
    endif
    father := FindParent(name2,male);set father of P1
    mother := FindParent(name3,female);set mother of P1
end HandleInputLine

Figure 6–22: Sketch of Input Line Semantics

6.4.5 Summary Information

Once you have prepared the specification of a module, you can derive summaries from the main information in a module specification. The specification of an interface procedure states what undesired events the procedure may report, and what value-returning procedures it affects. It is useful to present this information the other way around. If several interface procedures report exceptions, compile a table, sorted by name of exception, showing what procedures report each exception. This is especially useful if several procedures report the same exception. Similarly, compile a table with an entry for each value-returning procedure saying what procedures affect its value.

Whenever you report the same information in multiple places (such as in a specification and the corresponding summary), you run the danger of having one of them be incorrect. It is best if you can use a program to produce the summaries from the original specifications, which may require that you impose some formatting restrictions on the specifications.

6.5   Restricted Interfaces

A specification defines an interface to a module; it gives information about the module that is unlikely to change. If client modules depend only on the specification, then they should not need to change if the secret hidden by the module changes.

Sometimes information in an interface is likely to change. For example, a module may define an interface to a device; you may plan to replace the current device eventually. Some control functions for the current device may not be applicable on the new one; you may be unable to use the methods of Section 6.1.1 to hide the differences. The only way of limiting the effects of changes to these functions is to label them as restricted. You mark the interface procedures in some way, and say that only certain modules may call them. When the device changes, the device interface module and any clients of the restricted procedures must change. Ideally only one module must change when an implementation changes, but restricted interfaces at least force you to document what else must change. The module will likely export many nonrestricted procedures; clients of these procedures need never change.

Another reason for restricted interfaces arises when a module implements some type, and one (or at most a few) client modules require an extended version of the type to represent a relationship among objects of the type, or between those objects and objects of different types. For example, a module might represent the *is enrolled in* relation between students and courses. Quickly finding a student's courses may require storing information about courses in the object representing a student. However, only the enrollment module should make use of the interface procedures having to do with courses, since those procedures would disappear if the maintainer decided to represent the information differently.

For another example, the Find algorithm of Figure 6–12 on page 74 requires the procedures NumWaysRelated, AddRelation, and Distance defined on Persons. No other client of the Person module needs these procedures, and they might change or disappear if the Find algorithm changes. Section E.6 in the Appendices specifies the Person module; only the Find module may call certain procedures. I have marked their names with an "(R)."

You might object that Find should build its own auxiliary data structures to provide the information it gets via these restricted procedures. However, Find does not know the details of how to represent Persons; the procedures must be part of the Person module to record information directly with the representation of Persons. Without the IndexPerson/IthPerson pair of procedures, there is no way to build auxiliary data structures to store information about Persons.

Further Reading

Parnas (1977a) discusses using specifications in software development. I based Section 6.1.1 on his papers on designing abstract interfaces [Parnas 1977b], and on designing device interface modules [Britton et al. 1981].

Exercises

6–1   Write a small program that reads an unsorted sequence of numbers from a file, then repeatedly asks the user to choose from the following commands.

- Print the largest element of the sequence.
- Print the smallest element of the sequence.
- Report where in the sequence a particular number occurs.

As part of your program, design a sequence module that implements the following capabilities.

- Test whether the sequence is empty.
- Append an element to the end of the sequence.
- Iterate over members of the sequence.

Implement this program twice, once with sequences based on arrays, and once with sequences based on linked lists. Ensure that you do not change any code outside the sequence module while swapping implementations. If your implementation language supports separate compilation, compile your main program and your sequence module separately.

6–2   Extend the sequence package of Exercise 6–1 to include an editor that supplies the following operations.

- Insert before the current element. After the next *Advance*, the current element should be the newly inserted element.
- Insert after the current element. After the next *Advance*, the current element should be the newly inserted element.

- Delete the current element. No further operations on the current element are legal. After the next *Advance*, the current element should be the one after the deleted element.

Be sure you consider boundary conditions, such as deleting or inserting at the beginning and end of the sequence.

6–3   If a module exports an editor for a collection, is there any reason clients would want an iterator over the same collection?

6–4   As part of a program for generating multilevel indices, you are designing modules to implement references to entire sections. One input is a file of table-of-contents information, where each line is of the form

$$\text{level title page}_1 \text{ page}_2 \text{ section}$$

"Level" means the depth of section (1 for a chapter, 2 for a section within a chapter, and so forth). "Title" is the title of the chapter or section, enclosed in double quotes. "Section" is the number of the chapter or section (for example, 4.2.5). "Page$_1$" and "Page$_2$" are page numbers. For obscure implementation reasons, page$_1$ is the number of the last page of the previous section, and page$_2$ is the number of the first page of the section described by the line in question. They are identical unless the section title appears at the top of the page, in which case page$_2$=page$_1$+1.

A second file contains section references, of the form

$$\text{information section}$$

where "section" is a chapter or section number as in the table-of-contents file; you will use it as a key to connect the information from the section reference file to the page numbers of the table-of-contents file. Your job is to generate an output file of the form

$$\text{information page}_A \text{ page}_B$$

where page$_A$ and page$_B$ are the first and last pages of the section whose number appears on the input line. At the moment, the requirements document for your system says that a reference to a section includes all the pages of subsections it contains. However, you expect that certain clients may insist the definition change to exclude contained subsections.

Design a module to hide the definition of page ranges for section references, so that only this one module need change if the requirement changes. Describe in a few sentences how other modules in the system will use the one you design.

Project Exercises

6–5   Determine what subset you will implement of the project you began in Chapter 4, and what subset of the modules from Chapter 5 you will need.

For each of these modules, assign a person to write the specification of the module, and a different person to implement the specification. If your group has enough members, assign a third person to write the unit test plan for the module (see Chapter 8). This gives you maximum incentive to write clear specifications.

Compile a list of what interface procedures your module should export, with their parameters and results. Give a brief English description of what each procedure should do. Review your list with the person who will implement your module, and with the people who will specify and implement modules that depend on your module.

6–6   Refine your English descriptions from Exercise 6–5 into a precise specification. Use a method from Part III (preferably Chapter 12 or Chapter 13) if possible. See Appendix E for examples.

_____ Chapter 7 _____

Module
_____ Implementation _____

So far you have seen how to

1. Determine and record the requirements a large system must meet.
2. Break up a large system into modules.
3. Specify what functionality a module must provide.

You must now

1. Represent each module as a unit in your implementation language.
2. Determine how to cast the specification into our implementation language.
3. Design the implementation of the module.
4. Code the module.

Sections 7.1 through 7.4 discuss each of these issues in order.

7.1 Representing Modules

Chapter 5 said that the key idea of a module is a collection of related programming-language entities such as procedures and types. Each module should be small enough to understand on its own, and small enough to form a suitable work assignment for a single person. Each module should restrict its relations with other modules to reduce the complexity of the system.

With any programming language you have some way to represent modules. At the low end, the language has no module facilities of its own, and you must make do with simple tools outside the language. At the high end, the language has full facilities for defining modules as separate units, describing relations among modules, and combining modules into systems. The following sections discuss three important points on this scale.

7.1.1 No Module Facilities

Some languages have no built-in facilities for dividing programs into modules. You can still write your program as a collection of separate files, and combine the files to form the full program. You should try to find and use a file inclusion program to

---

```
program Main(input,output);
const
%INCLUDE module1.const
%INCLUDE module2.const
%INCLUDE module3.const
type
%INCLUDE module1.typ
%INCLUDE module2.typ
%INCLUDE module3.typ
var
%INCLUDE module1.var
%INCLUDE module2.var
%INCLUDE module3.var
{ forward declarations for all procedures }
%INCLUDE module1.fwd
%INCLUDE module2.fwd
%INCLUDE module3.fwd
{ bodies of procedures }
%INCLUDE module1.body
%INCLUDE module2.body
%INCLUDE module3.body
begin
calls to appropriate initialization routines
call top-level procedure of program
end.
```

Figure 7–1: Pascal Inclusion Skeleton

---

assist in putting the pieces together. Such a program takes an input file containing ordinary text and copies it to its output. Some lines of the input file contain file inclusion commands naming other files. Each such command tells the inclusion program to replace the line with the contents of the other file.

Figure 7–1 shows the skeleton of a Pascal program with three modules. Because of Pascal's rules about order of declarations, each module consists of five files. X.const contains constant declarations for module X. X.typ contains type declarations. X.var contains its variable declarations. X.fwd contains **forward** declarations for all procedures and functions of the module that you might refer to from other modules. You need it only if your *uses* hierarchy has cycles; otherwise you could simply topologically sort the *uses* relation, and include the files in the reverse order. Finally, X.body contains the bodies of the procedures and functions.

This scheme does let you build and test subsets of a large system. However, it requires much effort to recompile the whole system when you change any part of it. Also, it provides no distinction between names that should be local to a module and those that should be visible to other modules. Thus you need to impose strict naming conventions to avoid having one module define an internal procedure that conflicts with one from a different module.

The only help that this scheme gives to information hiding is that placing things in separate files makes it clear where you believe the module boundaries should go. There are two important classes of violations of information hiding that you must check manually.

1. The implementor of a module can write code that calls any procedure of any other module (or at least, of any module that appears before his or her module).

2. Any code that can declare a variable of some type can access the representation of the type.

The listing typically shows no sign of the original %INCLUDE substructure. To make the boundaries between included files clear, place comments at the beginning and end of each file giving its name. For example, at the start of X.typ you might say

    { start of types from module X }

7.1.2 Separate Compilation

Compiling a large program can take a long time. If you change a small section, it is wasteful to recompile all the other unaffected portions of the program. Thus many languages have facilities for compiling programs in several separate sections. If a language lacks such a facility, compiler implementors have often tacked on some form of it. Although separate compilation started as an efficiency measure, you can use it as a modularity mechanism.

When you compile a program as a unit, each procedure can call any other procedure you declared before it. When you split the program into separate sections, you must tell the compiler what procedures from other sections you intend to call. Typically, if procedures in module X want to call procedure P from module Y, you must place a declaration of the form

procedure P(parm$_1$: type$_1$; $\cdots$; parm$_N$: type$_N$); **external**;

in module X. You must usually also place it in module Y, so that the compiler knows it must arrange to make P accessible to other modules. You can combine this with the file inclusion facility of the previous section; Figure 7–2 shows the skeleton of module3, which uses module1 and module2. The module file starts with some keyword (such as **segment**) other than **program**. It typically has no **begin/end** block, unlike a main program (but some extensions use such blocks to contain module initialization code). The included files have some differences from those of Figure 7–1 on page 88. The X.const, X.typ, and X.proc files contain only those constants, types, and procedures that module X exports. Things that module X uses internally appear directly in the file containing module X.

```
segment module3;
const
%INCLUDE module1.const
%INCLUDE module2.const
%INCLUDE module3.const { constants exported from module3 }
{ constants local to module3 go here }
type
%INCLUDE module1.typ
%INCLUDE module2.typ
%INCLUDE module3.typ { types exported from module3 }
{ types local to module3 go here }
var
... { module 3 variables go here }
{ external declarations for all procedures imported and exported }
%INCLUDE module1.proc
%INCLUDE module2.proc
%INCLUDE module3.proc
{ bodies of procedures for module3 go here }
```

Figure 7–2: Pascal Separate Compilation Skeleton

These facilities make information hiding a little easier. You must explicitly decide what procedures to allow other modules to call. However, any code that declares an object of some type can still manipulate the representation of the object.

7.1.3 Module Constructs

Several languages that appeared in the late 1970s have explicit constructs to represent modules. The details (and even the names) of such constructs vary from language to language, but they have three common characteristics.

1. You can explicitly bracket and name a collection of declarations to draw a distinction between what is inside a module and what is outside.

2. You can permit the code within a module to perform operations forbidden to clients of the module.

3. The language constructs let the compiler check your restrictions automatically.

The two primary examples of the second characteristic are that you can restrict access to the representation of a type (for example, you can prevent clients from fetching components of a record or array), and you can declare procedures that you can call from within the module that clients cannot call.

In addition to the first three common characteristics, some of the modern languages have additional facilities that help with modular decomposition.

4. You can represent the *uses* relation explicitly (such as via Ada's **with** clause).

5. You can physically separate the specification of the module (the list of characteristics outsiders can depend on) from its implementation (for example, Ada separates a package specification from a package body). Thus you can tell whether to recompile clients of a module by looking at the date of change of the specification.[1]

6. You can give a body of initialization code, which the language implementation will execute for you automatically.

To be useful for dividing work among several people, the language must also provide a separate compilation facility or a file inclusion facility so programmers can work independently on modules in separate files.

7.2 Casting Specifications into Implementations

With most specification techniques you have several choices about how to represent items from the specification in your implementation languages. You must at least

---

[1]You may have more complex decision criteria, but this simple one often gives reasonable results.

decide how to represent each interface procedure, and how to detect and report undesired events.

7.2.1   Interface Procedures

The syntactic specification of an interface procedure gives its signature (parameters and return types). One specification technique may require you to say

> Name: Add
> Parameters: complex a,b
> Result: complex c

while another requires

> Add: complex $\times$ complex $\rightarrow$ complex

In implementation languages one adds the complexities of parameter passing modes, side effects, and limitations on parameter and result types. In most programming languages there are four possible ways to implement interface procedures: functions, procedures, constants, and macros.

If an interface procedure returns a result, consider implementing it as a function. Thus the above interface procedure specification might become

function Add(a,b: Complex) : Complex;

However, some languages place restrictions on what results a function may return. Most Pascal implementations do not allow records or arrays as return types. You might therefore recast the function as a procedure with a result parameter:

procedure Add(a,b: Complex;
        var c: Complex);   { output parameter }

Furthermore, efficiency considerations might dictate that you pass large objects like arrays and records by reference, to avoid the cost of making a local copy within the procedure. Thus you might write

procedure Add(**var** a,b: Complex;   { input parameters }
        var c: Complex);   { output parameter }

In both cases the comments tell a reader what is really going on.

Few implementation languages allow functions to return multiple results. In these languages you have three choices:

1. You can implement the interface procedure as a procedure with multiple result parameters.

2. If the language allows functions to return records, you can build and return a record with one component for each result.

3. If the language allows functions to have output parameters, you can pick one result to return as the value of the function and return the others as output parameters.

Lookup: key $\rightarrow$ boolean, ItemType + {undefined}
Initially: $\forall$ k, Lookup(k) = (false, undefined)

Enter: key k, ItemType i
Effect: Lookup(k) = (true, i)
           $\forall$ i$\in$key, i$\neq$k $\rightarrow$ Lookup(i) = 'Lookup(i)'
procedure Lookup(k: key; **var** Found:boolean; **var** Val:ItemType);

type LookupResult = **record** Found:boolean; Val:ItemType; **end**;
function Lookup(k: key) : LookupResult;

function Lookup(k: key; **var** Val: ItemType) : boolean;

Figure 7–3: Representing Multiple Returned Values

Figure 7–3 shows these three possibilities. The third is especially common if one result is undefined when the distinguished parameter has a particular value. For example, the ItemType result of the Lookup procedure is undefined if the boolean result is false.

If an interface procedure takes no parameters, returns a single result, and is unaffected by calls on any other interface procedures, you might implement it as a constant. Typical interface procedures of this sort specify some maximum or minimum value.

When first exposed to information hiding, many people claim that all those procedure calls would cost too much. There are two counterarguments to this.

1. Usually only a few procedures have a strong effect on performance. Designers are often wrong in predictions of where the performance bottlenecks will be; the only sure way to find inefficiencies is to measure them. Most often, a performance improvement comes from changing an algorithm or data structure, and this is exactly the type of change that information hiding makes easy.

2. In some languages, such as Mesa and Ada, you may request that the compiler expand certain procedures inline. This means that you have all the efficiency of directly coding the body of the procedure at the point of the call, with all the benefits of information hiding. In languages without such a facility you may have a macro processor or preprocessor, which can provide similar benefits.

7.2.2 Namespace Control

Many programming languages let you use the same name for different things in different contexts. Unfortunately, most linkers impose a flat name space. If any name is visible outside the module that defines it, no other object may have the same name. To avoid accidentally duplicating names, you may need to impose namespace control early in the project. You may need to do this as early as the time you write the specification, since the procedure in the implementation should have the same name as the procedure in the specification.

The classic technique for controlling name space is to assign a short one-character or two-character prefix to each module, and ensure that all procedures in that module have names that start with that prefix. Unfortunately, some linkers still impose severe restrictions on how many characters an externally visible name may have — sometimes as few as six. This leaves few characters left over to give readable names. A partial solution, if your language has a macro preprocessor, is to define long names as macros that expand to the short names. Unfortunately, any debugging or cross-reference aids of your language system will present information using the cryptic short names.

7.2.3 Undesired Event Handling

Most specification techniques have some way of saying that under certain conditions an interface procedure cannot proceed normally. It is an *undesired event* or *exception* whenever an interface procedure detects that something has gone wrong. You might want to call such events *errors*, but people generally regard "error" as meaning a program bug. For clarity, this textbook avoids the term "error," using *exception* to mean a detected undesired event, and *defect* to mean a flaw in the program. Figure 7–4 gives an example of an exception. It shows a procedure for entering a

---

Name:	Enter
Parameters:	key k, Element e
Effect:	Lookup(k) = (true, e)
	$\forall$ i$\in$key, i$\neq$k $\rightarrow$ Lookup(i) = 'Lookup(i)'
	NumInTable = 'NumInTable' + 1
Exceptions:	if 'Lookup(k)' $\neq$ (false, undefined) then
	ErrAlreadyPresent
	if 'NumInTable' = MaxInTable then ErrTableFull

Figure 7–4: Specification of Exceptions

---

new element into a fixed-size table that reports an undesired event if the element already exists or if the table is full.

There are currently six methods for communicating information about exceptions between a module and its clients.

1. Use a language-specific exception reporting mechanism.

2. Return a status result from the interface procedure.

3. Call an exception-reporting procedure passed to the interface procedure.

4. Call a global exception-reporting procedure.

5. Set a status variable.

6. Ignore the possibility of exceptions.

Not every language allows all these possibilities. The following paragraphs discuss them in more detail.

```
type EnterStatus = (EnterOK, EnterFull, EnterAlready);

procedure Enter(k:key; e:element; var Code:EnterStatus);
   begin
      if key already in table then
         Code := EnterAlready
      else if room left in table then
         begin
            Code := EnterOK; put element in table
         end
      else Code := EnterFull
   end;
...
{ caller }
   var ret : EnterStatus;
   ...
   Enter(key1, value1, ret);
   case ret of
      EnterOK:     proceed normally
      EnterFull:    report no room in table
      EnterAlready: report in table already
   end;
```

Figure 7–5: Exception Reporting via Returning a Status

```
type TableStatus = (TableOK, TableFull, TableAlready, ...);
var Status: TableStatus; { hidden from callers }

function GetStatus:TableStatus;
   begin GetStatus := Status end;

procedure Enter(k:key; e:element);
   begin
      if key already in table then
         Status := TableAlready
      else if room left in table then
         begin Status := TableOK; put element in table end
      else Status := TableFull
   end;
   ...
{ caller }
   Enter(key1, value1);
   case GetStatus of
      TableOK:        proceed normally
      TableFull:      report no room in table
      TableAlready:   report in table already
      TableNotFound:  can't happen
   end;
```

Figure 7–6: Exception Reporting via Global Status

A status code is a value from an enumeration type, corresponding to a particular undesired event. You might have one enumeration type for each interface procedure, or one enumeration type for the whole module. The first is preferable on the principle of separation of concerns; it lets you consider each interface procedure separately from every other. The second may be appropriate if several interface procedures report overlapping sets of exceptions, or if there are many interface procedures in the module. You must use a global status type to report exceptions by setting a module-wide status variable. If a procedure reports only one exception, you might choose to return a boolean status code. If you do so, you should try to be consistent from procedure to procedure (and module to module) about whether **true** means that the exception happened, or that the procedure returned normally. Figure 7–5 shows an implementation of the Enter procedure of Figure 7–4 by returning a status code. Figure 7–6 shows an implementation using a global status code; clients access the status by calling a function, so that they cannot change the status. The case statement examining the status should have an entry for exceptions that Enter should not report; it is amazing how often "impossible" exceptions really happen.

Languages like Ada have mechanisms designed for reporting undesired events. Figure 7–7 shows how to report undesired events via Ada exceptions. If the call to Enter succeeds, the system executes the statements after the call up to the keyword **exception,** then proceeds with whatever follows the keyword **end**. If Enter executes a **raise,** the system abandons the execution of Enter, then goes to the exception handler at the end of the block containing the call on Enter. It then executes the **when** clause corresponding to the exception that Enter raised, or the **when others** clause if Enter or something it called raised some other exception. Ada exceptions are considerably more complex than this, but the example shows a constrained use of the facility.

```
exception EnterFull;
exception EnterAlready;

procedure Enter(k:key; e:element) is
begin
    if key already in table then raise EnterAlready
        elsif room left in table then put element in table
        else raise EnterFull
    end if
end Enter;
...
-- caller
    begin
        Enter(key1, value1);
        proceed normally
    exception
        when EnterFull  = >      report no room in table
        when EnterAlready = >     report in table already
        when others  = >         can't happen
    end;
```

Figure 7–7: Exception Reporting via Special Construct

If the implementation language allows it, you can pass procedures as parameters to the interface procedure. Figure 7–8 shows a Pascal example. When it detects an undesired event, the interface procedure calls the appropriate parameter, which can take any action it chooses. This mechanism is flexible. The interface procedure can pass parameters to the exception procedure to give it more detailed information on what has gone wrong. The exception procedures should not return to the interface procedure; otherwise they are part of a recovery mechanism, which may be considerably more complex than simple exception reporting. In Figure 7–8, the exception-reporting procedures use a nonlocal **goto** to exit the block in which the undesired event occurs. Some people do not like the idea of nonlocal **goto**s. Tennent (1981) shows an alternative mechanism called sequencer procedures; you could look on Figure 7–8 as a simulation of this higher-level facility.

In languages that provide them, the interface procedure might call a procedure variable to report an undesired event. Figure 7–9 shows an example in the C language. This might be appropriate if there is a particular action that is usually

```
procedure Enter(k:key; e:element;
      procedure EnterFull; procedure EnterAlready);
   begin
      if key already in table then EnterAlready
      else if room left in table then
          put element in table
      else EnterFull
   end;

  ...
{ caller }
   label Done;
   procedure ReportFull;
      begin report no room in table; goto Done end;
   procedure ReportAlready;
      begin report in table already; goto Done end;
   begin
      Enter(key1, value1, ReportFull, ReportAlready);
      proceed normally;
   Done:
   end;
```

Figure 7–8: Exception Reporting via Exit Procedures

best for recovery from certain undesired events, but the details of the recovery vary from program to program. The module would provide a default value for the procedure variable; callers might supply a different value, and might save and restore the old value to temporarily override the current value. You should take care in using this scheme, since your program becomes harder to understand when it has a dynamically changing procedure calling relation.

Sometimes it may be appropriate to call a fixed procedure rather than a parameter. For example, a catastrophic failure might force you to abort the whole program. This scheme has almost no flexibility; you cannot easily make the procedure specific to particular callers.

Finally, you might decide not to check for undesired events and thus not report them. This makes sense only for events corresponding to program bugs. It is common to have checking in debugging versions of the system, but to turn it off in

---

```
int DoNothing() { return(0); }
int (*EnterFull)() = DoNothing,
   (*EnterAlready)() = DoNothing;
Enter(k,e)
   key k; element e;
{  if (key already in table) (*EnterAlready)();
   else if (room left in table)
      put element in table;
   else (*EnterFull)();    }
...
/* caller */
static int OK;
static int ReportFull()
   { report no room in table; OK = 0; }
static int ReportAlready()
   { report in table already; OK = 0; }
...
EnterFull = ReportFull; EnterAlready = ReportAlready;
...
OK = 1; Enter(key1, value1);
if (OK) proceed normally;
```

Figure 7–9: Exception Reporting via Procedure Variables

---

production versions for improved performance. This is dangerous, since few delivered systems are free of bugs. Nevertheless, some systems have extremely severe performance requirements, and the developers may feel forced into this approach. If you can prove that clients never invoke an interface procedure in a way that causes an exception, you can safely remove the checking. For example, if all callers of the Enter procedure already check whether the key is present, there is no need to check within Enter itself.

7.2.4 Undefined Values

Sometimes a specification will refer to special undefined values. For example, the Lookup procedure of Figure 6–16 on page 78 and Figure 7–3 on page 93 returns undefined for its second result if its first result is false. It is usually wrong for an implementation to try to use an undefined value. Callers of Lookup can avoid trying to use the second result if the first is false, since for Lookup the specification is clear about when the result is undefined.

Figure 7–10 is an example of a specification where a procedure may return an undefined value; it is an undesired event if this happens. GetParam is initially undefined, and only SetParam changes it. This means that some client must call SetParam before any client calls GetParam. If you have some way to guarantee this (such as some tool or validation procedure that examines the code to prove that someone calls SetParam before anyone calls GetParam), you can ignore the question of implementing this undefined value and the ErrParamUndefined exception. In the absence of such a guarantee you may decide to implement the checking at runtime, which means you must implement the undefined value. GetParam and SetParam are a fetch/store procedure pair that you might implement using a global variable (invisible to callers). You might represent the undefined value as a constant outside the legal range (such as 0 or 101). Module initialization (see Section 7.2.5) would set the variable to this value, and GetParam would check whether the current value is this special undefined value. If the representation does not permit an extra value

---

Name:	GetParam	Name:	SetParam
Results:	1..100 + {undefined}	**Parameters:**	I ∈ 1..100
Initially:	Undefined	**Effect:**	GetParam = I
Exceptions:	if GetParam = undefined then ErrParamUndefined		

Figure 7–10: Undefined Return Value

(such as when any integer is a possible value), you might add a boolean flag to the representation to record whether any client has called SetParam.

7.2.5   Initialization

Often there is some work to do before clients may call any of the interface procedures of the module. Typically one needs to initialize data structures. Sometimes the specification explicitly names an initialization procedure. This can be confusing; you need to distinguish between once-only initialization, done at program startup, and reinitialization, done each time clients begin some particular activity.

Ideally, your implementation language provides some facilities for automatic initialization. Some languages allow you to initialize variables explicitly at the point of their declaration. The body of an Ada package can specify a sequence of statements to execute during initialization.

If your language lacks such a facility, you need to simulate it. If you call your module X, add an interface procedure InitX whose body contains all the appropriate initialization code. Your main module should call an initialization procedure whose purpose is to call all the initialization procedures of the other modules in the correct order. This would make your main module depend on all other modules; you might want to create a separate initialization module to save recompilation time when module specifications change.

It can be hard to determine a reasonable initialization order. If your *uses* relation has no loops, you can use any of its topological sorts. If *uses* has loops, try defining and sorting the *initcalls* relation. Module X initcalls module Y if the initialization procedure of module X calls procedures of module Y; if module X has no initialization procedure, it doesn't initcall any other modules. If even this relation has loops, your last hope is to see if you can eliminate some arcs from initcalls. Eliminate the arc from X to Y whenever module X initcalls module Y, but X's initialization only calls procedures of Y that do not really depend on whatever Y's initialization does. All this peering into the insides of modules is perilous, since it gives results that might change whenever you modify a module's implementation. You are much better off making sure the *uses* relation is loop-free in the first place.

7.3   Module Design

You are probably proficient in designing the implementation of small modules, given the detailed specifications of previous design steps. Because of information hiding, no decisions at this stage affect the functionality of the system. Thus under time pressure to get a working system, you can use any implementation decision that meets the specification. This is one approach to prototyping: design module interfaces carefully, then use any implementation with the correct functionality, ignoring performance and capacity requirements. For example, if the final implementation of some large data structure must include complex software memory management and data overlaying, implement the first version with a small memory resident table.

When not prototyping, you cannot entirely ignore performance, or any of the other resource constraints you budgeted for back in module decomposition (Section 5.4). At the start of the implementation phase, you can check your resource budget by writing and measuring one (or a few) modules, then using the ratio between measured and estimated resource consumption to calibrate your resource estimates. If this brings you close to (or over) any of your limits, you must take action to ensure you will meet your budget, by trimming functionality or paying closer attention to the design of those modules with tight budgets.

As with any other design decisions, a developer should record those that are part of the module implementation. As with module specifications, the exact format of the record will vary depending on the size of the project and conventions of the development organization. You might collect all the module implementation descriptions into a single document, with one module per chapter; Appendix G gives an example of such a document. You might have one document per module (typically called a *module development folder*), with the specification, module implementation description, and current listing all together. If the implementation description of a module is simple, you might simply record it in comments at the start of the listing. However, if the description requires diagrams or extensive pseudo-code this might be difficult.

You should consider the possibility of implementing portions of some modules in hardware, especially if you expect to reuse those modules widely in different systems. For example, the operating system for the message switching multiprocessors of DATAPAC (developed at Bell-Northern Research) provided a message queue module. Several processes running in parallel on separate machines might try to access the queue independently. The designers implemented the module as a collection of simple cover procedures that invoked operations on a hardware list processor, which maintained several independent queues. The hardware took care of synchronizing parallel attempts to use the queues, and managed an internal data structure for representing queues.

7.4 Coding

The primary purpose of the coding step is to create a representation for a module that implements the specification according to the method outlined in the implementation description. Any junior programmer should be able to do this. Software engineering concerns impose some constraints on the resulting code.

Coding standards have two purposes: reducing the chance of making mistakes in the implementation, and making it easier for someone to modify the code later. The three major classes of coding standards are style conventions, commenting conventions, and usage conventions. The suggestions in this section may seem too low-level, but you might not be able to see their value without placing them in the context of a large project where someone else will need to read your code months later. Appendix H shows a sample listing.

7.4.1 Style Conventions

Style conventions constrain program layout (indenting, use of blank space to separate sections, one procedure per listing page) and choice of names to make the module easier to understand.

Indenting styles are rules about where to put keywords and how much to indent statements from the beginning of a line. Figure 7–11 shows three different styles of indenting Pascal **if** statements. Variations include

- whether the **end** keyword should line up with the statements in the block it ends, or with the keyword (such as **if** or **else** that began the clause)

- whether **begin** should be on a separate line

- whether it is important for the statements of a **then** clause to line up with those of the **else** clause

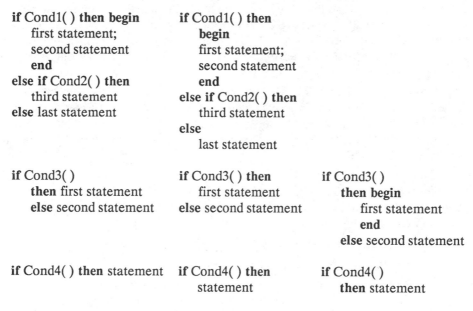

Figure 7–11: Indenting Styles for If Statements

- whether to allow a single statement on the same line as **then** and **else** or to force it to a new line

- how many spaces to indent each level

Many programmers intensely favor one particular indenting style, to the point where they find any other style hard to read. Whatever the merits of individual styles, it is much harder to read code written in a mixture of styles. Thus when you maintain code written by someone else, you should struggle to keep the same indenting style.

7.4.2 Commenting Conventions

Commenting conventions specify how to document the module. I have found the following conventions to be useful.

The first page of the module should state its purpose; the best statement of purpose is a quote from the module decomposition document of what secret the module hides. If the module is in an *is composed of* hierarchy (see Section 5.1.1), it should state what other modules it contains and what modules contain it. If part of the specification is that clients should call procedures in a particular order, this should come next. These three items are what the average user of the module might want to know about the whole module.

After this client-oriented material are comments intended for the maintainer. First should be a change log. Each entry contains the date of a change, the name of the person who made the change, and a brief statement of the change. You need not make the first entry before the first time someone else besides you sees the module. Thus the first comment might be "ready for code walkthrough" or "first version released to users."

Following the change log is a summary of the module design information discussed in Section 7.3. This typically includes brief descriptions of any design information not confined to a single procedure of the module. For example, you might say that your data structure is a list of records sorted alphabetically by some particular string-valued field.

Each procedure, especially the interface procedures, should have comments giving information needed by clients and maintainers. Figure 7–12 gives a sample procedure header comment for the Enter procedure of Figure 7–4 on page 94. The comment contains the following information:

- A brief English statement of the purpose of the procedure.

- Some form of the specification of the procedure.

- Descriptions of all the parameters. State any restrictions on parameter values that are not obvious from the parameter type. For example, a string-valued parameter containing a name might require the extra description

  Person's name, in the form "LastName, First Middle, title" with no extra blanks between parts. Valid titles include ...

```
procedure Enter(var k:key; e:element; var Code:EnterStatus);
{------------------------------------------------------------
{ Enter a new key/element pair into the table.
{
{ Parameters:
{   k,e as under Side Effects.   On normal exit, Code=EnterOK.
{ Side Effects:
{   After Lookup(k1,B1,E1); Enter(k,e,XX); Lookup(k2,B,E)
{     for k2=k we have B=true, E=e
{     for k2=k1<>k we have B=B1 (always), E=E1 (if B1 true)
{ Exceptions:
{   If key already in table (Lookup(k,B,E) gives B=true) set
{     Code to EnterAlready
{   Otherwise if table full (NumInTable=MaxInTable) set
{     Code to EnterFull
{   In either case the table is unchanged
{     (forall k, Lookup(k,B,E) yields same B and E before
{       and after)
{------------------------------------------------------------}
```

Figure 7–12: Procedure Heading Comments

Comments should state how the procedure uses a **var** parameter: for efficiency as an input parameter, to return results, or to modify an actual
parameter in place (an in/out parameter).

- Descriptions of the results of the procedure.

- Descriptions of any side effects of the procedure, other than modifications of
  result parameters. These might include input, output, changes to global variables, or calls to storage allocators.

- Descriptions of undesired events the procedure detects, including how it
  reports them to clients.

- Descriptions of known bugs in the procedure. Normally one simply fixes the
  problem. However, if the fix is difficult or shows up only in restricted circumstances, one sometimes simply documents the bug, if the cost of fixing
  the problem is higher than the benefit. For example, the algorithm used in
  some procedure might fail in obscure circumstances, but the implementor
  might not know a better algorithm.

All these comments should be easy to find. One typically sets them off in a *block
comment* separated from the rest of the program by a line of asterisks or dashes.
Figure 7–13 shows block comments in several languages. In many languages the

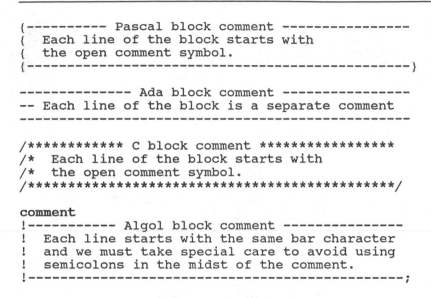

```
{---------- Pascal block comment ----------------
{   Each line of the block starts with
{   the open comment symbol.
{------------------------------------------------}

-------------- Ada block comment ----------------
-- Each line of the block is a separate comment
-------------------------------------------------

/*********** C block comment *****************
/*   Each line of the block starts with
/*   the open comment symbol.
/*****************************************/

comment
!---------- Algol block comment ---------------
!   Each line starts with the same bar character
!   and we must take special care to avoid using
!   semicolons in the midst of the comment.
!-----------------------------------------------;
```

Figure 7–13: Block Comments in Several Languages

opening comment delimiter may appear inside a comment; the block comment is more visible if the open comment delimiter appears at the start of each line. You might also choose to have an end-of-line marker on each comment line, making a rectangle of the whole block, but this may be difficult to keep lined up using some editing programs.

7.4.3 Usage Conventions

Usage conventions constrain how to use the implementation language. Every programming language contains constructs that coders can misuse to write programs that are difficult to understand. Usage conventions forbid certain constructs, or specify that coders should use the constructs in certain ways. Some typical conventions proposed over the years include the following.

1. Use **goto** only to simulate some higher-level control construct. Figure 7–14 shows a Pascal fragment that uses a **goto** to simulate an Ada **exit**.

2. Do not allow side effects from functions. That is, do not assign to global variables from functions, or call procedures that do so. Do not allow **var** or **out** parameters on functions. People reading a program expect a function to simply return a value, and make mistaken assumptions about what is happening if the functions have side effects.

```
-- Ada fragment
loop
    GetNextItem(x,IsPresent);
    exit when not IsPresent;
    ProcessItem;
end loop;

{ Pascal fragment with repeated code }

GetNextItem(x,IsPresent);
while IsPresent do begin
    ProcessItem; GetNextItem(x,IsPresent)
    end;

{ Pascal fragment without repeated code }

while true do
    GetNextItem(x,IsPresent);
    if not IsPresent then goto Done;
    ProcessItem
    end;
Done:
```

Figure 7–14: **Goto** for Loop Exit

3. Order all parameters so that input parameters are first, in/out parameters second, and output parameters last. The order is not as important as the grouping of similar modes, and the consistency from one procedure to the next.

I do not use all these conventions; for example, I believe there are reasonable uses of side effects in functions. Each development organization, or perhaps each project within an organization, might have its own conventions.

Exercises

7–1   Specify a module whose procedures report several different undesired events (such as the Table module of Figure 6–16 on page 78). Design a small program that uses the module. Implement the module and its client twice, with two different exception reporting methods from Section 7.2.3. Compare the two implementations. Which was easier to write? Which is easier to understand?

7–2   Pick any specification you wrote as part of the exercises or project from Chapter 6 or Chapters 11 to 14. Cast these specifications into two different implementation languages, preferably two that differ widely. Compare the results with each other. How close is each result to the form of the original specification?

7–3   Find reference manuals or textbooks describing several different modern languages with module facilities (such as Ada, Alphard, Clu, Mesa, Modula-2). Write a five- to ten-page essay (1,000-2,000 words) comparing these facilities with each other. What are their similarities and differences? How well does each support the software engineering activities discussed in this book?

7–4   Find any program of moderate size (500-1,000 lines) you wrote more than a year ago. Time how long it takes you to determine, in detail, what each procedure does. Keep a log of particular points that puzzled you. How close do the comments in this program come to the standards of Section 7.4? To what extent would following such standards have reduced the time you took to understand the program? What puzzles would still remain? What other coding standards would have helped with these remaining puzzles?

7–5   This exercise requires that you did Exercise 7–4, and does not fit within the time frame of a regular college course. The next time you write a program of similar size and complexity to the one of Exercise 7–4, follow the coding principles of this chapter. A year later, repeat Exercise 7–4 with your new program. Have the coding standards reduced the time it takes you to understand your own program? What other factors complicate trying to compare the two programs?

Project Exercises

7–6   Write a module implementation description for each module you will incorporate into your subset. See Appendix G for examples.

Chapter 8

Testing

Debugging is the search for the cause of defects; it often involves much detective work. *Testing* has much broader scope, and usually assumes you have finished most of the debugging. Testing may uncover problems, which may lead to further debugging. For a large system, the developers must carefully plan the testing.

There are three main kinds of testing. *System testing* involves verifying that a system meets its requirements. However, you must start testing before you put all the modules of your system together. If you link together a large collection of untested modules, when the inevitable defects show up, you will have so many places to look for problems that it will take you a long time to fix the problems and get back to further testing. Thus in a large system you may need to *unit test* single modules in isolation, and slowly build up larger collections of modules to test during *integration testing*.

Testing must try to detect several classes of defect. *Logic defects*, the classic "bugs" you usually think of in debugging, are only one type of defect that testing tries to discover. *Overload defects* are failures that occur when something exceeds the capacity of the system. Testing for this type of defect can be difficult, because it involves generating large amounts of data or many service requests in a short time. *Timing defects* happen in concurrent systems when some event occurs at an unexpected time; they are hard to find because they are hard to repeat. With *performance* or *throughput* problems, the system responds correctly but too slowly. Finally, the *hardware* or *operating system* on which the system relies may fail. Often software systems ignore this class of defect as being outside their control. However,

```
program TableTest(input,output);
   const InitialItem = ...;
   var k:Key; i:Item; Cmd:char;

   { procedures used in DoEnter, DoLookup, etc. }

   procedure GetKey(var k:Key);    ... { read a key from the terminal }
   procedure PrintKey(k:Key);      ... { write a key to the terminal }
   procedure GetItem(var i:Item);  ... { read an item from the terminal }
   procedure PrintItem(i:Item);    ... { write an item to the terminal }

   { Command implementation procedures }

   procedure DoEnter;              ... { see Figure 8-2 }
   procedure DoLookup;             ... { see Figure 8-2 }
   procedure DoInit; begin InitTable end;
   procedure DoDelete;             ... { similar to above }
   procedure DoShow;               ... { see Figure 8-3 }
begin { main program }
   InitTable;  i : = InitialItem;
   write('Initial item '); PrintItem(i); writeln;
   repeat
      read(Cmd);
      if Cmd in ['D','E','I','L','Q','S']
         then case Cmd of begin
            'D': DoDelete;
            'E': DoEnter;
            'I': DoInit;
            'L': DoLookup;
            'Q': { do nothing };
            'S': DoShow
            end
         else writeln('No such command as ',Cmd);
      readln;
   until Cmd = 'Q';
end.
```

Figure 8-1: Test Driver for Table Lookup

designers of systems that manage sensitive or critical data may need to protect against this class of problems.

8.1 Scaffolding

Generally, all but the highest-level modules in a system need some other module to call them. Thus unit testing and integration testing require some form of *scaffolding* to simulate the environment in which the module or collection of modules will run. Scaffolding is software that is not part of the final system; you write it simply to help you test. The term comes from analogies with building construction.

Software scaffolding includes *test drivers* and *stubs*. A test driver reads test data, calls interface procedures of the module you are testing, and reports results or checks for correctness. A stub is an abbreviated version of a module called by the one you are testing.

8.1.1 Test Drivers

To test a module, you need some way of calling its interface procedures and reporting the results of such calls. A test driver is a program that does this for you. A simple test driver might call a subset of the interface procedures in a fixed order; to do different tests, you would edit the driver, recompile, relink, and run the new driver. A more complex driver might allow flexible testing without recompilation by providing a collection of commands you could type from a terminal to invoke tests.

Figure 8–1 shows the skeleton of test driver for the table lookup module of Figures 6–16 on page 78 and 6–20 on page 80. Procedure *main* reads single-character commands from the terminal and selects a procedure to implement each command; a more complex test driver might have a more complex user interface. Figure 8–2 shows the bodies of some of the command implementation procedures. Procedure *DoEnter* is typical. It reads command line arguments corresponding to the input parameters of the *Enter* procedure, calls *Enter,* and reports the results. Procedure *DoLookup* is similar. It always prints the Item result to verify *Lookup* doesn't change it when *Lookup* returns **false**. *Main* reads an Item to ensure that what *DoLookup* prints is never undefined.

It sometimes happens that debugging requires additional interface procedures not needed by most clients. For example, in debugging the table module, the *DoShow* procedure should print all entries in the table, to ensure that an *Enter* or *Delete* affected no other entries but the ones passed as parameters. The interface of Figures 6–16 and 6–20 gave no way to do this; perhaps the intended clients did not need such a procedure. Thus debugging requires an AllTable interface procedure so you can write the DoShow debugging procedure; Figure 8–3 illustrates both of them.

8.1.2 Stubs

Suppose module M1 calls module M2, and you wish to try to debug M1 without the real version of M2. You must write a *stub* for M2 that has the same interface procedures, but provides simpler (or perhaps just different) behavior. This can happen for several reasons.

```
procedure DoEnter;
    var result:Status;
  begin
    GetKey(k); GetItem(i);
    Enter(k,i, result);
    write('Key '); PrintKey(k); write(' item '); PrintItem(s);
    if result=EnterOK
        then writeln(' entered OK')
        else writeln(' already present');
  end { procedure DoEnter };

procedure DoLookup;
    var result:boolean;
  begin
    GetKey(k);
    write('Key '); PrintKey(k);
    result := Lookup(k,i);
    write(' item '); PrintItem(i);
    if not result then write(' not');
    writeln(' found');
  end { procedure DoLookup };
```

Figure 8–2: Command Test Routines for Table Lookup

- The behavior of M2 is complex, but M1 does not really depend on the full behavior to work properly. For example, M1 might be a command dispatch module, and M2 contains procedures implementing a collection of complex commands. A stub for M2 might simply contain procedures that print their names and arguments on the terminal. This lets you ensure that M1 parses arguments correctly, and that it correctly invokes the appropriate action routines.

- The real version of M2 exhibits unrepeatable behavior. This makes debugging extremely difficult; the stub allows debugging by giving predictable behavior. For example, a game program might contain a procedure that chooses randomly among several alternatives. The stub might always pick a particular alternative, or might read alternatives from a file, or might interact with you at your terminal to choose an alternative.

{ within Table module }

...

procedure AllTable(**function** Each(k:Key,i:Item):boolean);
{ Call procedure Each for each key/item pair in the table. Stops early if Each
returns **true**. }

...

{ within main procedure of test driver (Figure 8–1) }
procedure DoShow;
   var Count:Integer;
   function PrintEach(k:Key,i:Item):boolean;
     begin
       PrintKey(k); write(' : '); PrintItem(i); writeln;
       Count : = Count + 1;
       PrintEach : = **false**;
     end;
   begin
     Count : = 0;
     AllTable(PrintEach);
     writeln(Count:1,' entries');
   end;

Figure 8–3: DoShow Procedure, Using AllTable Iterator

- The real version of M2 might interact with peripheral devices that do not
  exist on your test system. This poses problems similar to the previous case.
  The stub might interact with your terminal rather than the actual device, or
  might read input from a file instead of from the actual device. Stubs involving interrupt handling in realtime systems are of this sort.

8.2 Unit Testing

Unit testing involves a single, isolated module. Ideally, you unit test each module
before trying to integrate that module with others. Testing low-level modules
requires drivers to provide input and output; testing high-level modules requires
stubs for missing lower-level modules.

    The entire purpose of unit testing is to reduce the effort of integration testing.
The effort to develop stubs to unit test high-level modules might swamp the benefit
gained by testing them in isolation. Thus, it is common to do pure unit testing only

for the lowest-level modules, or for high-level modules like command dispatchers, where the stubs are easy to write.

Although you might not unit test all modules, you must plan a module test for each module. The plan is simply what data to provide to the module, and what results to expect. You need this plan whether working with the module in isolation, or testing it together with other modules as part of integration. If you have a test driver whose commands correspond exactly to the procedures of your module, you could think of the module test plan as a system test plan for the test driver.

The primary source for test cases for a module test plan is the module specification; some people refer to this as *black box testing*. A module is typically small enough that you can do some *white box testing* as well. In the latter, you look at the code of the module and design test cases that force it through particular statements or patterns of statements in a module. For example, for an **if** statement, you create one test that forces it to execute the **true** part and one test that forces it to execute the **false** part. For a **while** statement, you might create tests that force the loop to execute zero, one, and several times. For a simple, small procedure, you might be able to test all possible paths through the procedure. This gets expensive quickly. For example, a procedure with five consecutive **if** statements and a **while** loop that might execute up to six times has $2^5 \times 7 = 224$ possible paths.

8.3   Integration Testing

The module dependency document (see Section 5.5) guides the plan for integrating modules together. The integration plan specifies the order in which to combine modules into partial systems. Each partial system is a contiguous subgraph of the module dependency graph, possibly with stubs in place of some modules, and probably including a test driver for the top-level module of the partial system. At each stage you take the result of some previous stage (or an empty partial system) and add a collection of modules to form another partial system (possibly replacing some stubs with their corresponding real modules). You might have several independent partial systems undergoing tests simultaneously, as long as they contained disjoint sets of undebugged modules. At the last stage of integration, the "partial system" includes all the modules, and it is ready for system testing (see Section 8.4). Appendix F shows a sample integration test plan.

8.3.1   Styles of Integration

There are two dimensions along which to chose styles of integration: direction and quantity.

The direction of integration is either *top-down* or *bottom-up*. In bottom-up testing, you test the lowest-level modules first, then integrate them with their callers one level up in the hierarchy. In top-down testing, you test the highest-level modules first, then integrate them with the modules they call. Pure top-down testing needs no test drivers; pure bottom-up testing needs no stubs. Mixed strategies may make sense: you might integrate a large portion of the system bottom-up, but supply stubs for some modules that implement functions you do not intend to test immediately. This may be especially useful if you are developing a subset of the full system.

The quantity of integration is either *incremental* or *phased*. In incremental integration, you add only one new module to the partial system at a time. In phased integration, you add a group of related modules. Incremental integration gives the fewest changes at a time, thus making it more likely that the new module causes any any newly discovered bugs. Phased integration requires fewer integration steps, but makes it more difficult to track down defects because there are more new modules that might cause them.

Incremental bottom-up testing is popular because it is the simplest form of debugging to plan. Some people believe in top-down incremental testing, because it uncovers high-level design defects earlier. However, low-cost stubs for many modules can be hard to design and write. Furthermore, you can get some of the same benefits by building a subset system bottom-up, with the additional advantages described in Section 4.5. I typically use incremental bottom-up testing for most modules, but sometimes combine this with top-down testing of command dispatch modules. The main thing is to have some sensible plan for integration.

8.3.2 Unit Testing versus Integration Testing

A software project schedule usually puts severe time pressure on the developers, which leads them to try to cut corners and eliminate some testing. Some people try to skip unit testing of low-level modules, feeling that they can toss a large collection of modules together and catch module-level bugs as well as problems of integration. This usually leads to disaster, because when a bug occurs there are too many places to look for it.

Sometimes there is little unit testing that makes sense for higher-level modules. If a stub must have nearly the complexity of the module it replaces, there is little point in writing the stub. Stubs should be so simple that they almost never contain bugs. For this type of module, the best test might be bottom-up integration. However, the integration tester must take special care to debug the lower-level modules before integrating the higher-level module that did not go through unit test. Furthermore, the developers should take special care during a code walkthrough of the untested module (see Section 18.3.3).

8.4 System Testing

System tests are tests designed to verify that the finished system meets its requirements. There are three kinds of system testing. *Alpha testing* is system testing performed within the development organization. *Beta testing* is system testing performed by a select group of friendly customers. They get early delivery of a system, perhaps at reduced prices, in return for feedback to the developers on how the system works. *Acceptance testing* is system testing performed by a customer to determine whether to accept delivery of the system.

System testing requires careful planning. Since the main purpose is to verify that the system meets its requirements, the major source of ideas for test cases is the requirements document. As soon as appropriate managers approve the requirements document, the testing organization should begin planning for system tests.

A large system may require many test cases. Thus you need some structure to organize and keep track of tests; such an organized collection of test cases is called a test suite. Since most of the tests come from the requirements, you might group tests according to chapters, sections, and subsections of the requirements document. Since the requirements might change, and you presumably structured the requirements document to make such changes easy, structuring your tests this way makes it easier to change the test suite as the requirements change.

You may need to impose additional structure on the tests.

- You might group tests into major categories, such as whether they will work normally or will produce exception messages. Other categories depend on the application. For example, compiler tests might divide into those expected to produce compile-time messages and not run, those expected to compile correctly but not run, those expected to produce runtime messages when run, and those expected to work correctly when run.

- You might subdivide the tests to follow the subsetting strategy outlined in the life-cycle considerations (see Sections 4.3.1 and 4.5). Testing of early subsets can proceed in parallel with development of later subsets. Test cases for facilities added in later subsets might presume that the facilities from earlier subsets still work. For example, tests of output-producing commands might presume that the input commands work.

Of course, although the *test cases* might presume earlier subsets work, *testers* should not: they should rerun previous tests when starting to work with a new subset.

Appendix C shows a sample system test plan for the genealogy program of Appendix A. This system is small enough that the document can describe the entire collection of tests.

8.5   Regression Testing

Regression testing is not a separate category from unit, integration, and system testing. Instead, it is a separate dimension to all forms of testing. Regression testing is the practice of rerunning old tests after a change, to ensure that system facilities you did not mean to change still work the same way.

All large systems change. Information hiding limits the effects of changes, and configuration management tries to control changes. However, in even the best-designed systems, a change in one area may have surprising effects on other areas. Thus it is a good idea to rerun all the tests, even if the maintainer believes the change should not affect them.

Regression testing requires considerable resources. All the old tests must be available; the maintainer must have scaffolding to help run the tests and verify that they produce the same results as last time. The organization must be able to afford the computer time required for all the tests.

8.6 Personnel

To a programmer, a test is successful if it shows that the program works. To a software test designer, a test is successful if it uncovers the presence of a bug. A good test set is one that defines test cases that maximize the likelihood of uncovering bugs. As Section 15.3.1 shows, programmers have psychological difficulty in accepting that their programs have bugs, and therefore may not have the right outlook to design successful (bug-revealing) tests.

Any one person brings a particular mindset to the task of understanding and using a system. To fully exercise a system, you need people with several different points of view. Thus beta testing is extremely valuable, since it gets several real customers trying out their viewpoint on your system. Almost all software has a few bugs that crop up only after customers use it in the field.

You can improve your testing by trying to mimic customer-directed tests as much as possible during alpha testing. If your organization can set up a testing group composed of different people from the development group, you are more likely to design a successful test suite. Unfortunately, supposedly independent test groups are subject to political pressure. If the development group has a mandate to deliver a system by a tight deadline, and the test group has a mandate to reject systems with bugs, the development group is likely to try to sidestep the test group as deadline pressure mounts. This is a sad but natural tendency: if someone else is responsible for quality, and you are responsible for the deadline, you are likely to decide that your responsibility is more important than the other person's. Ideally, the person responsible for meeting the deadline should also be responsible for the quality of the product. The software development group and testing group for a project should each report to the same project manager, who can decide the appropriate tradeoff between the conflicting goals.

Exercises

8–1   As part of a game-playing program you have implemented a module representing a cavern containing caves numbered 1 to N. One operation on a cavern is to select a random cave not the same as some given cave. Early in the project your testing staff report they cannot plan tests effectively because they cannot predict what room this procedure will select. Sketch the portion of the Cavern module dealing with rooms, and any other modules you need to introduce, so that you can provide a stub that solves your testing group's problem. Write both the stub and the code it replaces. You may assume that the system library provides a random number generator

procedure draw(Low, High:integer; **var** Result:integer);

that sets Result to a random integer uniformly distributed in the range Low to High inclusive.

Project Exercises

8–2   Write a system test plan for your project. You may begin this as soon as you have agreed on the requirements for your project. See Appendix C for an example.

8–3   Write an integration test plan for your project. You may begin this as soon as you have agreed on the module decomposition for your project. Be sure that you integrate the modules needed for your earliest subsets as early as possible in your plan. See Appendix F for an example.

8–4   Write a unit test plan for each module in the subset you will deliver. As mentioned in Exercise 6–5 on page 85, try to avoid having either the specifier or implementor of a module write its test plan.

System
Delivery

The development organization's work is not over once it finishes building the product. Delivering the product to the customer, and maintaining it afterward, can require much work. This chapter discusses delivery; Chapter 10 discusses maintenance.

Delivery goes through several stages.

1. *Site preparation* gets the customer's place of business physically ready for the new system. This may take no effort for a pure software system, but may involve considerable effort for a joint hardware/software system.

2. *System setup* installs the system at the customer's site. If installation is simple, the developer need only provide instructions. For more complex installation, the developer may need to do the installation.

3. *User training* prepares the customer's operators and end-line users to interact with the system.

4. *System introduction* is the first real use of the new system.

5. *Cutover* is the point at which the customer abandons previous systems and becomes dependent on the new one.

9.1 Site Preparation

It is rare these days, but sometimes the software system you deliver is the customer's first use of a large computer system. Installing such a system can be a major construction job. The customer may do most of the work, or contract it out, but will usually need guidance from the developer.

The new system may need a computer room; most large computers require extensive cabling, which requires a raised floor to provide a way to keep the cables out of the way. Computers typically require air conditioning, often of much greater capacity than typical office air conditioning. The room may need higher air pressure than surrounding halls and offices, to minimize dust. Computer equipment draws much electrical power; the customer may not only need to install electrical conduits, but may need to order additional capacity from the power company.

The computer room may need special fire detection and extinguishing equipment. The high value of the contents of a computer room may require automatic fire extinguishers, because of the damage that can occur before a fire department would respond. Since many fire extinguishing systems, such as sprinklers, damage electrical equipment, a computer room may need chemical systems. Some of these are poisonous, requiring special alarms and delay systems to allow personnel to evacuate the computer room before the automatic system triggers.

Computer peripherals such as terminals may not have such stringent physical requirements. However, the customer must carefully plan where to locate the peripheral equipment. Most peripherals have cable length limits. Exceeding these limits may require additional equipment, such as repeaters or telecommunications hardware.

The customer may need to connect the new system with others at the same site via a local area network, or with distant sites via a communications network. Some workplaces permit (or even encourage) employees to do some work from home. This requires modems and telephone lines, perhaps including special arrangements for a *hunt group* of telephone lines, where someone need only dial one number to get any one of several dial-in lines.

Small computer systems may not have all the requirements of large ones, but may still need some preparation. Many small systems are still large enough to need a separate desk or table; credenzas designed for typewriters are usually not big enough for terminals or small computers. Office microcomputers or minicomputers may be sufficiently noisy, with disk drives and air circulation fans, to need sound baffling. If you can separate the keyboard and display for a noisy micro from the main system, the customer might collect the systems in a separate, soundproofed room and run cables to the terminals in individual offices. This leads right back into the preparation needed for large systems.

9.2 User Training

As mentioned in Section 4.2.1, the people who interact with the system include operators and end-line users. Both may need training in using the system.

Operators need to know how to interact with the system. They may need to fill in forms, enter data, make queries, and so on. Operators may have little technical training; typically they need tutorial material that assumes no familiarity with computer systems.

End-line users are typically managers. They may never interact directly with the system, but may study reports that it produces. They need to know how to interpret the reports, but may not need much training; the reports may be similar to those from the old system. Each class of users may need their own tutorial, introductory, and reference manuals (discussed in Section 4.4) tailored to their own needs. Each may find it useful to read the Functional Description.

Both sorts of users may need procedure manuals as well as user manuals. A user's manual says how to interact with the system; a procedures manual says how to do one's job in the context of the new system. A user's manual may describe individual commands; a procedures manual may say what combination of commands to use to do typical tasks. Ideally, an introductory user's manual includes both kinds of information.

9.3   System Introduction

There are three main strategies for introducing a new system at a customer's installation.

1. *Immediate replacement* installs the new system and immediately cuts over to it. This has low cost and brief instability, but requires high confidence that the new system works and little effect from user unfamiliarity. Customers often install new hardware this way, especially if they can do it over a weekend. If all goes well, the system support staff have one hard weekend, and the rest of the employees have no troubles.

2. *Parallel running* uses both the new system and the old at the same time. This imposes high costs in time and money, since users must duplicate their work. However, this method may be necessary for customers who strongly depend on correct operation. Financial software or patient monitoring systems may need this method.

3. *Phased replacement* introduces one piece of the new system at a time, or introduces the system in one subdivision of the customer's business. Each piece might use either immediate replacement or parallel running. The users who gain experience with the new system may help introduce it to others.

Phased replacement may use two tactics to introduce the system more easily.

1. A *dry run* lets a select group of users operate with old, but real, data. For example, a new library catalog system might use the previous month's queries, if the old system kept a record of them. This requires extra work

from the users, but lets them get used to the new system before it becomes critical. They may be able to provide feedback to improve the system before it becomes fully operational.

2. A *mini-implementation* has a small group begin to use the system for its regular work. For example, one store in a chain might use a new cash-register system. The initial users may progressively introduce the system to their colleagues.

9.4   The Effect of Market Size

The size of the market for your product affects your system delivery strategy. Market size is a continuum, but there are three main classes of interest.

1. A single customer. Most of this text talks of "the customer" and of interaction with a particular customer during requirements analysis, so having a single customer is an implicit assumption. This has been the usual case in the past, and is still true of many large products.

2. A small market. There may be one or two prime customers, which may play the role of "the customer" as discussed in other sections. However, the developer may be able to market the product to other customers with similar requirements.

3. Mass market. Here there are many customers. Typically the product originates within the development organization, or its marketing division. The system architects may have no typical customers to interact with during requirements analysis. Much personal computer software is in this category.

With multiple customers, it is less likely that the developer will install the system at each customer site. Thus you must package the system so that customers can install it themselves.

Different markets have their own standard media for distribution. For mainframes, one often uses magnetic tape. For microcomputer markets, one typically uses floppy disks. Different operating systems have their own formats for tapes or disks. The wider your market, the more likely you will need to deal with a large variety of media.

Regardless of the medium, you need to tell customers enough that they can install the system and assure themselves that the software works. This typically means that you must supply an installation guide describing

*   the delivery medium. Be sure to mention recording density and format if there is any chance of variation among customer sites.

*   the minimum hardware configuration needed to run your system. This is the same information you had in the *Environment Characteristics* chapter of the requirements specification.

- how to run any automatic installation programs on the tape. Many operating systems provide command file facilities or batch facilities that you can use to reduce tedious work for the installer.

- the names and nature of any permanent files needed by your system. If the customer must create them, say how. If the installation programs create them, say so.

- how to customize the system according to local preferences.

- how to run test cases (which you should supply on the distribution medium), and what results they should produce.

_____ Chapter 10 _____

_____ Evolution _____

System delivery is not the end of the developer's involvement with a system. Every long-lived system changes; by some estimates, 40 percent of software effort is in maintaining and enhancing old systems. This chapter discusses what a developer needs to do to evolve an existing system.

10.1 Categories of Maintenance

The term *maintenance* is a little strange when applied to software. In common speech, it means fixing things that break or wear out. In software, nothing wears out; it was either wrong from the beginning, or you decided later that you wanted to do something different. However, the term is so common that we must live with it.

There are four major categories of software maintenance. *Corrective maintenance* fixes failures to meet the system's requirements. *Perfective maintenance* improves the system in areas not directly violating the requirements. *Adaptive maintenance* evolves the system to meet changing needs. *Enhancement* is adding facilities the original designers didn't anticipate.

Corrective maintenance includes fixing bugs (processing failures), meeting performance requirements (performance failures), and ensuring that the system matches the design (implementation failures). During the time pressure to meet a deadline, an implementor might cut some corners, implementing something that works too slowly, or usually works but doesn't always.

Perfective maintenance includes improving performance in areas not directly related to requirements, improving maintainability of the code by inserting comments or following usage conventions ignored during implementation. It might involve small changes that improve ease of use — though this may shade into meeting new requirements, which is adaptive maintenance.

Adaptive maintenance includes changing the system to match changes in the environment, such as moving it to new hardware or a new operating system. It may involve changes to data, such as new accounting categories for a bookkeeping system. A main purpose of the Changes section of a requirements document (see Section 4.3.1) is to plan for such changes, so that the module decomposition can isolate their effects to single modules (see Chapter 5).

Enhancement is different from the other kinds of change because, to do it properly, you must revisit all stages of the development process to incorporate the new requirements into the old design. The boundary between enhancement and adaptive maintenance is somewhat fuzzy. If the designers expected a particular requirements change, handling the change probably involves modifying a few modules, and is thus adaptive maintenance. If the designers did not expect the change, maintainers must study the original design to see where to fit in the new facilities, and may need to redo portions of the requirements document, module decomposition, module dependencies, and specifications, as well as modifying the implementation. Thus enhancement is more costly than adaptive maintenance, but much less costly than designing a new system to meet the changed requirements.

10.2   Levels of Support

Maintenance is easier or harder depending on how much support the development organization has kept around for the maintainers. With ideal support (Section 10.2.1), maintenance changes that do not violate fundamental assumptions are not difficult. Unfortunately, many existing development organizations give no support to maintainers (Section 10.2.2). If a system goes through a long period without proper maintenance support, you may be able to rebuild some of what the developers should have left you in the first place (Section 10.2.3).

10.2.1   Full Support

The best support for maintenance results from following the software development process outlined in earlier chapters, together with the configuration management discipline discussed in Chapter 17. The design documents become maintenance documents: they help a maintainer understand the system.[1] Configuration management practices ensure developers reflect each change in the appropriate documents.

---

[1] I do not believe a separate category of "maintenance documentation" is useful; if the designers don't use the documents themselves, they won't write them or keep them up-to-date.

Such support does impose some overhead. It of course imposes the overhead of doing the design documents in the first place. Beyond that, it requires that you keep machine-readable sources for all the design documents (possibly offline, in a well-known place), that you keep old test cases for regression testing, and that you have someone responsible for configuration management of delivered products. It requires that you take the time to go through the configuration management procedures whenever you change something.

A good deal of support for evolution is the steps you take during development. Chapter 4 discussed planning for evolution during requirements analysis, and organizing the requirements specification for maintainability. Chapter 5 discussed decomposing the system so each design decision for which you could not rule out a change is the responsibility of one particular module. Chapter 8 mentioned keeping tests around for regression testing.

This does not mean that all changes will be easy. A planned change should require only identifying where in the system the change fits, then changing or rewriting one module. If your modules are of appropriate size, this should take at most a few weeks. Unplanned changes may involve more work. For example, Section 6.2.1 planned for changes to the representation of a sequence, but didn't consider some particular representations that required a change to the module specification for efficiency. This led to changing code in all the modules that used sequences. Changes that violate fundamental assumptions are still more costly.

10.2.2 The Worst Case

Far too often a development organization sloughs off maintenance on inexperienced programmers, who do not even have access to the design documents (which might not even exist). If the development organization ever dropped configuration control procedures, you cannot trust the design documents to be accurate. When this happens, the best a maintainer can do is make changes wherever it seems appropriate, usually under too much time pressure to learn much about how the designers organized the system. Under these conditions, whatever structure the designers built in slowly disintegrates over time. Eventually the whole thing becomes unmaintainable; folklore tells of a large mainframe operating system where each release fixed about 1,000 bugs and introduced about 1,000 more.

It might seem like this could not be "the worst case," since you would get *some* maintenance. However, an unmaintained system is at least stable; it may have severe problems, but often you can discover them, work around them, and live with them. A poorly maintained system may be worse, since it keeps shifting out from under you.

10.2.3 Restructuring

If you have an old, poorly documented and poorly structured system, you may be able to restructure it, possibly incrementally. This can take much effort, and might be worthwhile only if you expect to have to maintain it for several years. This section gives some suggestions as to how to improve the structure of an old system.

Start by making a list of what modules make up the system, and what externally visible procedures each module contains. For each procedure, list what other externally visible procedures it calls (of its own module, as well as of other modules). This gives you a first draft of a module decomposition and module dependencies document. If you have only one large program with no visible divisions, proceed with the step dealing with internal structure of modules.

For each module, try to determine all the design decisions embodied in the module. If you discover several, try to split that module into separate modules, one per design decision. This may result in turning some internal procedures into externally visible ones. Each client module that depended on the unsplit module might now depend on all the subdivisions of the module; each subdivision might depend on all the modules on which the original module depended. However, look at the procedure call graph to see if clients really depend only on procedures in a subset of the modules, and if the subdivisions depend only on a subset of what the original module depended on. Modify the module decomposition and module dependencies documents accordingly.

A particular set of design decisions to look at is representations of data structures. If your system is in a high-level language with user-defined data types, this job is not too difficult. For languages that lack such facilities, you need to look for collections of variables that the module typically uses close together, and deduce an abstract type composed of those variables. For example, incrementing an integer variable and using it to index an array might mean that the integer and the array were part of some sequence type, like a stack or queue. For each data type, create a separate module to hide the representation of the type. Look at all the code that manipulates the representation of the type, and try to deduce what abstract operations the code is trying to do. Introduce interface procedures to perform those operations, and modify the code to call them.

Another set of design decisions that may be easy to identify is the ones having to do with the fixed interfaces. You may be able to get documentation on operating system calls or peripheral device interfaces. You can then begin looking for parts of the system that make those calls, or that interact with those devices. If one change you expect to make soon is to adapt the program to a similar peripheral, you have some basis for designing a device interface module that would work for both, and retrofitting your new interface module into the old system.

One fortunate aspect of this approach is that you do not necessarily need to understand the whole system completely to begin to restructure it. All you must be able to do is to identify chunks of it that make sense. As you pull cohesive chunks out of older modules, the task of analyzing the rest becomes easier. This should not be surprising; the difficulty of comprehending a program goes up more than linearly with the size, and so decreases more than linearly as you reduce the size.

10.3 Product Support

All kinds of maintenance and enhancement require a product support organization
to receive problem reports; distribute upgraded versions of the system; and keep
customers informed of problems, solutions, and new versions.

10.3.1 Problem Reports

A major activity of a product support organization is handling problem reports. A
problem report is a document used to report something requiring a change to the
system. Most organizations have problem report forms (sometimes called change
requests, or bug reports) for people to fill out when they detect a problem. A significant part of configuration status involves keeping track of these forms.

A problem report form goes through several stages. First, someone detects a
problem and fills out a form to describe it. Next, someone responsible for change
requests records the form, typically assigning it a number to use to keep track of it.
The configuration management organization determines an appropriate person to
analyze the form, typically someone from the portion of the development organization that is responsible for whatever area of the system appears to be involved in the
problem. The developer analyzes the problem and assigns it a disposition.

The developer typically classifies the report into one of three categories.

- *No action* means that the organization need not respond to the report (other
  than notifying the originator about the disposition of his report). A *no
  action* disposition means either that a fix for the problem is already in progress, or it is not a problem. *Not a problem* means that the reporter misunderstood something about the system; the development organization typically
  responds with an explanation.

- *Software change needed* means that the problem is a bug; the system does
  not do what the requirements specified.

- *Change request* means that the system met its requirements, but the problem
  reveals a genuine need to change the requirements.

For each of the latter categories, the developer may need to estimate the resources
needed to make the change. Management will then decide whether to make the
change, and how to fit it into the schedule.

It can be hard to distinguish between bug reports and requests for new features.
If a user and a developer have different interpretations of a requirement, the user
may view something as a bug when the developer views it as a change request.
Even if something is a bug, it may require so much effort to fix that you should
change the requirements instead. Of course, if the requirements are part of a contract, changing them requires approval from both the developer and the customer.

10.3.2 Multiple Releases

Since software systems evolve, delivery is not as simple as Chapter 9 outlined. You will likely deliver several successive releases of your system. The method of distribution varies a great deal.

- For small problems where the customer has system support staff, you can send them editing changes (for those with system sources) or binary patches (for those without). If you do this extensively with different customers, you rapidly build up problems keeping track of which customers have what updates. If you send all updates to all customers, many customers will install only those updates that relate directly to their own problems. It is best to limit this method to small changes that fix crucial problems.

- You might accumulate multiple bug fixes into a new major release, which you send to all those customers who have purchased maintenance agreements, or for whom maintenance was a condition of the original contract.

You could treat each release as the delivery of a completely separate product, but this is more costly and inconvenient to your customers than treating them as parts of the same product (since they need to pay for new manuals, and try to discover how the new ones differ from the old). Typically, the first release of your product should include complete user documentation for your system. You might package successive releases in two different forms. Customers whose first release is a later one should get complete documentation, as though theirs is the first release of the product. Customers who already have an earlier release should get updates to their documentation. An update contains

- a *release notice* summarizing important differences from the previous release

- copies of changed or new pages

- change bars along the margin of changed lines

The update process is easier if you have organized your document for ease of change in the first place.

If you have planned a series of subset releases in advance, you could choose to handle the documentation in one of three ways.

1. Treat the first subset as a complete release, and deliver documentation describing just the subset facilities. For later subsets, deliver changed pages.

2. Deliver documentation that fully describes the first subset, with placeholders for material from later subsets. For later subsets, deliver changed pages. This helps your customers plan for the future.

3. Deliver the documentation for the last subset, along with a release notice summarizing what you left out in the current release. Appendix I shows a release notice of this sort. The system you deliver ought to have stubs for the missing features (which might say "not yet implemented"), because

customers will forget about the release notice as they use your system, and will expect to find all the facilities they read about in the user documentation.

10.3.3 Distributing Information

For many customers an important part of product support is advice and information. Customers typically want news about known bugs, work-arounds for bugs, upcoming releases, nonobvious uses of existing facilities, and strategies for making better use of their product. News of known bugs can be especially important; it can be extremely frustrating for a customer to work hard tracking down a problem to report, only to be told the developer heard about that bug two months ago — especially if there is a simple way to work around the bug.

Distributing anything in the mass market can be enormously expensive. Sending a single letter costs several dollars in employee time; sending an identical letter to 100,000 customers costs tens of thousands of dollars in paper and postal charges alone. Some developers resort to information utilities and commercial bulletin-board systems to distribute updates. Most restrict newsletters to customers with maintenance agreements, or include a limited newsletter subscription with the purchase price.

10.3.4 Conversion Support

New releases of a system may have different formats for files they read or write. Customers will need to create new versions of these files to use with the new system. Ideally, you should make this process as painless as possible.

A poor approach is to force users to regenerate files from scratch. This can be tempting for a compiler writer who brings out a new object file or compilation library format, since in theory users can regenerate everything from source. However, sometimes people have object files without the corresponding sources. Even if they have the sources, it can take a long time (many hours or days) to rebuild a large system, which they may not be able to afford to do at the moment they install the new compiler.

A better approach is to provide a conversion program that reads the old format and writes the new. For many changes you can put together the conversion program by combining the file reader from the old system with the internal data structure manager and output writer of the new system.

Depending on a conversion program can leave users in a state where someone has failed to run the conversion program, and your system behaves strangely when it tries to interpret the old format files. Your system should be able to recognize its own input files. You might place a particular pattern at the start of the file, identifying it as input to (or output from) your system. You might also include a file format indicator, which could be as simple as an integer that you increment with each change in format. The module that tries to read an input file might then have two exceptions: "not a proper input file," and "unexpected file format." In the latter case, higher levels of the system might report to users that they need to run a particular conversion program (or series of conversions, if the format is sufficiently old).

The most painless approach for users, given that the files really must change, is for your system to convert the files for them. New software should be able to recognize old formats and read them, though it can restrict itself to writing the new format. Updating files in the old format is dangerous; you need to make sure the customer really wants to convert the files, and doesn't need to go back to using an older release of your system.

Further Reading

Glass and Noiseux (1981) give a detailed portrayal of maintenance. Swanson (1976) originated the taxonomy of maintenance activities I used in Section 10.1, except for my distinction between adaptive maintenance and enhancement.

Project Exercises

10–1   Write a release notice for the program you have built. See Appendix I for an example.

10–2   Have someone who was not a member of your group (preferably, your instructor) pick one of the potential changes you listed in your life cycle document. Make this change in your program. Record how much effort it took. Did your earlier planning help make this change easy?

10–3   Have someone who was not a member of your group (preferably, your instructor) change one of your requirements. Write a brief (2–3 page) report describing the implications of this change for your program.

Introduction to
_____ Specifications _____

Chapter 6 discussed module specifications in general. This chapter covers issues common to many formal methods. The following chapters discuss three specification techniques in more detail: algebraic specifications, trace specifications, and abstract model specifications.

11.1 Common Issues

Several issues are common to most specification techniques. Every technique must have some way of defining

- the *syntax* of interface procedures
- the *semantics* of interface procedures
- *exception* conditions under which the interface procedures cannot proceed normally

The syntax of an interface procedure specifies what parameters it takes and what results it returns. A typical syntactic specification has the form

$$\text{Name: parm}_1 \times \text{parm}_2 \times \ \cdots \ \text{parm}_N \rightarrow \text{res}_1 \times \text{res}_2 \times \ \cdots \ \text{res}_M$$

which means that Name is a procedure taking N parameters of types parm_i and returning M results of types res_j. Some techniques might require $M \leq 1$, limiting procedures to zero or one result. Some procedures might take no parameters. For example, an algebraic specification of an abstract data type typically has one procedure that has no parameters and returns a fresh object of the abstract type.

Some techniques, such as algebraic specifications, require that all interface procedures be pure functions. Others allow procedures with side effects. Either case requires some method of making a correspondence between the specification and the implementation; most implementation languages allow side effects.

If a specification technique allows side effects, a designer has a choice of two kinds of signatures for interface procedures. A module might implement a single object, or might export a type and allow the user to create many objects of the same type. In the latter case, the interface procedures must take a parameter of the exported type; in the former they need no such parameter. A specification of a module that exports a type might be more complex, because of the need to say that changing one object of the exported type has no effect on other objects of the same type. Sometimes you can presume that anything not mentioned remains unchanged; other times, because of details of how the particular formal method works, you need to say something explicitly.

11.2 Verification

Formal specification techniques show promise of helping with two important areas of quality assurance:

1. Ensuring that specifications are complete and consistent.
2. Ensuring that implementations meet their specifications.

People usually call the second area "proving programs correct." However, the whole subject is controversial, because many practitioners do not believe we will ever be able to prove the correctness of large systems. Regardless of opposing positions on this issue, formal specifications are valuable simply as precise communications between software developers.

At the moment most work in program verification depends on abstract model specifications. Guttag et al. (1985) propose a two-tiered approach to specifications. They use a method based on algebraic specifications to define language-independent mathematical abstractions, then build programming-language-specific abstract models on top of the abstractions.

11.3 Limitations of Specifications

As Chapter 6 noted, not all specification techniques are equally suited to information hiding. It is important to avoid unduly constraining implementations, or unduly favoring a particular implementation. In many specification techniques, one must introduce *auxiliary functions* to write the equations. These functions are not part of the interface; users may not call them. However, it is hard to avoid presuming that one must implement something corresponding to the auxiliary function.

A good specification describes behavior that all possible implementations must exhibit, and avoids unnecessary details. Sometimes it is much easier to write an overly constrained specification than one that gives the truly minimal constraint. For example, suppose you have a Set module, with operations including adding a member to the set, determining how many members there are in the set, and iterating over members of the set. You might represent the iterator as an operation to fetch the Ith member of the set, and forbid adding to the set in the midst of iterating over it. A simple specification of the meaning of Add might be

Create: (out s:set)
   Size(s) = 0

Size: (s:set) returns i:integer
   Value: determined by Create, Add

Fetch: (s:set; i:integer) returns e:elem
   Value: determined by Add
   Exceptions: if $\neg$(1≤i≤Size(s)) then ErrBadIndex

Add: (inout s:set; e:elem)
   Effect: if $\neg$ $\exists$i∈[1..'Size(s)'] | 'Fetch(s,i)'=e then
        Size(s) = 'Size(s)' + 1
        Fetch(s,Size(s)) = e

Items in quotes refer to values before side effects take place; values outside quotes refer to values after side effects take place. This specification overconstrains the implementation. It says that the newly added element goes at the end of the sequence generated by the iterator; it seems likely that the order of elements returned by the iterator is irrelevant, as long as it gives each element once. Fixing this problem gives a longer specification:

Add: (inout s:set; e:elem)
   Effect: if $\neg$ $\exists$i∈[1..'Size(s)'] | 'Fetch(s,i)'=e then
        Size(s) = 'Size(s)' + 1
        $\exists$i∈[1..Size(s)] | Fetch(s,i) = e
        $\forall$i∈[1..'Size(s)'] $\exists$j∈[1..Size(s)] | Fetch(s,j) = 'Fetch(s,i)'

The first equation remains the same; the second says that the new element exists somewhere in the sequence; the third says that all elements from the old sequence still exist somewhere in the new sequence, but their positions might have changed. Part of the length of this specification comes from the need to say that everything that used to be in the set is still there somewhere, but possibly in a different place. Compare it with the following, which is the same as the original but explicitly says that every item remains in its old place.

Add: (inout s:set; e:elem)
   Effect: if $\neg$ $\exists$i∈[1..'Size(s)'] | 'Fetch(s,i)'=e then
        Size(s) = 'Size(s)' + 1
        Fetch(s,Size(s)) = e
        $\forall$i∈[1..'Size(s)'] Fetch(s,i) = 'Fetch(s,i)'

Specifications of procedures that build variable-length data structures need to be concerned about limits on how big a data structure you can build. It is usually much easier to say that a structure has no bound than to give a bound. Some implementation strategies make it difficult to say anything about what the bound is. For example, a linked-list implementation of a stack can grow to fill all dynamic memory. There is no good way of saying how big a stack you can safely build. Typically you need to use an existential quantifier, such as $\exists N > \text{Lower} \mid P(N)$, where $P(N)$ is some assertion that says that the structure can grow to size N and no larger. With an implementation that allocates all dynamic memory out of a common pool, you might not be able to set any lower bound larger than zero.

All formal specification techniques require mathematical sophistication; this limits the number of people who can read and understand them. Moreover, no existing technique is suitable for specifying all possible modules. Thus formal specifications are not widely used in industry. Nevertheless, formal specifications satisfy the need for precision. As Section 6.3 points out, an imprecise specification can lead to ambiguity and misunderstanding. Thus software engineers should struggle to master existing techniques and apply them, while researchers try to extend the techniques to new areas.

Further Reading

Several texts discuss ideas of program verification. Most of these books discuss verification methods, which many practitioners do not believe will ever be able to prove the correctness of large programs. Few sources discuss the need for precise specifications, even in the absence of verification methods.

Berg et al. (1982) discuss the role of verification in software development. Chapter 8 of their text introduces algebraic and state-machine specifications. Bartussek and Parnas (1977) introduced the idea of trace specifications; McLean (1984) gave a formal specification of the method.

Chapter 12

Algebraic
Specifications

Algebraic specifications define the meaning of a collection of interface procedures via equations. Each interface procedure is a pure mathematical function without side effects.

12.1 Outline of a Specification

Figure 12–1 gives an algebraic specification of a stack of elements. An algebraic specification has four sections.

1. The *types* section says what types the specification defines, and what existing types it uses; Figure 12–1 defines a type *stack* and uses types *element* and *boolean*.

2. The *exceptions* section gives names to exceptional conditions used later in the syntax and equations sections.

3. The *syntax* section defines the signatures of the interface procedures. For example, *Push* takes a stack and an element and returns a new stack. Algebraic specifications often have interface procedures return large objects; all the interface procedures must be pure functions without side effects.

4. The *equations* section gives a set of rewrite rules defining the meanings of the interface procedures in terms of each other.

Names not mentioned in the syntax section, such as "s" and "e," are variables. By convention, each equation is implicitly universally quantified over all possible values

---

types
   defines stack
   uses boolean, element
exceptions *underflow, novalue*
syntax
   Push: stack× element→stack
   Pop: stack→stack + {*underflow*}
   Top: stack→element + {*novalue*}
   Empty: stack→boolean
   NewStack: →stack
equations
  1. Pop(NewStack) = *underflow*
  2. Pop(Push(s,e)) = s
  3. Top(NewStack) = *novalue*
  4. Top(Push(s,e)) = e
  5. Empty(Newstack) = true
  6. Empty(Push(s,e)) = false

Figure 12–1: Algebraic Specification of a Stack

---

of these variables. Thus, for example, the second rule of Figure 12–1 means

$\forall s \in$ stack $\forall e \in$ element Pop(Push(s,e))=s

The rewrite rules let you determine the meaning of any sequence of calls on stack functions. Thus in an expression such as

Push(Pop(Push(Push(NewStack,e1),e2)),e3)

you can eliminate the call on Pop by observing that it is of the form

Pop(Push(s,e))

which reduces to s by the second equation of Figure 12–1, where s is the stack

Push(NewStack,e1)

and e is e2. Thus the original expression reduces to

Push(Push(NewStack,e1),e3)

For an expression involving Empty or Top, you can eliminate all the calls to Pop, which will leave the expression in one of the two forms

f(Push(s,e))
f(NewStack)

where f is either Empty or Top.

You might wonder if this rewrite process terminates, and whether all choices about which rewrite rule to use next give the same final answer. The first property is called *finite termination*, and the second *unique termination*. The rewrite process is *convergent* if it has both properties. For arbitrary algebraic specification, convergence is undecidable. This means there is no algorithm for deciding whether rewrites always converge. However, restrictions on algebraic specifications to guarantee convergence allow most reasonable specifications one might write. For example, if the right hand side of each rewrite rule has fewer function calls than the left, the rewrite process must always terminate.

12.1.1 Exceptions

Equations 1 and 3 of Figure 12–1 are examples of *exception equations*. They say that you can't apply Pop or Top to a NewStack (that is, an empty stack). The syntax section said that Pop and Top returned either a stack or an exception value.

As written, the equations say that you cannot proceed after one of these exceptions, since *underflow* is not a stack and *novalue* is not a proper stack element. If you wanted to say that after an underflow the stack remained unchanged, you could say

    syntax
      ...
      Pop: stack $\rightarrow$ stack
    error functions
      underflow: $\rightarrow$ stack
    ...
      Pop(NewStack) = underflow
      underflow = NewStack

which means that after an underflow exception the resulting value is an ordinary empty stack.

12.1.2 Constructor Functions

Figure 12–1 shows a typical pattern for writing algebraic specifications. NewStack and Push are *constructor* functions; you can rewrite any combination of functions yielding a stack as a combination of NewStack and Push. Choosing suitable constructor functions can be a bit of an art, but typically you have at least one implementation in mind to guide you.

You may start by considering all the functions that return objects of the type your module defines. Typically there will be an "initial creation" function, such as NewStack, that takes no parameters of the type you are defining. You can then look over the other candidates, and eliminate those you know how to define in terms of other candidates. For example, suppose you are designing a module that defines complex numbers. You might have a function that creates a complex number from real and imaginary components, and several others that create complex numbers from other complex numbers (such as add, subtract, multiply, form conjugate). Here the first function is the only constructor you need.

Sometimes you have several candidates for constructor functions. For example, if you are specifying a double-ended queue, you might pick either AddFront or Add-Back as a constructor.

12.1.3 Auxiliary Functions

Sometimes a specification needs to introduce extra functions, not part of the interface, to define the meaning of some interface procedure. Figure 12–1 specified unbounded stacks; there was no restriction on how often you could push new items onto the stack. To specify a bounded stack, you need to add the Depth function of Figure 12–2, and say that Push returns either a stack or the special exception value "overflow." As shown, overflow is a fatal exception, since it is not a stack and all the other procedures require stacks as arguments.

If the specifier of the stack module wants to provide a Depth function, there is no problem. However, auxiliary functions often simply aid writing the specification and are not part of the interface. They strongly suggest that the implementation should have some measure of depth, and may strongly suggest how to implement the interface procedures. Thus for information hiding they are undesirable. Section 12.2 gives a more serious example in Figure 12–4, requiring auxiliary queue functions to define the meaning of an iterator.

12.2 Dealing with Side Effects

Since algebraic specifications deal with pure functions, it may seem difficult at first to say anything about procedures that have side effects. This section temporarily ignores the general problem, and shows techniques for writing specifications in

---

Push: stack $\times$ element $\rightarrow$ stack + {*overflow*}
Depth : stack $\rightarrow$ integer

Depth(NewStack) = 0
Depth(Push(s,e)) = Depth(s) + 1

Push(s,e) = *overflow* if Depth(s) $\geq$ Max

Figure 12–2: Auxiliary Function: Depth

---

several special cases. Chapter 14 deals with the more general problem of casting an algebraic specification into a programming language with side effects.

Some side effects create no problems. The primary example of this is procedures with reference parameters, where the procedure never reads from the parameter but simply writes to it (such as **out** parameters in Ada, some **var** parameters in Pascal). Here the side effect on the parameter is simply a way of returning a result from the procedure. The algebraic specification can simply state that the function returns a tuple containing multiple values.

You can deal with some other side effects simply by a change of point of view. Consider a module that maintains some internal state, where some of the interface procedures modify the state, but interface procedures have no side effect on any state outside the module (especially, no side effect on parameters). You can then

- Define a type to represent the internal state of the module.

- Add a parameter to each interface procedure representing this implicit internal state.

- Add a result to each interface procedure with a side effect, meaning that it implicitly yields a new internal state.

For example, consider the interface procedures

procedure Init;
procedure Push(e:elem);
function PopTop:elem;
procedure IsEmpty: boolean;

---

types
    internal state
    uses boolean, element
syntax
    Init: $\rightarrow$ state
    Push: elem $\times$ state $\rightarrow$ state
    PopTop: state $\rightarrow$ (elem $\times$ state) + {*underflow*}
    IsEmpty: state $\rightarrow$ boolean
equations
  1. PopTop(Push(e,s)) = (e,s)
  2. PopTop(Init) = *underflow*
  3. IsEmpty(Push(e,s)) = false
  4. IsEmpty(Init) = true

Figure 12–3: Algebraic Specification with Hidden State

---

for a module that implements a single, hidden stack. *Init* initializes the stack to empty, *Push* places an element on the stack, *PopTop* removes the last element and returns it, and *IsEmpty* reports whether the stack is empty. You can define type *state* to represent the internal state of this module, and define the syntax of the procedures as Figure 12–3 shows. You can then define the meaning of these procedures via equations involving both visible parameters and hidden state. The similarity to Figure 12–1 is instructive: the module of Figure 12–1 makes its internal state an explicit parameter, so that a client may declare many different stacks.

Extending these ideas allows specifications of certain styles of iterator. For example, Figure 12–4 gives an algebraic specification of an iterator over a sequence. The equations for the *Next* function require auxiliary functions *Remove* and *Front*,

---

types
    defines seq, seqiter
    uses elem, boolean
syntax
    NewSeq: → seq
    Append: seq × elem → seq
    Init: seq → seqiter
    Test: seqiter → boolean
    Next: seqiter → (elem × seqiter) + {*endseq*}
auxiliary functions
    Remove: seq → seq + {*endseq*}
    Front: seq → elem + {*endseq*}
equations
  1. Test(Init(NewSeq)) = false
  2. Test(Init(Append(s,e))) = true
  3. Next(Init(NewSeq)) = *endseq*
  4. Next(Init(Append(s,e))) = (Front(Append(s,e)),
                                      Init(Remove(Append(s,e))))

auxiliary equations
  5. Remove(NewSeq) = *endseq*
  6. Remove(Append(NewSeq,e)) = NewSeq
  7. Remove(Append(Append(s,e1),e2)) = Append(Remove(Append(s,e1)),e2)
  8. Front(NewSeq) = *endseq*
  9. Front(Append(NewSeq,e)) = e
 10. Front(Append(Append(s,e1),e2)) = Front(Append(s,e1))

Figure 12–4: Algebraic Specification of a Sequence Iterator

---

which treat the internal state of the iterator as a FIFO queue. The equations say

1. Doing a Next on an empty sequence raises an exception.

2. The element returned by Next is the first element added to the queue.

3. Doing a Next yields an iterator that behaves as though you had started with a different sequence, without the original first element.

Figure 12–4 used three equations instead of the expected two to define each of Remove and Front. You might instead have written equations 6 and 7 as the single equation

Remove(Append(q,e)) =
   if q = NewSeq
      then NewSeq
      else Append(Remove(q),e)

However, in reasoning with such an equation, you must remember that an expression not textually identical to "NewSeq" may still be equal to it (suppose q=Remove(Append(NewSeq,e))). The safest way to reason about a specification with such a conditional is to ensure that the arguments are in a normal form consisting solely of calls on constructor functions.

12.3   Reasoning About Algebraic Specifications

Section 12.1 showed that you can use an algebraic specification to determine the meaning of (that is, the value computed by) an expression involving the types defined by the specification. You can use the specification to prove more general properties of the type or the operations on the type. Such proofs may need to rely on some form of induction.

The principle of mathematical induction says that if you have some predicate
   P: integer→boolean
about nonnegative integers, you can prove it is true of all nonnegative integers by first showing $P(0)$ to be true, then showing that assuming $P(k)$ lets you prove $P(k+1)$. A similar principle holds for algebraic specifications; you can prove properties of a type by induction on the depth of nesting of calls in arbitrary expressions that return objects of the type. Furthermore, if you have organized your specification to use constructor functions, you can restrict your attention to expressions composed solely of the constructor functions, since any other expression yielding an object of the type is equivalent to one in the restricted form.

For example, Figure 12–5 defines addition and multiplication on integers. Given these equations, you can prove Plus(Zero,i)=i as follows

1. By construction (that is, since Zero and Succ are the constructor functions), "i" must be of the form $Succ^k(Zero)$, $k \geq 0$. Thus you need prove only

     $Plus(Zero, Succ^k(Zero)) = Succ^k(Zero)$

---

types
    defines integer
syntax
    Zero: $\rightarrow$ integer
    Succ: integer $\rightarrow$ integer
    Plus: integer$\times$integer $\rightarrow$ integer
    Times: integer$\times$integer $\rightarrow$ integer
equations
    1. Plus(i,Zero) = i
    2. Plus(a,Succ(b)) = Succ(Plus(a,b))
    3. Times(a,Zero) = Zero
    4. Times(a,Succ(b)) = Plus(Times(a,b),b)

Figure 12–5: Peano Axioms as an Algebraic Specification

---

2.   Basis step. For $k=0$, Plus(Zero,Zero)=Zero by equation 1.

3.   Induction. Assume

$$\text{Plus}(\text{Zero},\text{Succ}^n(\text{Zero})) = \text{Succ}^n(\text{Zero})$$

Then

$$\text{Plus}(\text{Zero},\text{Succ}^{n+1}(\text{Zero}))=\text{Succ}(\text{Plus}(\text{Zero},\text{Succ}^n(\text{Zero}))) \qquad \text{(equation 2)}$$

$$=\text{Succ}(\text{Succ}^n(\text{Zero})) \qquad \text{(hypothesis)}$$

$$=\text{Succ}^{n+1}(\text{Zero}) \qquad \text{QED.}$$

12.4 Advantages and Disadvantages

Algebraic specifications are powerful; for example, Figure 12–5 shows an algebraic specification giving the Peano axioms for defining arithmetic. They have a strong mathematical basis; you can view an algebraic specification as a heterogeneous algebra.

On the other hand, algebraic specifications cannot deal with side effects, and so can be difficult to integrate with typical implementation languages. An implementation of the stack type would typically have Push modify a stack, rather than returning a new one.

Algebraic specifications can also be hard to understand; changing a single equation can have a substantial effect on meaning. For example, Figure 12–6 gives

---

types
  defines set
  uses element, boolean
syntax
  NullSet: $\rightarrow$ set
  AddMember: set $\times$ element $\rightarrow$ set
  DelMember: set $\times$ element $\rightarrow$ set
  IsMember: set $\times$ element $\rightarrow$ boolean
equations
  IsMember(NullSet,e) = false
  IsMember(AddMember(s,e_1),e_2) =
      ($e_1=e_2$) $\vee$ IsMember(s,e_2)
  DelMember(NullSet,e) = NullSet
  DelMember(AddMember(s,e_1),e_2) =
    if $e_1=e_2$
        then DelMember(s,e_2)
        else AddMember(DelMember(s,e_2),e_1)

Figure 12–6: Algebraic Specification of a Set

---

an algebraic specification of a set. The constructors are NullSet and AddMember; you can think of DelMember as editing the expression representing a set to eliminate all calls on AddMember with the same element as the DelMember. A multiset is similar to a set, except that any element may be present multiple times. The specification of a multiset is identical to Figure 12–6 except in the second line of the second equation for DelMember, which would read

  then s

instead of

  then DelMember(s,e_2)

Thus changing one short line of the specification makes a major change to the type it defines.

Exercises

12–1 Using the specification of Figure 12–6, prove that, for any set s,
        IsMember(DelMember(s,e),e) = false

12–2 Extend the set specification of Figure 12–6 to include union and intersection.

12–3 Modify the specification of Exercise 12–2 to define a multiset instead of a set. Add the function
     Count: multiset× element→integer
which returns the number of times the element is present in the multiset.

12–4 Using the specification of Exercise 12–3, prove that
     Count(Union(a,b),e) = Count(a,e) + Count(b,e)

12–5 Consolidate the examples of Figures 12–1 on page 138 and 12–2 on page 140 with that of Section 12.1.1 to give a specification of a depth-limited stack with recovery from underflow exceptions. Modify this specification to allow recovery from overflow exceptions in two ways.

     a. Pushing onto a full stack gives an overflow exception but leaves the stack alone.

     b. Pushing onto a full stack gives an overflow, throws away the bottom element of the stack, and pushes the new element.

Chapter 13

Trace
Specifications

As Chapter 12 showed, algebraic specifications cannot handle procedures with side effects. This chapter discusses techniques designed to deal with side effects. *State machine* specifications explicitly introduce procedures with side effects; *trace* specifications evolved from state machine specifications, and handle modules with complex history better.

13.1 State Machine Specifications

A state machine specification treats a module as defining an abstract machine. It divides the interface procedures into two classes.

- V-functions (for Variable or Value) report values. They have no side effects.

- O-functions (for Operations) change the state of the module. They do not return values.

Thus, unlike algebraic specifications, state machine specifications can handle side effects, and are more directly useful with typical implementation languages. Figure 13–1 recasts the table module of Figure 6–16 on page 78 as a state machine specification. Expressions in single quotes represent values before any effects take place. There is no InitTable procedure, since its sole purpose was to do the initialization implied by the **initially** clause.

---

vfun   Lookup: key → boolean, Item + {undefined}
  initially   ∀ k, Lookup(k) = (false,undefined)

ofun   Enter: Key k, Item i
  effect   Lookup(k) = (true, i)
  exceptions if ∃i | 'Lookup(k)' = (true, i) then ErrAlreadyEntered

ofun   Delete: Key k
  effect   Lookup(k) = (false, undefined)
  exceptions if ¬ ∃i | 'Lookup(k)' = (true, i) then ErrNotPresent

Figure 13–1: State Machine Specification: Table Module

A state machine specification may need auxiliary functions even more than algebraic specifications. An algebraic specification can represent some of the history of operations on a type as set of nested calls on interface procedures. State machine specifications cannot do so; instead, they must often introduce auxiliary functions simply to represent some aspect of the history of a sequence of operations. Figure 13–2 shows a state-machine specification of a stack. The auxiliary functions Depth and Items strongly suggest an array implementation.

13.2   Trace Specifications

Trace specifications make assertions about sequences of procedure calls. As with state-machine specifications, they define value-returning procedures and side-effect-producing procedures; they allow value-returning procedures to produce side effects. They provide assertions about values returned by the v-procedures. They also give assertions about legal sequences of procedure calls, and equivalences between sequences.

The following three rules define a *subtrace*.

1. The empty sequence, ϵ, is a subtrace.

2. Any syntactically valid procedure call is a subtrace. For example,

   $$X(p_1, p_2, \cdots, p_n)$$

   is a subtrace consisting of a call on procedure X with parameters $p_1 \cdots p_n$.

3. If T and S are subtraces, then T.S is also a subtrace. This represents the sequence of calls represented by T, followed by the sequence of calls represented by S.

---

ofun   Push: element e
  effect   Depth = 'Depth' + 1
          Items(Depth) = e
  exceptions   if 'Depth' $\geq$ Max then ErrOverflow

ofun   Pop:
  effects   Depth = 'Depth'-1
  exceptions   if 'Depth' = 0 then ErrUnderflow

vfun   Top: $\rightarrow$ element
  value   Items(Depth)
  exceptions   if 'Depth' = 0 then ErrEmptyStack

vfun   Empty: $\rightarrow$ boolean
  value   Depth = 0

auxiliary vfun   Depth: $\rightarrow$ integer
  initially   0

auxiliary vfun   Items: integer i $\rightarrow$ element
  initially   Items(i) = undefined

Figure 13–2: State Machine Stack Specification

A *trace* is a subtrace that begins at the beginning of time. That is, no calls on interface procedures occur before the start of the trace. Thus

    Push(5).Push(7).Top.Pop.Push(9).Pop.Pop.Top

is a subtrace; it is a trace if no other calls on Push, Pop, Top, or IsEmpty occur before it.

Legality assertions state that certain traces do not cause exceptions. L(T) means that no exceptions occur during the execution of trace T. L(ϵ) is always true, since legal traces always start from the initial state when no procedure calls have taken place. L(T.S) asserts that T.S is legal, which implies L(T). It does not imply L(S). If from the given legality assertions you cannot deduce that a trace is legal, then it is illegal.

A value assertion applies to a trace ending in a value-returning function. For example,

V(T.Push(a).Top) = a

gives the value of any legal trace ending in a Push followed by a Top. A value assertion does not of itself imply that the trace is legal; strictly speaking, each value assertion should occur in a context that implies its argument is legal. In the worst case,
you could modify the above example to say

L(T.Push(a).Top) $\Rightarrow$ V(T.Push(a).Top) = a

The assertion

$T_1 \equiv T_2$

says that T_1 and T_2 are equivalent. This means

$\forall S, L(T_1.S) = L(T_2.S) \wedge$
$\quad \forall F, L(T_1.S.F) \Rightarrow V(T_1.S.F) = V(T_2.S.F)$

where S is any subtrace, and F is a call on any value-returning function. That is, two
traces are equivalent if and only if you can substitute one for the other without
affecting legality or returned values. It is safe to call this "equivalence" since you
can prove it is an equivalence relation (that is, it is reflexive, symmetric, and transi-
tive). T_1 and T_2 may be of different lengths, and there is no guarantee that any prefixes of either are equivalent.

Figure 13–3 shows a trace specification for an unbounded stack. The syntax
section defines the calling sequences of the procedures; as with algebraic models of
side effects, "state" means a type representing the hidden internal state that is an
implicit parameter of most procedures, and an implicit result of side-effect-
producing procedures. Variables representing traces, such as T, implicitly range
over all possible traces composed of calls on procedures mentioned in the syntax
section.

To find the meaning of some long trace, use equivalence 6 to eliminate any call
on IsEmpty not at the end of a trace; this assertion means that IsEmpty has no side
effects. Equivalence 2 lets us eliminate any Pop immediately after a Push. Assertions 2 and 3 imply that Top is legal immediately after a Push, and that you can
eliminate any such calls (just like calls to Pop). All these operations together let you
turn any legal trace into a series of Push calls, possibly followed by a Top or
IsEmpty. Assertions 5, 7, and 8 determine the final value.

A trace beginning with Top or Pop is illegal, but this is not immediately
apparent from the specification. The only assertions from which you can deduce
legality of Pop or Top are 2 and 3. The first says that you can eliminate Pop from a
trace if a call on Push immediately precedes it. From the properties of equivalence,
you can deduce

L(T) $\Rightarrow$ L(T.Push(a).Pop)

since assertion 1 implies that you can append a Push to any legal trace. This
together with equation 3 implies

L(T) $\Rightarrow$ L(T.Push(a).Top)

---

syntax
   Push: element × state → state
   Pop: state → state
   Top: state → element
   IsEmpty: state → boolean
assertions
   1. L(T) ⇒ L(T.Push(e))

   2. T.Push(e).Pop ≡ T

   3. L(T.Top) = L(T.Pop)
   4. L(T.Top) ⇒ T.Top ≡ T
   5. L(T) ⇒ V(T.Push(e).Top) = e

   6. T.IsEmpty ≡ T
   7. V(IsEmpty) = true
   8. L(T) ⇒ V(T.Push(e).IsEmpty) = false

Figure 13–3: Trace Specification of a Stack

Since no other equations say anything that lets you deduce legality of Pop or Top (you can't run implication 4 backward), you can deduce only that these procedures are legal after a Push. Since you cannot deduce that a Pop or Top is legal if not preceded by a Push, you can deduce that a trace consisting solely of a Pop or Top is illegal.

Figure 13–3 used variable T to represent any possible prefix of a trace. Sometimes you might need to restrict assertions to apply only to traces of a particular form. For example, suppose the programming language required explicit initialization of every module, rather than the implicit initialization that Figure 13–3 presumes. Then the only legal traces would be ones that start with a call on a special *Init* procedure. Thus Equation 1 might become the two assertions

   L(Init)
   (T=Init.T1 ∧ L(T)) ⇒ L(T.Push(e))

13.3 More Complex Traces

Some problems that are difficult to specify using other techniques are easy with trace specifications. Some additional notational conveniences make certain common situations easier to specify. You can abbreviate a trace of the form

$$p(a_N).p(a_{N+1}) \cdots p(a_M)$$

to $p_{i=N}^{M}(a_i)$. You can further abbreviate $p_{i=1}^{M}(a_i)$ to $p_i^{M}(a_i)$. This notation is especially good for expressing legality constraints that depend on the length of a trace. For example, to specify a bounded stack instead of the unbounded one of 13–3, you can replace legality assertion 1 with

$L(Push_i^{M}(a_i))$

or possibly

$L(Init.Push_i^{M}(a_i))$

if you need a module initialization procedure. This says that a trace of Max calls on Push is legal, and therefore any trace of less than Max calls on Push is also legal. This eliminates one reason for auxiliary functions such as Depth.

Sometimes you need a subroutine to deliver a unique value. Commonly, such a routine returns a number one higher than the last number it returned. However, if all you want is to say that each value is different, this gives too many constraints. Figure 13–4 shows an alternative trace specification. Equation 1 says that any number of calls is legal, up to some limit NumElements. Equation 2 says that if one trace yields the same value as another trace, the two must have the same length; thus each successive call yields a distinct value.

The specification of Figure 13–3 cheated slightly by defining the procedures to operate on a single, hidden stack. This avoided having to say that operations on one stack do not interfere with operations on any other stack. You can still implement the procedures to take a stack as a parameter, using the standard trick mentioned in Section 12.2 of passing the entire state of the module as an extra parameter. If you did not do this, you would need to make an entire collection of assertions like

$s1 \neq s2 \Rightarrow T.Push(s1,e1).Push(s2,e2) \equiv T.Push(s2,e2).Push(s1,e1)$

---

syntax
 UniqueElement: $\rightarrow$ element
assertions
 1. $L(UniqueElement^{NumElements})$
 2. $V(UniqueElement^M) = V(UniqueElement^N) \rightarrow N=M$

Figure 13–4: Trace Specification of Unique Element Generator

---

since otherwise you would not be able to reorder these calls to get Push and Pop on
the same stack together. You typically need one such equation per pair of interface
procedures. You could reduce the writing task by introducing special notation, such
as

$$\forall P_1, P_2 \in \{Push, Pop, Top, IsEmpty\} \quad \forall s_1, s_2 \in stack$$
$$s_1 \neq s_2 \Rightarrow T.P_1(\cdots s_1 \cdots).P_2(\cdots s_2 \cdots) \equiv T.P_2(\cdots s_2 \cdots).P_1(\cdots s_1 \cdots)$$

This is unsatisfying because of the imprecision about what " $\cdots$ " means.

13.4   Normal Forms for Traces

From the assertions of Figure 13–3, you can deduce that all legal traces are
equivalent to a trace in one of the forms

> T
> T.IsEmpty
> T.Push(a).Pop
> T.Push(a).Top

where T consists solely of zero or more Push operations, by induction on the length
of the trace. However, the proof is tedious.

Traces consisting solely of a sequence of Push calls are in *normal form*. Normal form traces are important for the same reason that constructor functions in
algebraic specifications are important: they help us organize our specifications more
clearly. The set of normal form traces for a module is a subset of all possible traces
such that every trace is equivalent to some normal form trace.

Any module has at least the trivial normal form consisting of all possible traces.
A good normal form is one that simplifies the specification, typically by restricting
the trace to using a subset of the possible interface procedures. It is especially useful if all normal form traces are legal. Finding a normal form for traces is an art,
just as finding constructor functions can be an art; in the worst case you may have to
live with the trivial normal form.

In defining normal forms you may need to make assertions about what calls the
trace contains. To make this easier, you can use some predefined functions on
traces. For any trace T, **length**(T) is its length, that is, the number of calls it contains. For any trace T and interface procedure P, **count**(T,P) is the number of calls
to P in T. The assertion **all**(T,P) means that T consists solely of calls on procedure
P (that is, that **count**(T,P) = **length**(T)). Thus the assertion that a stack trace is in
normal form is **all**(T,Push).

To structure a trace around a normal form, consider each trace of the form
T.P, where T is in normal form and P is a call on an interface procedure.

1.   If T.P is illegal, ignore it. Otherwise continue with the following steps.

    2.   Define the normal form trace to which T.P is equivalent.

    3.   If P returns a value, assert what the value is.

Applying these principles to the stack example gives Figure 13–5. You need not add equations such as L(T.Top) and L(T.Pop), since you can deduce these from Assertions 1 and 2. For example, Assertion 1 says

    T.Pop ≡ T1

From the prior conditions you know L(T) and T=T1.Push(e). Thus you know L(T1) by the property of legality of prefixes of legal traces; by the properties of equivalence you can deduce L(T.Pop).

In addition to structuring the specification a little better, the normal form let us give a simpler definition of IsEmpty in equation 5 of Figure 13–5. You could convert this to a specification of a depth-limited stack by changing the first line to

$$\forall\, T\ normal(T) \Rightarrow (\ (\ L(T) \Leftrightarrow length(T) \leq Max)\ \wedge$$

Auxiliary functions like these can help in writing assertions like the reordering assertions mentioned at the end of the last section. For example, you can introduce

---

syntax
    Push: element × state → state
    Pop: state → state
    Top: state → element
    IsEmpty: state → boolean
predicates
    normal(T) ⟺ **all**(T,Push)
assertions
∀T normal(T) ⇒ (L(T) ∧
    T=T1.Push(e) ⇒
        1. T.Pop ≡ T1

        2. T.Top ≡ T
        3. V(T.Top) = e

      4. T.IsEmpty ≡ T
      5. V(T.IsEmpty) = (**length**(T)=0)
)

Figure 13–5: Normal Form Trace Specification of a Stack

---

a built-in function **callname**(T), applicable to traces of length one, which returns the name of the procedure called in the trace.   You can extend **callname** to longer traces by having it return the set of names of procedures in the trace.   You can define your own auxiliary function stackarg(T), also applicable to traces of length one, via the equations

stackarg(Push(s,e)) = s   stackarg(Top(s)) = s
stackarg(Pop(s)) = s   stackarg(IsEmpty(s)) = s

If you had arranged things so that all the appropriate interface procedures had the stack argument in a particular position, you could define similar generic built-in operations such as arg1(T) or arg2(T), and use them; defining your own lets you adapt to having the relevant parameter in different places.   You can then rewrite the old equation as

$\forall$ P$_1$,P$_2$ (**callname**(P$_i$)$\in$ {Push,Pop,Top,IsEmpty} $\wedge$
     stackarg(P$_1$) $\neq$ stackarg(P$_2$)) $\Rightarrow$ T.P$_1$.P$_2$$\equiv$T.P$_2$.P$_1$

When defining auxiliary functions like these, make sure you do not fall into the trap of adding functions that imply special implementation properties.   The ones I have shown above all define properties you can determine by simple inspection of a trace.

13.5 Advantages and Disadvantages

Trace specifications allow assertions about sequences of procedure calls, and thus make it easier to talk about the history of calls on procedures from a module.   However, it is difficult to talk about passing the value returned by one procedure as a parameter to another.   Figure 13–6 shows an attempt at a state machine

---

vfun   IsMale: person $\rightarrow$ boolean

vfun   NamePerson: person $\rightarrow$ name

?fun   NewPerson: name n$\times$ boolean s $\rightarrow$ person
     value new person p distinct from all others with
                NamePerson(p) = n
                IsMale(p) = s

Figure 13–6: State Machine Specification for NewPerson

---

specification of a module for representing some information about persons. NewPerson creates a new person; the specification gave no good way of stating this except by resorting to English. Furthermore, NewPerson is not really either a v-function or an o-function. It returns a value, but must have some side effects to guarantee that it returns a person distinct from all others. On the other hand, in an algebraic specification it would be easy to say

NamePerson(NewPerson(n,b))=n

Figure 13–7 shows a trace specification of the same module. It is longer and more complex, simply because it has to say things like

$p = \text{NewPerson}(n,b) \Rightarrow V(\text{NamePerson}(p)) = n$

You might get around this by adding machinery for translating nested calls into sequences of calls. Thus you might treat

$V(T.\text{NamePerson}(\text{NewPerson}(n,b))) = n$

as an abbreviation for a longer assertion such as

$V(T.\text{NewPerson}(n,b)) = p \Rightarrow V(T.\text{NewPerson}(n,b).\text{NamePerson}(p)) = n$

Another disadvantage is that trace specifications do not explicitly state the conditions under which undesired events occur; you must deduce them from the legality and equivalence assertions. You can lessen this problem by following the guidelines of Section 13.4.

---

syntax

      IsMale: person $\rightarrow$ boolean

      NamePerson: person $\rightarrow$ name

      NewPerson: name$\times$boolean$\rightarrow$ person

assertions

  1. $L(T) \Rightarrow L(T.\text{NewPerson}(n,b))$

  2. $V(\text{NewPerson}_i^N(n_i,b_i)) = V(\text{NewPerson}_j^M(n_j,b_j)) \Rightarrow N = M$

$T = T_1.\text{NewPerson}(n,b).T_2 \land L(T) \land V(T_1.\text{NewPerson}(n,b)) = p \Rightarrow$

    3. $T.\text{IsMale}(p) \equiv T \land$

    4. $V(T.\text{IsMale}(p)) = b \land$

    5. $T.\text{NamePerson}(p) \equiv T \land$

    6. $V(T.\text{NamePerson}(p)) = n$

Figure 13–7: Trace Specification of NewPerson

Further Reading

Bartussek and Parnas (1977) introduced trace specifications; McLean (1984) gave a formal definition of the method. Hoffman and Snodgrass (1986) introduced the idea of using normal forms.

Exercises

13–1 Prove that $\equiv$ is an equivalence relation.

13–2 Give a trace specification of a queue, with operations Add (to the end), Front (returning the front element), Remove (from the front), and IsEmpty.

13–3 Give a trace specification of a double-ended queue, with operations Add-Front, AddBack, Front, Back, RemoveFront, and RemoveBack. Use a normal form consisting of zero or more calls on AddFront.

13–4 Consider both AddFront and AddBack to be queue constructors. The trace specification of Exercise 13–3 was asymmetric, in that it picked one particular procedure as the constructor. Give a trace specification of a double-ended queue, but allow a normal form consisting of mixed calls on AddFront and AddBack. Treat AddFront and AddBack as symmetrically as you can.

Chapter 14

Abstract
Modeling

Abstract modeling defines the meaning of a module by specifying its interface procedures via operations on well-known mathematical objects such as sets, sequences, multisets, trees, and graphs. From an information-hiding purist's point of view, an abstract model may be undesirable because it strongly suggests the implementation ought to follow directly from the model, and thus may unduly constrain possible implementations. However, abstract modeling is important, since it is the main way of proving programs consistent with their specifications (that is, proving program "correctness").

14.1 Overview of Verification

Teaching verification is beyond the scope of this book, especially since many lower-level undergraduate courses now introduce some aspects of it. I intend this section to serve as a reminder to those who already know something of verification, and as an introduction to the key ideas for those who do not. Readers who want to understand verification in greater depth can consult the suggested readings.

The basic idea of verification is to prove that, given certain initial conditions, a program or portion of a program establishes certain final conditions. The *state* of a program at any point in time is the values of all the variables in the program (including components of arrays and records). Any program transforms some initial state into some final state (or set of possible final states, if the program is nondeterministic). You can describe a set of possible states via a *condition* or *predicate*, a boolean expression describing properties of some of the variables. The expression **true** represents all possible states; the expression **false** represents no states.

Instead of viewing a program as transforming states, you can view it as transforming a predicate describing an initial state into a predicate describing the corresponding final state. A *precondition* is a predicate describing the set of possible states before a program executes; a *postcondition* is a predicate describing the set of possible states after the program executes. The assertion

> {P} S {Q}

means that, given precondition P, program S establishes postcondition Q. Thus

> { true }
> **if** x ≤ y
>   **then** M := x-1
>   **else** M := y-1
> { M < x ∧ M < y }

means that, given any initial conditions, the **if** statement assigns M a number smaller than either x or y. As with any predicates involving a change in state, you might enclose subexpressions of Q in quotes to show you mean the value of the expression before the statement executes.

To prove a program correct, you have to show how statements in the programming language transform one predicate into another. You can do this in one of two ways. You can work forward from the precondition, showing how each statement transforms it into a new condition, then show how the condition you finish with implies the postcondition. Alternatively, you can work backward from the postcondition, determining the weakest (least constraining) condition that must be true before each statement to establish the condition you want to be true afterward, then show how the precondition implies the weakest precondition of the whole statement. For example, in working forward,

> {P(E)} x := E {P(x)}

characterizes the meaning of an assignment statement. This means that if some predicate is true of expression E before the assignment it is true of x after the assignment. In working backward,

> wp(x:=E,P(x)) = P(E)

means that, if you want P(x) to be true after the assignment, you must establish P(E) before the assignment. For example,

> wp(x:=x+1, x>7) = (x+1)>7 = x>6

It usually works out better to work backward from the postconditions via weakest preconditions.

14.2 Overview of Abstract Modeling

To prove a program correct, you need to work with predicates at the level of the programming language and variables in the language. Unfortunately, working at this level prevents you from using the abstractions you need to keep a problem intellectually manageable.

Abstract modeling tries to alleviate this problem. You first plan the meanings of your operations at a higher level, then translate our predicates to a lower level for the actual proof. You model the concrete data structures your programs manipulate via abstract mathematical objects such as sequences and sets, and describe the meaning of the interface procedures via predicates on these abstract objects. Later, when you develop the concrete representation of the abstract model, you establish a correspondence between the abstract and concrete representations via

- an *abstraction function*, which maps a concrete data structure into an abstract model of the data structure, and

- a *representation function*, which maps an instance of the abstract model into the set of all possible concrete representations of the abstraction. This is a one-to-many mapping because there can be several representations of the "same" abstract value. For example, in an array-based stack implementation, the values stored in the array past the stack pointer are irrelevant to the abstract stack the array represents.

The steps involved in proving a program correct via abstract modeling are as follows.

1. Define an abstract model of the data the program manipulates. For example, you might define a queue as a type of sequence. Include an *abstract invariant*: a predicate that is always true of instances of the abstract type that model instances of the concrete data type. For example,

    Length(q)$\leq$Limit

    says that sequences representing queues might always be shorter than some limit.

2. For each interface procedure, define preconditions and postconditions giving the meaning of the procedure using the abstract model. These are the *abstract specifications* of the procedures. For example, the meaning of Add-Front might be

    procedure AddFront(**var** q:queue; e:element);
       pre Length(abs(q)) < Limit
       post abs(q) = <e> ~ 'abs(q)'

    which means AddFront changes q, forming a new value that corresponds to concatenating a sequence containing just the element e with the sequence representing q before the AddFront.

3. Prove that the abstract specification of each procedure establishes the abstract invariant. That is, given the invariant and the precondition, show that the postcondition implies the invariant. For example, for AddFront you have to show

(Length('abs(q)')≤Limit∧ Length('abs(q)') < Limit ∧
abs(q)= < e > ~ 'abs(q)')   ⇒ Length(abs(q))≤Limit

4. Define a concrete representation of the data the module manipulates. For
   example, you might represent the queue as a doubly-linked list, with
   pointers to the first and last elements.

   type
   qElem = **record** elem:element; Forward,Back: ^qElem **end**;
   queue = **record** Head, Tail: ^qElem **end**;

5. Define the abstraction function, abs, and the representation function, rep.
   For a collection like a queue, this may involve a recursive definition. For
   example,

   abs: queue→sequence
   addEnd: sequence× qElem^→sequence

   abs(q) = addEnd(< >, q.Front)
   addEnd(s,p) = **if** p=**nil** **then** s **else** addEnd(s~ <p^.elem>,p^.Forward)

   defines the relationship between queues and sequences.

6. Translate the abstract specifications (invariant, preconditions, and postconditions) into concrete specifications. This may require that you prove some
   abstract expressions are equivalent to corresponding concrete ones.

7. Write the bodies of the interface procedures.

8. Use the concrete specifications and the method of weakest preconditions to
   prove the bodies correct.

You can stop at the third step if you just want to specify the meaning of the interface procedures.

14.3   Relation to Algebraic Specifications

The introduction said that abstract models may use only operations on well-known
mathematical objects such as sets and sequences. The three reasons for this restriction are

1. you must know the precise meaning of the operations you use;

2. for ease of mathematical manipulation, the operations must be pure functions without side effects;

3. the operations should be familiar ones, so you understand how to use them.

Any algebraic specification defines operations with the first two properties. If you
already have an algebraic specification of some module, you can use it directly in the
proof of correctness of its implementation. The remainder of this section is an
extended example, showing how to use an algebraic specification of a stack to prove
the correctness of an array-based stack implementation.

types
   defines stack
   uses boolean, element
syntax
   Push: stack× element→stack + {*overflow*}
   Pop: stack→stack + {*underflow*}
   Top: stack→element + {*novalue*}
   Empty: stack→boolean
   NewStack: →stack
auxiliary
   Depth: stack→integer
equations
  1. Pop(NewStack) = *underflow*
  2. Pop(Push(s,e)) = s
  3. Top(NewStack) = *undefined*
  4. Top(Push(s,e)) = e
  5. Empty(Newstack) = true
  6. Empty(Push(s,e)) = false
auxiliary equations
  7. Depth(NewStack) = 0
  8. Depth(Push(s,e)) = Depth(s) + 1
  9. Push(s,e) = *overflow* if Depth(s)$\geq$Max

Figure 14–1: Algebraic Specification of a Depth-Limited Stack

Figure 14–1 shows the algebraic specification of a depth-limited stack. It combines the original unlimited stack of Figure 12–1 on page 138 with the auxiliary Depth function of Figure 12–2 on page 140.

Figure 14–2 shows abstract preconditions and postconditions of the concrete stack operations, with one concrete operation per abstract operation. An alternative is to combine the abstract Pop and Top operations into a cTop function that pops the stack as a side effect. Each condition in the algebraic specification that results in an exception becomes part of the precondition of the concrete operation. Thus

   Pop(NewStack) = *underflow*

becomes the precondition

   abs(s) $\neq$ NewStack

to cPop. The abstract postcondition of an interface procedure is that the result returned, or the value of the variable modified by a side effect, is the same as the

---

invariant $\forall s \in$ Stack, $0 \leq$ Depth(abs(s)) $\leq$ Max
procedure cPush(**var** s:Stack; e:element);
    pre Depth(abs(s)) < Max
    post abs(s) = Push('abs(s)',e)
procedure cPop(**var** s:Stack);
    pre abs(s) $\neq$ NewStack
    post abs(s) = Pop('abs(s)')
function cTop(s:Stack):element;
    pre abs(s) $\neq$ NewStack
    post result = Top(abs(s))
function cEmpty(s:Stack):boolean;
    post result = Empty(abs(s))

Figure 14–2: Abstract Specifications for Stack Operations

---

value of the corresponding abstract operation applied to the abstract values corresponding to the input parameters.

Figure 14–3 shows a Pascal type declaration for an array-based stack representation. Abs and rep are the abstraction and representation functions. They capture the typical intuitive description of this implementation: the stack is the elements of the array between 1 and the stack pointer, in the order they were pushed, with the top of the stack at the place indexed by the stack pointer. AddN is an auxiliary function; AddN(a,N) is the stack formed by pushing elements 1 through N of a.arr onto an empty stack.

You must prove that abs and rep really are inverses of each other. This is easy to do, by induction on the depth of a stack. First, let us allow the notation

$$abs(rep(X)) = Y$$

as an abbreviation for

$$\forall x \in rep(X), abs(x) = Y$$

Then, proving

$$abs(rep(NewStack)) = NewStack$$

is trivial; rep(NewStack) is all those concrete stacks with stack pointer 0.

$$\forall a \in rep(NewStack), abs(a) = addN(a,a.sp) = addN(a,0) = NewStack$$

Now assume that for some stack S, abs(rep(S)) = S. Pick some arbitrary $a \in$ rep(Push(S,e)). Then

---

const Max = ...;
type cstack = **record**
                   arr: **array** [1..Max] **of** element;
                   sp: 0..Max := 0;
                   end;

abs: cstack → stack
rep: stack → $\mathbb{P}$(cstack)
addN: cstack×integer → stack

abs(a) = addN(a,a.sp)
addN(a,0) = NewStack
$\forall N \geq 1$ addN(a,N) = Push(addN(a,N-1), a.arr[N])

rep(NewStack) = { a∈cstack | a.sp=0 }
rep(Push(s,e)) = { a∈cstack | a.arr[a.sp]=e∧
     $\exists b \in$rep(s) | (a.sp=b.sp+1 ∧ $\forall 1 \leq i \leq$b.sp, a.arr[i]=b.arr[i]) }

Figure 14–3: Abstraction and Representation Functions for Array-Based Stack

---

a.arr[a.sp]=e ∧ $\exists b \in$rep(s) | (a.sp=b.sp+1 ∧ $\forall 1 \leq i \leq$b.sp, a.arr[i]=b.arr[i])
Thus a.sp$\geq$1, so

$$\text{abs(a)} = \text{addN(a,a.sp)} = \text{Push(addN(a,a.sp}-1),\text{a.arr[a.sp])}$$
$$= \text{Push(addN(a,a.sp}-1),\text{e)}$$

Now all that remains is to prove addN(a,a.sp$-$1)=S. You know that a.sp$-$1=b.sp; you can easily prove by induction that

$$\forall 1 \leq n \leq \text{b.sp, addN(a,n)=addN(b,n)}$$

since $\forall 1 \leq i \leq$b.sp, a.arr[i]=b.arr[i]. Thus

$$\text{addN(a,a.sp}-1) = \text{addN(b,b.sp)} = \text{abs(b)} = \text{S}$$

Next, you must translate the abstract specifications into concrete ones. Figure 14–4 shows the results of this translation. To do this, you have to show that

Depth(abs(s)) = s.sp
Top(abs(s)) = s.arr[s.sp]
abs(s)=NewStack$\equiv$ s.sp=0

which are straightforward.

---

invariant $\forall s \in$ Stack, $0 \leq s.sp \leq Max$
procedure cPush(**var** s:Stack; e:element);
   pre s.sp $<$ Max
   post s.sp $=$'s.sp $+ 1$' $\wedge$ s.arr[s.sp] $=$ e
procedure cPop(**var** s:Stack);
   pre s.sp > 0
   post s.sp $=$'s.sp-1'
function cTop(s:Stack):element;
   pre s.sp > 0
   post result $=$ s.arr[s.sp]
function cEmpty(s:Stack):boolean;
   post result $=$ (s.sp $= 0$)

Figure 14–4: Concrete Specifications for Stack Operations

Finally, you write implementations of the bodies of all the interface procedures, and prove that they are correct with respect to the concrete specifications. For a simple data type like the stack, this last step is trivial; the bodies of the procedures are simple statements that correspond almost exactly to the specifications.

Further Reading

Wulf et al. (1981a) give a more detailed explanation of verification techniques, and how to use them with abstract modeling. Some introductory computer science texts now introduce the basics of verification [Goldschlager and Lister 1982]. Dijkstra (1976) introduced the idea of weakest precondition, and shows how to develop small programs from their specifications. Gries (1981) extends this work.

Exercises

14–1   Using the algebraic specification of sets from Figure 12–6 on page 145, write an abstract model of sets of small integers (that is, integers between 0 and K for some K).

     a. Develop an implementation using boolean arrays, where AddMember and DelMember modify their first argument in place.

     b. Translate your abstract specification into a concrete one.

     c. Prove your implementation correct.

14–2 Write the equivalent of Figures 14–3 and 14–4 for a stack represented as

type

    stackElemP = ^stackElem;

    stackElem = **record** Next:stackElemP; Elem:element **end**;

    cstack = **record** Top:stackElemP; CurrentDepth:integer **end**;

Chapter 15

_____ The Workplace _____

This chapter documents a few areas in which typical industrial jobs differ from what a new recruit might think. Programmers typically work in teams; Section 15.1 describes some typical team organizations. To work together, people usually have to hold meetings; Section 15.2 talks about different types of meetings and how to run them. Section 15.3 talks about several psychological considerations for professional programmers. Section 15.4 suggests you keep a log to record what you work on, and what you learn from your work.

15.1 Team Structure

Any organization has both a formal and an informal structure. The *informal structure* of an organization is whatever communication patterns happen to evolve. Much of this communication is social chit-chat, but amidst such apparently unproductive conversation, a surprising amount of technical communication and learning takes place. While relaxing over a coffee break, someone gripes about his current difficulty, and a fellow worker points out some tool that solves the problem easily.

Brooks (1975) points out that any successful group needs

- a goal
- a division of labor
- a leader

A leader is responsible for ensuring that the group she manages meets its goals. Typically someone higher in the organization sets at least the major goals of the group. The leader ensures that the group can work effectively: that they have the resources they need, their goals are clear, they are well-motivated, and misunderstandings are rare. The leader also monitors progress, and perhaps reports it to higher-level managers.

A group needs both technical leadership and administrative leadership, which it might get from different people. Variations in formal group structures are principally different ways of dividing labor, combined with smaller differences in ways of providing leadership.

Most team organizations try to address conflicting needs. On the one hand, requirements analysis and preliminary design require a small group of experienced people. On the other hand, the work involved in detailed design, coding, integration, and testing is so large that it requires many people. Good team organizations integrate few designers with many implementors.

15.1.1 Small Teams

If a project is small enough that a small (2–5 person) group can complete the work in reasonable time, and if the group consists of people with roughly similar ability, it may be possible to avoid formal structure by forming a *democratic team*. Typically a manager would provide administrative leadership, and at different times different members of the group might provide technical leadership. The members of the group would divide the work among themselves, and each person would be responsible for one or more subsystems of the project. Design reviews and code walkthroughs would ensure that several members of the group understood each subsystem; if one person left for any reason, there would be at least one other person who could take over the work.

Unfortunately, it is rare to find enough people of similar levels of ability for this organization to work. Furthermore, if the members of a team are equal in authority, the team may waste much time in internal squabbles. Such teams may still need a leader to arbitrate when the team cannot reach a consensus. Which person is leader may vary from time to time.

Commonly, a small project might have one experienced programmer and several less experienced programmers, who would form a *simple team*. The experienced programmer would become team leader, and would divide work among the others. Depending on individual abilities, the team leader might do most of the preliminary design, or might have a team member of intermediate experience assist. Some team members might be able to do their own detailed designs, which the leader would review. Others might require that the leader or a more experienced programmer do the detailed design for them.

Larger projects require multiple teams, and thus require further organization to coordinate the teams.

15.1.2 Chief Programmer Teams

With chief programmer teams, the system designers are a small group of experi-enced programmers. The chief programmers divide the system up among them-selves, and each is responsible for designing, coding, integrating and testing his or her own subsystem. The collection of chief programmers may act in some ways like a democratic team.

The term *chief programmer team* does not refer to the collection of *chief pro-grammers*: it refers to the group of people assigned to support the work of a chief programmer. Team compositions vary; the key similarities are that the chief pro-grammer is completely in charge of the team, and is free to make all the technical and administrative decisions for the team. Typical team members include

- an *assistant programmer*, whose chief responsibility is to understudy the chief programmer and be ready to take over if the chief leaves the project. The chief may assign the assistant particular design, coding, or testing responsi-bilities.

- an *editor*, responsible for taking draft documents (of the sort listed in Figure 2–1 on page 8) from the chief programmer and making them ready for pub-lication.

- an *administrator*, who relieves the chief programmer of day-to-day adminis-trative details.

- a *librarian*, responsible for entering programs and test cases and installing them in the appropriate libraries. This person handles the day-to-day details of configuration management, though the chief programmer makes all deci-sions about when to update previously stable libraries.

- a *toolsmith*, who adapts the existing tools to the needs of the team, and writes small special-purpose tools for specialized jobs. This person needs to be an expert on the host system used for program development.

- a *language lawyer*, who can advise the chief programmer on the best way to use facilities of the implementation language.

- one or two *secretaries*, to support the work of the editor and administrator.

Some projects adopt an approach more-or-less like chief programmer teams, but try to reduce personnel by eliminating some of the team positions, or making several of the team members responsible for multiple projects. Sometimes this works out well. Brooks (1975) reports that the language lawyer can serve several teams. If they have convenient programming development tools, some programmers find it easier to enter their own programs than to use a librarian. This reduces the librarian's duties to the point where one can serve several projects.

Sometimes eliminating team members does not work out well at all. Some projects try to eliminate the administrator, only to find the chief programmer neglects administrative duties. Managers sometimes fail to understand why a group needs its own toolsmith, thinking that a standard collection of tools or a company-wide tool support group should suffice. Chapter 19 discusses the role of tools in software development.

A project may also need a chief architect to oversee the chief programmers.

15.1.3 Chief Programmer/Chief Engineer

Some aerospace projects modify the chief programmer team approach by adding a chief engineer, responsible for specifying the requirements of a subsystem and designing tests. The chief engineer acts in some ways like a customer for the team. The project manager needs to make sure to give appropriate credit to each of the two leaders.

15.1.4 Designer/Team Leader

Chief programmer teams have an extremely specialized division of labor that some people feel makes everyone but the chief programmer feel like second-class citizens. It is common for a project to have a few experienced programmers and a larger collection of less experienced programmers. The experienced programmers form a small design team; when the design is complete, each becomes team leader for a subproject responsible for some collection of modules. Each team might have a different organization, but simple teams like those of Section 15.1.1 are common. This approach worked well during Bell-Northern's development of DATAPAC in the late 1970s.

15.2 Meetings

When several people work together, they need to meet to coordinate with each other. Unfortunately, people commonly regard meetings as unproductive interludes that take them away from their real work. To some extent this arises from short-sightedness: meetings are like many disciplines that have easily visible short-term costs and less visible long-term benefits. Largely, however, the perception arises because most meetings are run poorly. Running successful meetings is an important skill for managers and team leaders.

A successful meeting should have five characteristics.

1. It must have a clear purpose, one that requires the presence of all the participants. As much as possible, a meeting should do the minimum needed to achieve the purpose, and let people get back to their individual work.

2. It must stick to the purpose. Almost always, this requires having a chairperson whose main job is to keep the meeting on track. A team leader or manager would normally chair the meeting; a group of equals without an obvious leader should select a chairperson.

3. It must start and end on time. Starting late encourages lateness and wastes people's time. If it goes on too long, people get tired and their attention wanders; they may leave because of other commitments.

4. Participants should come prepared to address the purpose. The type of preparation depends on the type of meeting, discussed in the following sections.

5. If the meeting makes any decisions, someone should record them. If the meeting reveals any information that people not at the meeting should know, someone should record it. Thus at most meetings one participant should keep and circulate a set of minutes.

There are two major categories of meetings. A *status* meeting simply reports status. An *action* meeting solves a particular problem, or designs a particular item, or reviews some particular document. Action meetings divide into *decision-making meetings* and *brainstorming sessions*.

15.2.1 Status Meetings

The purpose of a status meeting is to bring the participants up to date on the state of other people's portions of a project. Participants are those who will report status, and those who need to hear it. A meeting is necessary only if the people who need to hear the status need also to interact with those reporting it, or if it is faster for everyone to do it that way than to write up a short status memo for circulation.

A status meeting needs an agenda, normally consisting of reports from particular people on the work they are responsible for. Everyone should keep new business to a minimum. If status shows that you must choose some action, do so at a separate meeting — but perhaps immediately after the end of the status meeting. Typically only a subset of the people who need to hear status reports need to be at a meeting to solve problems that show up in the report; mixing the two wastes the time of all the others.

Ideally, status meetings are short — ten to fifteen minutes. Folklore tells of one manager who kept status meetings brief by holding them in a room that had no chairs.

15.2.2 Brainstorming Sessions

The purpose of a brainstorming session is to come up with a variety of possible solutions to some particular problem or set of closely related problems. Participants are all those who might have some ideas to contribute — which may include junior people as well as experienced designers. One holds brainstorming sessions because ideas one person suggests often inspire ideas in other people; a group that interacts well together in this way can be much more creative than any one person in the group.

A standard danger in brainstorming is to throw away ideas too soon. You must evaluate your ideas eventually, but in a separate step once all the ideas are in the open. Even ideas you eventually reject may stimulate other ideas, and may have good properties you can try to incorporate into the solution you accept.

A person can quietly reject his own ideas because he fears criticism, or because he expects to be ignored. Thus participants at a brainstorming session have to be especially careful to encourage new ideas. Possible ground rules for encouraging people include the following:

- Never dismiss or criticize a suggestion (until a separate evaluation phase, later).

- Before stating a new idea of your own, restate what the previous speaker said to his or her satisfaction.

- Before stating a new idea of your own, find at least one good thing to say about the previous idea.

Think tanks specialize in brainstorming, and have evolved techniques for stimulating creativity. One approach is to require each participant to write down many ideas in too a short time to think about any of them in detail. This prevents people from taking the time to evaluate their ideas, which means more ideas get into the later discussions.

At the end of the brainstorming session, or in a separate meeting, you need to evaluate all the ideas that came out of it. This evaluation should take the form of measuring all the ideas according to a common set of criteria. An idea that fails several criteria may turn out well on others. Performing this evaluation may cut out several ideas, but may also suggest modifications to some ideas and may suggest new ideas.

15.2.3 Decision-Making Meetings

Decision-making meetings ought to be uncommon. Normally, a decision falls into some particular person's area of authority, and there is no need to meet to agree on something. However, sometimes a decision is not clear-cut, and the decision-maker wants suggestions or advice from others affected by the decision.

A common type of decision-making meeting chooses between several alternative designs. Individual designers, or the minutes of a brainstorming session, might propose alternatives. Participants at a decision-making meeting compare and evaluate the alternatives, and try to choose among them. Participants should prepare for such a meeting by reading the alternatives.

15.3 Programmer Psychology

The psychology of programmers and programming groups is too large a topic to cover in this book. However, there are a few ideas that every professional programmer should be aware of. Each of them corresponds to a problem area that you can do something to improve.

15.3.1 Ego

We have all heard of temperamental artists and performers, and understand they have ego invested in what they create. Software engineering involves creativity, too, although perhaps of a different sort. Whatever the differences between the individual areas, they have the common thread that when we create something, we view it as an extension of ourselves. It is extremely hard to step back and examine our creations objectively.

The particular way in which ego shows up in creating software is that programmers finds it difficult to see bugs in their own programs or flaws in their own designs. Finding a bug involves accepting that our work has flaws, which involves accepting that we have flaws. "Everyone makes mistakes," but unconsciously we refuse to believe it of ourselves until forced to by outside circumstances.

Fortunately for our products (but not for our egos), other people have much less difficulty finding flaws in what we do. The best way to find a problem in a design is to have someone review it who didn't create it. The best way to ensure a program is well-written, and a good way of finding bugs, is to have someone else read it. Often, simply having to explain our programs to someone else gives us just enough objectivity to find out what went wrong. This observation is the basic idea behind code walkthroughs (see Section 18.3.3). Some shops go further, and encourage programmers to think of code as belonging to the group, rather than the individual. This is called "egoless programming," because it tries to avoid having programmers invest much ego in the programming they do.

15.3.2 Programmer Variability

Innumerable works on programmer productivity point out that individual programmers differ by factors of ten or more in how fast they produce code, and by factors of two to five in how efficient the code runs. It is easy to throw up your hands and say that this results from innate differences. However, there are some things you can do to improve your own abilities.

Psychological studies show that expert programmers are not necessarily better at abstract thinking than novices. Primarily, they *encode* problems better. Encoding is the mental process of finding patterns in a problem and representing the problem as a structure of *chunks*. People can keep only 7 ± 2 chunks in short-term memory at one time. Experts have encountered more patterns than novices, and so can represent the same amount of information in fewer (but larger) chunks. Thus a key benefit of "experience" is not simply years of work, but exposure to a variety of different problems.

To some extent you get more experience by programming at your regular job. You can improve on this by trying to get yourself assigned to projects outside your main area of familiarity every so often. You can get wider exposure to different problems by reading other people's code, primarily by participating in walkthroughs. However, the best programmers often became the best by programming a lot, beyond what they had to do to get their immediate job done. This is true of other fields, too. Chuck Yeager, the ace pilot who first broke the sound barrier, says that if he were a better pilot than anyone else, it was because he flew more airplanes more hours than anyone else. Flying was his recreation as well as his job [Yeager and Janos 1985].

15.3.3 Group Psychology

One side effect of working together with other people is that you often begin to develop ties to the group. Some of this is healthy, and can lead to higher productivity. A bad aspect of group ties is *group think*. If other members of the group adopt a particular view, it is hard for you to express a contrary view. Sometimes other group members actively discourage diversity of opinion, but most often the process is unconscious. While harmony within a group is generally good, finding good solutions requires uncovering, expressing, and considering alternatives. Group think erodes your ability to examine a problem critically.

15.4 Personal Logs

In a professional career you build up more knowledge than you can keep in your active memory, and it is often knowledge you can't look up easily in standard references. You use a system, find problems, develop ways of working around those problems. You leave the system for a while, forget your work-arounds, come back to it, and re-encounter the same problems.

A good way to keep track of things you learn on the job is to keep a log. Typically, a log has three types of entries: descriptions, explanations, and prescriptions. *Descriptions* record what you did and how long you spent doing it. How much detail you go into depends on how much analysis and reflection you intend to do. If all you intend to do is fill out your employer's end-of-month time sheets, all you may need to do is record how many hours you spend on each billing category. If you intend to analyze your own productivity, you may need to go into further detail, such as how much time you spent planning, entering code at a terminal, debugging, or attending meetings. You might choose to keep descriptions in a daybook, separate from the rest of your log.

Explanations record reasons for things. In this type of entry you might explain a bug that you spent several hours tracking down. You might outline several approaches you tried to solve some problem, and the reason you picked a particular solution.

Prescriptions represent reflections on what you ought to do in future. These range from notes on what you plan to do tomorrow, to issues to bring up at some meeting, to changes you should make in your work habits, to ideas you might try to investigate later.

Further Reading

Brooks (1975) gave the description of chief programmer teams on which I based Section 15.1.2. Weinberg (1971) wrote the classic reference on psychological aspects of programmers and programming. Curtis (1984) summarizes more recent results.

Chapter 16

Scheduling and
Budgeting

The project schedule and budget are two documents a manager uses for planning, and for control of a large project. The schedule describes when various activities must finish; the budget describes what they will cost.

Both documents start early in the project planning stages. As the project progresses, the manager assesses progress, compares it with predictions, and takes corrective action if necessary. For small discrepancies, no action may be necessary. For medium-size discrepancies the manager may need to interfere by reassigning personnel, reallocating resources, changing the definition of some task, and so on. For large discrepancies, the manager may need to notify higher management.

16.1 Schedules

A schedule is a plan for when tasks should start and when they should finish. Each task has several properties.

1. The task *duration* is the length of time it takes. During planning, durations are always estimates. Section 16.3 discusses making estimates.

2. The *resources* needed to complete the task include personnel, machine time, supplies, equipment rental, and so on.

3. An *ending milestone* gives a clear criterion for telling when the task is over.

4. The *dependencies* of the task are other tasks that must finish before it starts.

5. The *planned completion date* is the date you expect the task to finish.

6. The *promise date* is the last date you changed the planned completion date.

Schedules are dynamic. As you work through the schedule, you discover that some tasks are behind schedule, and thus you adjust planned completion dates. The promise date for a task is the date you last changed its planned completion date. As you complete each task, you retire it from the schedule, and record the difference between the promise date and the actual completion date; the larger this is, the further ahead you were able to plan.

Many projects miss their deadlines because the managers did not realize they were behind schedule. A prime reason for this is that intermediate tasks did not have clear-cut milestones, so that the managers could fool themselves about whether the project was on schedule. The main thing about a milestone is that it is precise. For example, "coding 90 percent complete" is not a milestone; "18 of the 20 modules passed all unit tests" is a milestone — or a collection of 18 milestones. With the second milestone, a manager knows to investigate the status of the other two modules. Typical milestones include

- a document enters configuration control
- a document passes a review
- a module passes a code walkthrough
- the system passes all tests of a certain category

The task dependencies define a *partial order* among tasks. One task depends on another if it cannot start until the other finishes. If you think you have a task T_1 that can start when T_2 is "80 percent done," you must split T_2 into T_{2a} and T_{2b}, then have T_1 and T_{2b} depend on T_{2a}. You must also have a milestone for what "80 percent done" means, to determine the end of T_{2a}. Given a set of tasks, their durations, and their dependencies, you can draw a chart showing when each task must start and finish. Figure 16–1 shows a simple case with three tasks, where one depends on the other two. Tasks A and B may proceed in parallel, but C must wait for both to finish. Task A may slip up to one week (into the dotted region) without impacting the completion date, while neither B nor C may slip.

The path B–C from the start of the chart in Figure 16–1 to the end is a *critical path*, since every milestone on the path is critical to meeting the project deadline. Every schedule has a critical path, and managers watch the path closely to ensure it keeps on schedule. If necessary, a manager may switch resources from a noncritical task to a critical one.

This simple analysis leads to an ideal schedule with maximum parallel activity. Two problems complicate the picture. First, an initial schedule with large-sized tasks may take too long. The manager may need to break large tasks into smaller ones, expecting to find more parallelism, which could lead to a shorter schedule.

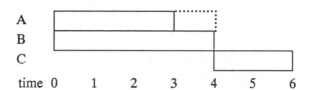

Task A: 3 weeks
Task B: 4 weeks
Task C: 2 weeks, depends on A and B
Critical Path: B–C

Figure 16–1: Sample Critical Path

Second, the project may not have enough resources to allow the ideal schedule. If at some time the ideal schedule calls for five tasks, but the project has only three programmers, some tasks that might go in parallel must instead proceed serially. This usually lengthens the schedule. There are tools that will figure out the critical path in an unrestricted schedule, but figuring an optimal schedule with resource limitations with many highly parallel tasks is an exponentially hard problem.

The classic problem with schedules is unrealistically short deadlines. Often higher-level management or marketing demands set the schedule. Most customers are happier to have accurate schedules rather than short ones (though, of course, they would like accurate, short ones). A good way to encourage accuracy is to have the people who will do the work set the schedules. Some might ensure accuracy by making long estimates, but this is often better than making unrealistically short estimates that you need to lengthen later.

16.2   Budgets

At a first glance, budgeting is straightforward. From the schedule and project plan, you can obtain information about the resources needed to do the project. Resources include salaries, equipment purchase, equipment rental, and supplies. To determine the budget, you multiply the estimates of resources by their price — personnel needed times salary, number of units of equipment by purchase price, and so on.

You typically divide the schedule into periods such as months and figure costs for each period. As the project progresses, the you compare estimated expenses with real ones, and take action if they do not match.

The budget must also reflect *hidden costs*. Personnel costs include not only salaries, but also fringe benefits and inflation and salary increases. Hardware costs may include installation fees and maintenance costs. Furthermore, the development organization incurs overhead costs such as rent for its building, utility charges (electricity, water, telephones), supplies such as paper and staples, and so on. Some people (such as secretaries, clerks, typists, computer operators, janitors, and some managers) support work that spreads across several projects; you usually include a fraction of their salaries in overhead.

16.3   Estimating Time

Estimating how long it will take to do a given task has five parts.

1. Determine some measure of how large the task is.

2. Determine how many people could usefully work on the task.

3. Determine the typical productivity of the sort of people who will work on the task, in units of work per month or per week. Take into account the loss of productivity caused by communicating among the number of people determined in the previous step.

4. Multiply productivity by size of task to get the "person-months" needed for the task.

5. Divide by the number of people to get calendar months.

The last step is fraught with danger; people and months are not interchangeable. That is why the second step said to determine how many people could cooperate on the task. If a task does not break easily into two parts, two people cannot work any faster than one.

Both amount-of-work and productivity estimates are fuzzy. One typically gets productivity estimates by collecting data from old projects. Similarly, past experience with similar software guides amount-of-work estimates. You can improve productivity estimates by gathering data more specific to the particular programmers who will work on the project. You can improve work estimates by breaking large tasks into smaller ones. Thus the module decomposition can help with estimates of programming time.

Amount of work is almost universally measured in lines of code, and productivity in lines of code per person-month. No one is particularly happy with such an inexact measure, but to date no one has come up with a more widely acceptable estimate. Using lines of code as a productivity measure has several flaws.

- It gives numbers that vary with coding style, unless you are careful to impose a uniform style or count language tokens instead of lines.

- It focuses on the coding activity, including the other stages only by amortizing the output of coding over the life of the project. A tool that doubles coding productivity (100 percent improvement) really improves project productivity by only 10 percent (by halving the 20 percent of the time that went into coding).

- It correlates poorly with product quality. As with good writing, it may take longer to create a smaller, cleaner program. The result is a more valuable product (more maintainable, more efficient, and so forth). The team that takes the time to do this comes out looking less productive, unless the care in coding significantly improves testing time.

- It penalizes higher-level languages. Early reports claim that people produce about as many lines of assembly code per month as high-level language lines, but a single high-level language line translates into several lines of assembler. The high-level-language programmer can thus code a much larger system in the same time. Furthermore, since high-level-language lines tend to represent more complex operations than assembly language lines, a programmer typically produces somewhat fewer of them per month and looks even less productive.

To make such a measure work, you must be consistent about how you measure.

- Always include executable code.
- Decide whether to include comments and data definitions.
- Decide whether to count source lines, statements, or tokens.
- When reporting productivity of a project, decide whether to include only new lines of code, or whether to include code from libraries and previous versions of the program.
- When reporting company-wide productivity, decide whether to include canceled projects and activities not related to programming.

Typical industry productivity figures are much lower than a typical student programmer (or computer scientist) might think — a few thousand lines per person per year. Extrapolating from the time an amateur programmer takes to write a hundred-line program gives tens or hundreds of thousands of lines per year. The reasons for the apparently lower industry figures include communication time among team members, training time, time for planning and documentation, and "hidden costs" such as sickness, vacation, and interruptions. Typically a professional programmer spends only about half of each working day "productively"; folklore captures this as the rule-of-thumb, "make the best estimate you can, then double it."

Further Reading

Sweet (1986) describes the dynamic nature of schedules, and how to measure people's planning ability as the difference between promise date and real completion date. Jones (1986) analyzes methods of measuring productivity and gives detailed guidelines on how to apply them.

Exercises

16–1   Arrange the following eleven tasks into a schedule.

Task	Length	Depends on	Task	Length	Depends on
A	2	K	B	3	H
C	4		D	2	F, G
E	1	D, I, J	F	3	B
G	3	C, K	H	3	
I	2	A, F	J	1	F
K	2	H			

- Identify the critical path.
- What is the minimum time to complete this schedule?
- What tasks are allowed to slip, and by how much?
- How many activities may proceed in parallel?

16–2   This question assumes you have been keeping a personal log like the one described in Section 15.4, and that you have been taking part in a group project. Summarize from your log how much time you spent on the group project, with subtotals for each phase of the project. Combine this with the information from your colleagues who worked on the same project. Count the number of lines of code in all modules of the program you produced, using a tool if one is available. Do not include lines of code from test drivers and stubs.

    a.   Determine your group's productivity in lines of code per hour. Extrapolate to lines of code per day and per year, assuming four productive hours per day and 1,000 productive hours per year.

    b.   Determine what percentage of your time you spent on each of the project's phases.

Chapter 17

Configuration
Management

To make progress, developers need a careful mixture of stability and change. You must eventually fix bugs and introduce new features, but you must ensure you don't interfere with your co-workers. *Configuration management* is a discipline for controlling changes to a system to avoid confusion, misinterpretation, and interference. A *software configuration* is a collection of related documents, source files, and tools used in designing and implementing a software system.

Configuration management consists of three activities. *Configuration identification* decides what pieces of the system you need to keep track of. *Configuration control* ensures that changes to a configuration happen smoothly. *Configuration status and accounting* keeps track of what changed and why it changed.

17.1 The Need for Configuration Management

A large software project needs configuration management simply to keep track of the many objects that make up the system, and how to put them together. A project of any size, large or small, must also deal with multiple *versions* of the same software. A new version of an object is a *revision* if you intend it to completely replace the object from which it came; a module revision might fix a bug, or introduce new functionality for all possible versions of a system. A new version of an object is a *variant* or *variation* if you intend it to co-exist with the object from which it came; the two variants represent different members of the same program family (see Section 5.2.1). Formally, you can define a history relation, *is version of,* between objects, and split it into two subrelations, *is revision of* and *is variant of.* In general, these relations form a directed acyclic graph, since you might create a version that merges several others.

Variants cause at least two kinds of problems. First, suppose you have several variants of the same module, and find a bug in one of them. If the bug is in code common to the variants, you need to fix it in them all, and thus must be able to find them all. Second, suppose two people each create variants of a base module to add new functionality; often, one eventually wants to merge both sets of changes back into the main line of revisions. If neither person knows about the other, each can try to update the main revision stream simultaneously, and one set of changes will be lost.

Even in a system where all versions are revisions can have problems. If a fellow programmer is debugging module M1, your changing M2 can change the symptoms of the bug. The hardest thing about some problems is to reproduce them consistently; changes in apparently unrelated code can make the bug behave differently, because the code is a little larger or smaller, or because the pattern of data in memory is different.

With modern programming languages and tools, the relationships between configuration elements become more complex. Certain kinds of changes to a module may force you to recompile some clients of the module. A source file may be input to some tool, whose output becomes input to a second tool, and so on through several steps before you get object code that is part of the running system. When a tool changes, you may need to regenerate its output files. You need to identify these relationships, and carefully manage rebuilding of the system when some parts change. To make progress, developers need a careful mixture of stability and change. You must eventually fix bugs and introduce new features, but you must ensure you don't interfere with your under co-workers.

17.2   Configuration Identification

Configuration identification is the process of deciding what things need to be placed under configuration control, and what the relationships between them will be.

17.2.1   Objects

Any object is in one of three categories. *Controlled* objects are under configuration control; there are formal procedures you must follow to change them. *Precontrolled* objects are not yet under configuration control, but will be eventually. *Uncontrolled* objects are not and will not be subject to configuration control. *Controllable* objects include both *controlled* and *precontrolled*.

Typical controllable objects include

- Any of the design documents from Figure 2–1 on page 8. The configuration manager might decide to split some of these objects into individual chapters, controlled individually.

- Tools used to build the product, such as compilers, linkers, program component generators (such as the lexer and parser generators used in most compiler-building projects).

- The source code for each module.

- Input to tools other than source files, such as command line arguments, command files, and system libraries.

- Test cases. Changes to tests may be less likely, but during the coding and testing phase an ill-considered change might impede progress. For example, one developer might be using a particular test case to track down some complex problem.

- Problem reports (see Section 10.3.1). These are a primary source of requests for changes.

The Configuration Management Plan, written during the Project Design stage, lists what objects to control. The managers who develop the plan must strike a balance between controlling too much, and thus impeding development, and controlling too little, thus leading to confusion when something changes.

Some typical documents that might not be subject to controls include personal logs and minutes of meetings. The first belongs to the individual keeping the log; likely no one else would read it. The second would never change, and so needs no change controls. Minutes have an intermediate place between uncontrolled objects such as logs and controllable ones such as source code; someone must keep track of them, so that developers can refer to what happened.

17.2.2   Relationships

The conventional English meaning of "configuration" includes not only a collection of components, but also relationships among those components. In software, "configuration management" has come to mean primarily managing multiple versions of components. The more recent term *system modeling* covers the other half of the English meaning.

When you build a piece of software, you start with objects you build by hand, pass those objects through tools to derive new objects, and combine those derived objects into one (or at most, a few) objects you deliver to customers. For example, you write two Pascal modules, compile each of them into relocatable files, and link the relocatables into an executable program. The original objects are *source* objects, and the output from the tools are *derived* objects. The objects you deliver to customers are *exported* objects; normally they are derived objects such as executable programs, but some source objects might also be exports. The system model describes the process by which you generate the exported objects from the source objects.

Formally, a system model is a directed acyclic graph with two types of nodes: objects and processing steps. Objects and processing steps alternate in the graph; each processing step takes one or more objects as inputs and produces one or more objects as outputs. Processing steps are simply placeholders in the graph. Objects include familiar things such as the source and derived files mentioned previously, but also include tools (such as compilers and linkers), command line arguments for invoking them, "hidden" files read automatically by the tools (such as standard module libraries), and even such data as the value of the time-of-day clock, if any outputs depend on them. With this view, derived objects are simply the outputs of processing steps, and source objects are inputs to some steps that are not outputs of any other steps.

The idea of a system model is that if you begin with the same source objects, and run through the same processing steps, you would get the same output. This is important if you ever need to regenerate an old system to track down a customer's problem. The idea of including tools, command line arguments, and hidden files is important. Experienced developers allude to the idea of "software rot": you try to recreate a program after some months or years, only to discover that it no longer works. What has usually happened is that a system library has changed, or someone has installed a new release of the compiler; what you thought of as unchanged source really has changed, because you did not preserve all inputs to the system building process.

To be serious about system modeling and reproducible system building, you must treat source objects as immutable. Instead of changing an object, you create a new object (a version of an old object). Instead of changing a file and rebuilding the system, you substitute new versions of some source objects, and re-derive all the appropriate derived objects. As of the mid-1980s, most file systems and database systems did not provide enough support for system modeling. Some tools, such as SCCS and RCS under UNIX, could keep track of versions of source files. Experimental systems with much better support for the full process showed promise of coming into production use within a few years.

17.3 Configuration Control

Configuration control is the process of managing changes; it is the piece of configuration management that most directly affects day-to-day operations of developers.

Each controllable object starts off as precontrolled; the people assigned to work on it may make whatever modifications they choose. When the object is reasonably complete, the developers (or, more likely, their team leader or manager) places it under configuration control, and it becomes a controlled object.

Details of when to make something controlled vary between projects; the Configuration Management Plan should define criteria for making such a decision. When someone other than the creator needs to refer to it is a typical time. For example, a design document might go under configuration control when its authors circulate a first draft to reviewers. Source code might go under configuration control just before testers need it during integration.

17.3.1   Baselines and Updates

The whole reason for configuration control is that people need a stable environment to make progress. If you are trying to integrate module A with modules B and C, you cannot make progress if the developer of module C keeps changing it out from under you; this is especially frustrating if a change to C forces you to recompile A. Thus before anyone who depends on a particular object need to use it, the configuration manager *freezes* it; no one may change the frozen object. This establishes a *baseline* for others to use and depend on. The term comes from surveying; surveyors carefully measure a baseline, then make all other measurements relative to that line.

Freezing a configuration may involve archiving everything needed to rebuild it. Archiving means copying to a safe place such as magnetic tape. An archival tool examines a system model, writes a representation of the model to tape, then copies all source objects to tape. Some of these "source objects" may actually be programs used to generate derived files. A partial archive saves the executable programs; a full archive saves enough to rebuild them. This process recurs with programs used to build the programs, and so forth; it stops by saving the executable form of programs considered immutable (such as a compiler from a particular old release tape from a manufacturer).

It usually does become necessary to change a baseline at some point. For example, those who review a document need a baseline so that they know they are all referring to the same document. However, their review usually leads to changes in the document. What happens here is that developers copy the baseline document, then change the copy. When a reviewer says "change page 4, paragraph 7" a developer may need to translate this to page 6, paragraph 2 of the new document, but both people share a standard reference point. This process of changing a copy is the basis of immutability.

At any given time a programmer may pay attention to three versions of a configuration:

1.   the current baseline configuration
2.   an updated configuration
3.   the programmer's private version

A large enough project may have several distinct updated configurations, one per subproject plus a master updated configuration. There may be one private configuration per programmer; a developer may make whatever changes she chooses to her own private configuration. Moving objects from a private version to the updated configuration requires approval from a manager responsible for change control. Objects never move into a baseline configuration; instead, every so often the configuration manager freezes the updated configuration and declares it to be the new baseline. A developer who needs stability uses the current baseline configuration.

One who needs the most recent version uses the updated configuration, but must live with the consequences of frequent changes.

17.3.2 Change Control

Once an object goes under configuration control, any changes require management approval. Approval usually certifies several things about the change:

1. The change is well-motivated.
2. The developer has considered and documented the effects of the change.
3. The change interacts well with changes made by other developers.
4. Appropriate people have validated the change (for example, someone has tested a code change, or has verified that a requirements change is consistent with other requirements).

The amount of work involved here depends on the size of the change and the importance of the changed object. For source code, you might be able to describe both motivation and effects by a short statement like "Fixes problem report 17, callers need to be recompiled." A manager might disallow a change made from motivations such as "changed spelling of all original author's identifiers," or with effects such as "requires extensive editing of all modules containing calls on procedure X." If a manager approves a change with such large effects, the configuration control procedures should notify all the appropriate people of the need to make such a change. A configuration manager needs to be extremely hard-nosed; it is hard to convince someone who wants a bug fixed today to wait a week, accepting a short-term loss of personal productivity in return for a gain in group productivity.

17.3.3 System Rebuilding

When you update a source object in a configuration, you must regenerate the derived objects that depend on it. With older systems this meant compiling the source file and placing the resulting object file in a library. Modern systems are complex enough to require tools to manage the system rebuilding process.

A system rebuilding tool takes as input a system model and a list of files to substitute for some of the objects (normally, source files) of the model. It reruns those processing steps that depend on the changed objects, then reruns those steps that depend on changed derived objects, and continues until it has regenerated all derived objects that depend directly or indirectly on anything that has changed. The most widely known system rebuilding tool is the UNIX *make* utility. Each object is a file; it deduces that an object has changed by the "date of last change" maintained by the file system, and rebuilds a derived object when its date is less than that of anything on which it depends. More recent experimental tools compare the new object to the old. For example, adding a comment to a source file might not require any rebuilding. For another example, if a tool produces several outputs, a change to its source file may affect only one output. Eliminating unnecessary regeneration steps can greatly reduce the time to rebuild the system, especially if the comparisons are fast or the output of a tool becomes input to many other tools.

17.4 Configuration Status and Accounting

Status and accounting ensures that developers, managers, and users know the history and current state of controllable objects. A particular developer or customer may need to know when a particular problem is fixed; managers may need to know how often changes are happening. The two major types of object for which people need to know status are individual modules and *problem reports* (see Section 10.3.1).

Several distinct types of information contribute to the status of a module. The configuration identification activity may separate these into distinct objects, but for status purposes it is more useful to group them together. A common practice is to create a *module development folder* for each module. In its simplest form this is a physical file folder. The folder contains

- the requirements the module implements (if it is a behavior-hiding module)

- the current specification, design, and code listing

- a log identifying all changes to the specification, design, or code, including date of change and who made the change

- the unit test plan for the module

- records of test case results

- copies of problem reports that affect the module

- notes about the module by the specifier, designer, and coder of the module

- a cover page with summary information, such as planned and real dates for completion of the specification, design, and code, with a place for signatures for the person responsible for verifying completion.

Status reporting involves analyzing and summarizing information about changes. The simplest report is the status of some collection of problem reports: who is responsible for handling them, what their current disposition is, what progress is being made on changes needed to fix the problems, and so on.

Managers also need summary information. For example, frequent change requests may suggest adding more resources to handle them, or may suggest improving quality control procedures. If you classify many problem reports as misunderstandings, you may need to improve user documentation. Finally, analyzing what changes people request may lead to better planning for change in future systems.

17.5 Configuration Hierarchy

So far this chapter has presented a system as one large configuration, with a single manager responsible for configuration control. This may be true of a medium-sized project, but is probably not true of a large one.

A large project may consist of several small projects, each with its own development schedule and configuration control. For example, a project may have several subprojects for developing individual pieces of the system, plus subprojects for developing or maintaining in-house tools such as compilers, simulators, or test-case generators. The manager responsible for each small project may have configuration control responsibility for his own project.

Typically, changes to widely visible portions of a system may require approval from a *configuration control board*. Such a board would consist of representatives of both developers and customers. For example, changes to requirements require negotiation and joint approval because they involve changes to a contract. In a more complex contractual arrangement, there may be operating and sponsoring agencies distinct from customers; they should have representation too. Changes to a major in-house tool such as a compiler might require approval from the compiler developers as well as the principal users of the compiler within the development organization. All representatives should be fully capable of committing their organizations to accepting whatever decisions the board makes.

Further Reading

Babich (1986) gives a highly readable explanation of configuration management based on modern industrial experience. Glass' books include many tales of computing disasters, some of them attributable to poor configuration management [Glass 1977, Glass 1978, Glass 1979, Glass 1981].

Quality
_____ Assurance _____

Quality assurance is the process of raising a developer's (and possibly a customer's) confidence that a system is of high quality. It is a planned, systematic activity. The two major thrusts of quality assurance are building in quality and measuring quality. Most of Part II discusses building in quality; this chapter concentrates on measurement and analysis. A related topic, *verification*, demonstrates that specifications are consistent and complete, and that implementations meet their specifications. Part III, on specification techniques, discusses verification issues. Chapter 8 discusses testing.

18.1 Measures of Quality

Software quality has several aspects. Some of these we can measure readily; for others, we can measure something that seems related to the quality we're looking for; for others, we currently can judge only subjectively. The following sections discuss several aspects of software quality. During requirements analysis, you should consider this list of qualities, define requirements for the measurable ones, and define goals for trading off the immeasurable ones.

There are two criteria with which to judge how well you can guarantee that a system is good according to a particular measure of quality. The first is the degree to which you can measure the quality; the second is the degree to which you can build your systems to embody the quality.

For any quality, the ideal case is to have a clear observer-independent measure of the quality, so that different people can agree on the degree of quality a system has. For example, there are well-known techniques for measuring performance. The next best case is to have measures that correlate with quality. For example, the number of well-designed test cases a system passes correlates with correctness. The worst case is to have no measure at all besides subjective judgment.

Ideally, associated with each quality there should be a set of design strategies for maximizing that quality, means of predicting what value the quality will have, means of measuring to what degree the final system possesses the quality, and strategies for cheaply modifying the system if the measures show that the quality is lacking. For example, folklore says that performance matters only for a small portion of a system. Analytic models or simulations can predict performance. You can measure performance, and modify the few sections of the program whose performance is weak.

An important research area since the early 1980s has been to define and validate measures of software quality. The principle behind such efforts is to find things to measure that correlate well with intuitive ideas of quality. For example,

- You might measure *ease of use* by how long it takes a user to do typical tasks. Cognitive scientists have begin to define measures that correlate with intuitive notions of human factors quality.

- You might define *portability* as the number of lines of code you need to change (or the cost of such changes) to move the software from one system to another, compared with the total size (or cost) of the system. Since you usually want high numbers to be good, and it is unlikely that the change could cost as much as the original development, you might define the measure as one minus this quantity.

The practices outlined in earlier chapters aim at building in quality. During requirements analysis, you try to make the system easy to use and easy to learn, and try to plan for changes and responses to undesired events. During module decomposition, you concentrate on portability and adaptability. During detailed design you concentrate on correctness. During testing you try to measure correctness, and possibly other qualities such as performance.

18.2 Validation

Validation is the process of ensuring that software meets its requirements. Chapter 8 discusses testing, which is currently the major activity in validation. However, software defects can appear at many stages in the development process, from requirements analysis through coding. Defect removal is the process of eliminating defects throughout development and maintenance. You can view requirements reviews, design reviews, code walkthroughs, testing, and use by customers as a series of defect removal filters.

The *defect removal efficiency* of any filter is

$$\frac{\text{defects removed} - \text{defects introduced}}{\text{total defects}}$$

The most accurate way of determining total defects is to collect data for the first couple of years of operation of the system, along with records of all the defects found by the filters. Some people advocate seeding the system with bugs, measuring how many of them the filters find, and comparing this with the number of unseeded bugs the filters find to estimate total defects. This "bebugging" process works only if the kinds of bugs you introduce mimic the kinds of bugs that really occur.

Paying attention to defect removal in early development activities reduces total system cost by reducing testing and debugging time.

18.3   Reviews

Part of building in quality is subjecting documents to review. A review involves gathering together several people to examine and evaluate a document or group of documents. There are several kinds of reviews; requirements reviews, preliminary design reviews, detailed design reviews, and code walkthroughs are the most common. They differ in who attends the review and what the reviewers look for.

The different kinds of review have several features in common.

- To get around the ego-related inability to see flaws in your own work, find some reviewers who have not contributed to creating the item under review.

- For an effective review, distribute the relevant documents in advance, and expect the reviewers to read them in advance. Give them some incentive to do this, or they won't get around to it.

- If a review finds significant problems, fix the problems, then have them reviewed again.

A review meeting is like an extended status meeting (see Section 15.2). It should thus have a clear-cut agenda, and someone should take notes so you can distribute minutes. For a large document, you might break the review into several sections, each responsible for a clearly identified portion. If the review finds problems, you should avoid the temptation to try to solve them during the review unless the solution is obvious; instead, record an "action item" in the minutes, to deal with the problem later. For example, a requirements review might show that the designers misunderstood some important customer needs; you should schedule separate action meetings to resolve such a problem. A code walkthrough might discover a subtle bug; an action item might require the implementor to go think about possible solutions, possibly with the help of some of the reviewers.

You need not necessarily hold a meeting. A review of a large document or group of documents might take several days; it might me more productive to conduct reviews of such documents via mail (especially if you have good electronic mail facilities). Here the "minutes" might simply be a list of all the problems discovered during the review.

18.3.1 Requirements Review

A major thrust of requirements reviews is to ensure that, if the developers build a system that meets the requirements, it will meet the needs of the users. This can be difficult to do with a set of words on paper, which is why some people recommend building a prototype instead of specifying requirements. There are some techniques that can help in the absence of a prototype. For example, reviewers can hypothesize typical scenarios for trying to use the system, and work through what the requirements say about how they would interact with the system. Such scenarios might include the ones used during requirements analysis, but might include fresh ones.

Requirements may suffer from several problems.

- *incorrectness*. The requirements demand something that the customers do not want.

- *incompleteness*. The requirements may fail to say anything about some important customer need. This is the commonest form of failure, since it is usually harder to detect the absence of something correct than the presence of something incorrect.

- *ambiguity*. A requirement is imprecise enough that it has several possible interpretations.

- *inconsistency*. Two requirements contradict each other. Some reviewers tend to classify inconsistencies as ambiguities, since both imply multiple ways of interpreting the requirements. It is better to distinguish the two: ambiguity is a problem of imprecision, possibly of a single requirement, while inconsistency involves multiple requirements that may say precise but contradictory things.

- *misorganization*. A requirement is in the wrong section of the document. You should deal with separate concerns in separate sections of the requirements. In particular, you should separate functional requirements, performance requirements, constraints, and goals.

Making the distinction among requirements, constraints, and goals can place customers and developers in an adversarial position. These distinctions are ones that affect developers most clearly at the beginning; for a customer they may all be "requirements" in the sense that they are all properties the customer wants the system to have. A constraint (that is, a property that strongly favors, or mandates, a particular implementation) is typically something a developer would like to remove; a customer may object to having something they want treated as "second-class." A goal is typically a property customers want for which there are no good quantitative measures; a customer may be unhappy that the developers claim they cannot tell whether they can meet such a goal.

It is especially important to review the fundamental assumptions and possible changes, since these will affect the evolution of the system. For example, the sample life-cycle considerations of Appendix B.2 on page 223 include the assumption that there is no need to consider "in-law" relationships in a genealogy system. This leads directly to the spurious behavior shown in the sample test plans (Appendix C);

- The program reports most relationships between two people twice, since a complete family tree has both a male and a female nearest common ancestor (except for half relationships, such as half-sibling).

- it shows Prince Charles as having several cousin relationships with Prince Philip (Figure C–6 on page 232), since Philip's being his father did not block tracing further relationships through Queen Elizabeth.

Developers and customers should both have high motivation to review the series of subsets, since any scheduling difficulties may force the developer to deliver a subset instead of the full system. The two sides should agree on the order of the subsets; a customer will typically have a priority ordering on features, while the developer will have an ease-of-implementing ordering. If some important facility is in a late subset, a customer may be unwilling to accept delivery of anything without it, which will remove some of the benefits of planning subsets.

18.3.2   Design Review

The term "design review" covers any review of design decisions that precede coding. Different life-cycle models prescribe design reviews at several stages, usually including at least a preliminary design review and a detailed design review. During any design review the primary questions are

- does the design meet the requirements?
- is the design consistent?
- is the design complete?

For the model I outline in this book, a preliminary design review means reviewing the module decomposition and module dependency documents. Reviewers should check that the designers have allocated each requirement to some module (preferably no more than one per requirement), that their design recovers adequately from undesired events, and that they have addressed quality issues such as modularity, simplicity, and reliability. You might use the scenarios you sketched during requirements analysis to check how information would flow through your modules.

For the model I outline in this book, there are two kinds of detailed design reviews: reviews of the module specifications, and reviews of the module implementation sketches. The more important is a review of the the specifications. You might best handle each as several reviews, one per module or one per group of related modules.

18.3.3 Code Walkthroughs

A code walkthrough involves at least two people, the implementor and one other person. Ideally (if the organization can afford the time) there are three or four, with the chairperson of the meeting being someone other than the implementor. The chairperson runs the review. The implementor should not volunteer information about how the module works, to avoid imposing the wrong mind-set on the reviewers. The implementor can answer questions of the other reviewers, and can point out problems.

Before the meeting, everyone should read the relevant background documents, which include the sections of the module decomposition and dependency documents that mention the module, the module's specification, and any implementation notes on the module's detailed design. Ideally some reviewer should be familiar with the way that at least one client uses the module; the reviewers may also need to be familiar with the specifications of any modules the one under review calls.

Some organizations use a standard checklist such as that of Figure 18–1 to guide a walkthrough. Any problems normally result in having the implementor change the module, but might involve a recommendation for changing earlier documents such as the specifications or implementation sketch. As with any review, a code walkthrough should produce a set of minutes, typically called a *code walkthrough report*, describing what happened during the review; Appendix H.3 shows a sample code walkthrough report.

Date, time, and duration of review
Name of module
Name of chairperson
       implementor
       other(s)
Results of comparing listing with implementation sketch
Results of comparing listing with module dependency document
    Missing dependencies
    Added dependencies
Results of comparing listing with specification
    Report separately for each interface procedure
Stylistic and commenting problems
Action items resulting from problems

Figure 18–1: Code Walkthrough Checklist

As with most quality assurance measures, approaching deadlines cause people to try to "save time" by canceling code walkthroughs. This is short-sighted. For every walkthrough that "wastes time" by finding no problems (or small problems that would have come out quickly in testing), there are several that find problems that would have required considerable time during testing and debugging.

Exercises

18–1 Pick one of the system qualities listed in the index, other than efficiency. Investigate what measures people have proposed for this quality and write an essay describing your findings. How useful are the proposed measures? To what extent do they correspond to your idea of the meaning of the quality? Are there techniques for designing a system that will score highly on these measures? Given a low score on a measure, are there techniques for improving the system to score more highly?

Project Exercises

18–2 Hold a meeting to review each of your project's major design documents (user's guide; life-cycle considerations; module decomposition and dependencies; module specifications; test plans; module implementation summary). Submit the minutes of these meetings as design review reports.

18–3 Perform a code walkthrough for a module written by another team member. Hand in a report similar to the one of Section H.3.

Chapter 19

Tools

A tool is an artifact that you use to make some task easier (or possible). It has no intrinsic value except in what it enables you to do. Most computer programs are tools; in this chapter I concentrate on those tools that help with the software development process.

19.1 Evaluating a Tool

In deciding whether to build, buy, or use a tool, you need to compare the benefits of using the tool with the costs. If a tool automates some task you were already doing, the comparison is straightforward.

1. Pick a time period over which to do the comparison (that is, over which to amortize the initial cost of the tool). Many tools, especially those that embody changeable procedures, have a maximum useful lifetime before you retire them.

2. Measure the time it takes to do the task manually.

3. Multiply by the frequency with which you would do this task over the trial period.

4. Multiply by the fully loaded salary (raw salary plus benefits plus overhead) of the person who currently does the task.

5. Measure the time it takes to do the task with the tool.

6. Multiply by the frequency with which you would do this task over the trial period.

7. Add the time it takes to learn to use the tool.

8. Multiply by the fully loaded salary of whoever would use the tool. This may be a different class of person than you are currently using; a tool might make it possible for a clerical person to do something that formerly required more technical experience.

You now have operating costs for using the tool (step 8) versus using the manual system (step 4). You may not have enough information in advance to do a detailed calculation; instead you might give yourself a range of numbers by making optimistic, average, and pessimistic estimates.

To compare total costs, you must decide how to deal with the startup cost of building or buying the tool. You need to take into account the opportunity cost lost in not spending the money for the tool on something else. A typical way of doing this is to consider the startup cost as an investment, calculate how much money the investment saves you in reduced operating costs, and convert the savings into a "return on investment." For example, suppose a tool costs $1,000 and saves you $300 each year over five years, after which it becomes useless. Simplistically, you earn $1,500 for a cost of $1,000, or a net gain of $500 in five years. This corresponds to earning about 8.4 percent interest on your $1,000 in that time.

A dollars-and-cents judgment may be too harsh on a new tool, because tools may have intangible benefits and costs. For example, a tool might encourage standardization of some aspect of a project, which eliminates the cost of considering nonstandard alternatives. A tool might make it easier to produce a higher-quality product, so that you improve standards. On the other hand, some tools force a particular work method on you. If the method is convenient, and you rarely or never want to do things some other way, this can be an acceptable price to pay for the results.

Some toolbuilders advertise that their tools give you great gains in productivity. You need to examine the details of such claims to see if they are sensible. For example, some tool might claim a 100 percent improvement in productivity. On inspection this might turn out to be a 100 percent increase in lines-per-month produced in the coding phase, without affecting any other phases. This means it takes half as long to produce the same amount of code; if coding took 20 percent of the time of a project, you have cut out 10 percent of the total project time. Such a tool might well be worth adopting, but 10 percent is much less impressive than 100 percent. Furthermore, many projects depend on unpaid overtime for success; the first 20 percent or so of a productivity gain might simply vanish because workers stay home on evenings and weekends. Of course, in the long term, global organization-wide productivity may be higher if workers are better rested, more alert and happier in their jobs.

19.2   Software Engineering Environments

A good tool accomplishes a single, well-defined task. Modern software construction is sufficiently complex that you need multiple tools. A collection of tools, each good when considered in isolation, might interact with each other poorly. They might have different usage conventions, require different file formats, and produce confusingly different styles of report. Since the late 1970s there has been considerable interest in developing and using collections of tools that interact well with each other. The typical buzzword is that such collections should be *integrated*.

The term *software engineering environment* should mean a collection of tools, practices, and working conditions supporting software engineering efforts. To date there is no general agreement about what tools are worth building. Researchers have spent considerable effort on tools to aid in coding, a small portion of the development process. There are a few tools for requirements analysis; some attempts at module-level design languages; some version control and configuration management tools. There are almost no maintenance tools, except insofar as development tools help with maintenance.

In my view, many such tools suffer from an attempt to impose unverified methods on the development process; many of the tools get in your way more than they help you. A safer approach is to observe what practitioners do, and find ways to help them do those things more easily. A tool might make a particular technique especially easy (and possibly make others difficult), as long as it doesn't make other sensible techniques impossible. For example, extensible text editors with facilities for supplying syntactic templates seem easier for many of us to use than syntax-directed editors, which require a new way of looking at program construction.

19.3   Reusable Components

You gain much productivity by reusing portions of earlier systems rather than developing them from scratch. If you reuse an earlier design, decomposition, or module, the cost you incur is the overhead of creating and maintaining the library, and of finding the item you want in it. You save the time to redevelop the item, such as to specify, document, code, and test a reusable module. Without a good index and good documentation for the library, it can cost more to reuse software than to redevelop it, for small low-level modules.

The easiest items to see how to reuse are subroutines and low-level modules. Subroutine libraries of mathematical, scientific, and statistical subroutines have been around for a long time. You can look at information hiding as a way of reusing a module decomposition and a large body of existing code. To produce a new version of the old system, you typically need to change one or a few modules, thus saving the work of producing all the other modules. Furthermore, even without reusing a particular module, you may be able to reuse the module's specification.

A few applications provide reusable designs. There are a half-dozen or so typical top-level decompositions of compilers and operating systems, known to practitioners in those fields. If you start building a new compiler, you know you will have a lexical analyzer, a parser, a symbol table module, a semantic analysis phase, a code generator, and so on. Furthermore, there is a body of well-understood techniques for dealing with the detailed design of these subdivisions. Other application areas have typically not yet got around to documenting the equivalent ideas — perhaps because it can be a hard problem to analyze the systems and deduce common patterns.

19.3.1 Module Libraries

A module library is an organized collection of reusable modules. The idea has been with us for a long time, as "subroutine libraries"; these days "module library" is a more appropriate term, since we now view a module as more than a collection of subroutines.

A library module should have a well-defined, widely applicable purpose. Any module designed with information hiding will have a well-defined purpose. Modules in the software decision category are more likely to be widely applicable than those in the behavior-hiding category, since they have no connection with particular requirements. Modules that implement low-level data structures and widely applicable algorithms are likely candidates for a library. Modules that hide device interfaces might be useful in other applications that use similar devices. Operating system interface modules may be useful in other applications on the same operating system, but modules that try to hide the differences between operating systems may need to be closely tailored to the needs of the particular application that uses them.

The easiest module to incorporate into a library is one that uses no other modules, or whose use of other modules is invisible to its clients (see the uses $_v$ relation of Section 5.1.2). This means a programmer can understand the specification of the module without having to look at any other modules, and without having to adapt the new program to their existence.

A key issue in how widely you can use a module is how easily you can parameterize it to cover the needs of different clients. For example, in FORTRAN you can write a library module to sort arrays of real numbers; in standard Pascal you probably would not, since you would need to write one routine for each length of array. In Ada you could go one step further and write a generic module to sort arrays of any type of element, and parameterize the method of comparing elements. In some experimental languages (such as Alphard), you can write modules that take other modules as parameters.

19.3.2 Program Generators

When a problem area becomes well understood, you can sometimes reuse most of the same module decomposition for each new version of the system. You may not be able to reuse much code directly; even though each module may fulfill the same function in each system, the details of what it must do may differ. Here, a module library may not help you much.

If you understand the problem area well, you may be able to capture the differences between the versions of certain modules in some easy-to-use descriptive notation, and write a program that generates the modules from the description. For example, compiler writers regularly describe their languages in Backus-Naur form, then use a parser generator to write the parser for them. Depending on how big a chunk of your system such a program emits, you might call it a module generator, a program component generator (for several related modules), or an application generator (for entire programs). Parser generators are usually module generators. Tools that emit coordinated lexers, parsers, and reserved-word-lookup procedures are program component generators. Fourth generation electronic data processing languages are application generators.

Program generators have two characteristic problems you should take into account when you design one.

- You might tend to believe that only a compiler need ever read the output of the generator, so you are not particularly careful that it be readable to humans. This is acceptable only if humans really never do need to read it. If you design one generator expecting it to interact with code produced by a second generator, and the second is not available, people will have to deal with your unreadable output to hand-generate the code that would have come from the second generator.

- You might tend to believe that the code you generate is in charge of things, rather than subordinate to some program-specific code that calls it. This can make it difficult for people to use what you generate. For example, most compilers assume a runtime system with certain program startup code; certain applications with different needs require different code. If you provide source for standard startup code, clients can change it; if the compiler generates the startup code as part of the main module, clients cannot change it.

19.4 Prototyping

Prototyping is a variety of methods for developing a program that gives you information to help you do a better job of developing the eventual system. It is most useful during an opportunity study or during requirements analysis, but can be useful in choosing between alternative designs. A common use for a prototype is to fully develop a user interface and partially develop some functionality to determine if the system behaves the way the user wants.

A prototype is useful only if the effort involved in building the prototype is much less than that of building the final system. To reduce cost, you may sacrifice some constraints, exception handling, reliability, parts of the user interface — any aspect of the final system where you have little need of additional information. Some "very high level" implementation languages are especially suitable for prototyping because they allow you to describe large amounts of functionality in a small amount of notation. What they sacrifice is performance, both in speed and in space. APL, NIAL, SETL, and the UNIX shell command language have all served as prototyping languages.

One long-established prototyping method is to build a simulation. If done early enough to affect the final hardware and software, it can provide useful information about the performance effects of different design decisions. Simulation can be expensive. To simulate a realtime system properly, you may need to use a microprogrammed machine ten to a hundred times faster than the final machine. Likely you can afford to do this only if you are designing hardware, where replication costs are high enough to dominate development costs.

Software prototypes have one danger that prototypes in other fields do not. In every other field, you expect to build a prototype, learn some lessons, and throw the prototype away. The second time around you build the system "the right way." Software is so malleable, and the construction defects so invisible from the outside, that it can be hard to convince customers or higher-level managers to throw prototypes away. Unfortunately, maintainability is probably something you sacrificed in building the prototype. In the long run, you are better off starting over.

19.5   Toolsmith and Tools Group

Section 15.1.2 said that each chief programmer team might need a toolsmith to adapt tools to the team's needs and to write small special-purpose tools. This approach has several advantages. A good toolsmith understands both the set of available tools and the individual needs of her group. She can thus save the group much effort by pointing out the right tools for the group's needs, and can write command scripts and small programs to adapt the input or output of the tools to the group's needs. On the other hand, unless toolsmiths of the individual groups communicate well with each other, they may collectively waste time developing the same small tools repeatedly.

It might seem that an organization could save time and effort by having a single tools group to meet the needs of all the development groups. Certainly, if a company wants to develop in-house tools, it will need to treat each tool as a product whose customers are the company's other development groups. The tool developers and maintainers may become a *de facto* tools group.

However, isolating a tools group from the development groups makes it prone to the classic problems of service organizations. It becomes harder for the toolsmiths to appreciate the needs of the developers. Since the tools group must respond to requests from several groups, it may need to delay responding to any one request, thus slowing down or blocking progress for the delayed group. If service is poor enough, the development groups may take matters into their own hands and turn some of their own programmers into toolsmiths.

Each company may need its own mix of toolsmiths and tools groups. If you have toolsmiths, make sure they communicate with each other (and with the tools group, if any) to avoid duplicate effort. If you have a tools group, make sure it moderates its own internal goals with a concern for the needs of the development groups.

Further Reading

Brooks (1975) pointed out that you ought to build a first system intending to throw it away, because you will anyway. Kernighan and Plauger (1981) discuss several software tools.

Chapter 20

Retrospective

In the Preface and Introduction I said that this book introduces the basic ideas of software engineering. Now that I have presented these ideas, we can back away from the details and look at the area as a whole.

20.1 Fundamental Themes

It would be wonderful if we had a magic technique that would let us build high-quality software easily and cheaply. Unfortunately, we don't have any such methods, nor are we likely to. The methods of this book provide big gains only in that they help reduce the likelihood of certain kinds of disaster. For example, if you take care to interact with end users to define your system's requirements, you are less likely to deliver software the customer can't use. If you take care to use information hiding to decompose your system, changing your system should take much less time and effort. If you plan your testing carefully, you are less likely to deliver software that fails to meet its specifications.

The core idea of this book is that producing high-quality software requires planning. Requirements analysis means deciding what your software should do before you build it. Module decomposition and configuration management involve planning for possible changes. Module specification means pinning down what a collection of procedures should do before you implement them; module implementation requires that you make design decisions before coding. Coding standards require that you plan for someone else to be able to read and understand your code once you've left it. Successful testing requires planning long in advance.

Planning is useless unless you record the plan for later use. Most of us cannot remember what we agreed on in a meeting last week unless we write it down. Thus, because planning is important, documentation becomes important. I have tried to show how all the documents I outline are useful during development; requiring people to write documents they will not use does not work.

Another key idea is that software systems constantly change, and that everything you do during the development process needs to take change into account. You need to

- structure the requirements specification for change
- decompose your system into modules that make the system easy to change
- write specifications that hide design decisions, so they remain valid when the decisions change
- write your code to use only the specifications of other modules, so you don't need to change your code when the things it uses change
- structure your test cases to allow for change, and keep them around for regression testing
- design user documentation so you can easily change it

20.2 What Else Is There?

No one book can cover all software engineering, just as no one book can cover all civil engineering. Ideally, we would have undergraduate programs that lead to a software engineering degree. This extends what an undergraduate would already get in a computer science program to approximate what such a degree would need.

I've left out many specific techniques that could fit into the earlier chapters. People have proposed languages for defining requirements, methods for writing module specifications, techniques for developing test cases, methods for measuring productivity, design methods likely to result in higher quality software (such as higher reliability or safety), and tools for assisting in a variety of programming and engineering activities. Psychologists have a large body of knowledge that bears on human factors in requirements analysis. Business administration can say a lot more about managing groups of people.

I have touched only lightly on the interaction of hardware and software, and on the needs of parallel and realtime systems. Some computer system designers may not agree with my discussion of how to split functions among hardware and software. I have ignored interactions with ideas from information systems.

20.3 Do People Really Do This?

A reasonable question, when faced with the disciplines outlined in this book, is whether real software builders do all this. Certainly not everyone does; in the mid

1980s we still saw recent software projects that failed to meet customer needs, didn't even live up to their own descriptions, and arrived late. We don't always get to see the internal processes that led to such a state, but often when we do we can trace the problem to a failure to follow some of the guidelines I've summarized.

The situation is improving. There is much interest in Professional Development seminars on requirements specifications, configuration management, test planning, and other issues in this book. Software engineering courses like the one for which I wrote this book are becoming more common, so more beginning programmers are at least learning what methods there are, and what type of problems they should solve.

The waterfall life-cycle model came under attack in the early 1980s. Some of the arguments against it derive from the simple observation that we often discover problems with early stages while trying to do later stages. Parnas and Clements (1986) argue that we should write our design documents as though we built them according to the waterfall model, even if we deviate from it in some ways. I agree with them; this is not the least bit dishonest or misdirected. A mathematician presents a proof as a single chain of deductions, even though it came from a convoluted set of partial attempts, blind alleys, and backtracks.

The idea of defining requirements in advance has been particularly controversial. The problem is that computers are such flexible tools that we often try to get them to do things no one has tried to do before. This often means we often do not know in advance what the software should do. Thus some people advocate methods for developing prototypes rapidly, to let customers interact with the system to see if it meets their needs. As far as it goes, this is a reasonable idea. Unfortunately, much of the work I have seen on such prototyping ignores the issue of evolving the resulting system.

Most developers believe that module decomposition is important, if only for dividing work up among different people. Not everyone accepts information hiding as the key method; however, it is gaining ground as people realize how important it is to be able to change old software. Abstract data types and object-oriented programming, which grew out of the idea of information hiding, are beginning to spread.

The two classic problems that still plague development projects are changing requirements and unrealistic schedules. When requirements change part way through a project, one usually has to throw away much of one's prior work. When a schedule is too short, one often cuts corners to meet the schedule. The first thing cut is usually the planning activities (like careful requirements analysis, information hiding, configuration management, and test planning) that promise long-term gain for short-term cost. The result is a lower-quality product.

Both problems arise from nontechnical issues. Requirements change because customers, or your marketing division, change their minds about what they want or because their needs change as you develop their software. Managers set unrealistic schedules because they had to promise those dates to get the contract, or because the customer's procurement procedures didn't let the developer take the time to do enough work to produce a realistic schedule.

Some techniques reduce the damage these problems cause. Agreeing on requirements and possible changes in advance gives a contractual basis for resolving change issues. Designing modules that hide requirements that might change reduces the cost of adapting to such changes. Planning subsets gives you a fallback position if you can't deliver the full system on the original schedule. All the planning activities reduce the likelihood of problems that would delay your development.

If the various disciplines I have outlined look like too much work to adopt all at once, I'd strongly advise that you at least adopt the following four.

1. Use information hiding for your module decompositions. This makes your system a lot easier to change, and can compensate for failures in other areas by limiting the effects of problems.

2. Design a series of subsets; it's a lot less embarrassing to be able to deliver *something* on time.

3. Make sure you allocate plenty of time for integration; if you've never had to do it before, it takes a lot longer than you think.

4. Listen to your customers. If they don't like your system, little else matters.

20.4   A Personal View

In the early days of computer science, many people did not regard it as a legitimate separate discipline. To some extent the field suffered from an inferiority complex; people agonized over whether it was a "real" science. Its image has improved over the decades; it is common to get a Ph.D. for a pure computer science topic, rather than mixing computing with some other discipline. Few people now bother to debate the meaning of the term.

Software engineering in the mid 1980s suffers from some of the same image problems that computer science did in the 1950s. People wonder whether it is "real" engineering. The term has become a buzzword, used by many people to make what they are doing more attractive. Despite these problems, it is emerging as a worthwhile discipline separate from computer science, and separate from other branches of engineering. I believe that this book contributes to this evolution, by summarizing and teaching the key ideas of the field.

Appendices

These appendices give examples of the documents one might produce for the project outlined in exercises from Part II. The program manages small genealogical databases. It is too small to be suitable for a one-semester course, but is large enough to illustrate some of the main things to do in each project document. The examples are not perfect; each illustrates in a small way the sort of flaws and compromises present in current real systems. My comments on flaws appear in footnotes.

Were these examples separate documents, I would not have included the introductory remarks before the first subsection of each of them. Each would include a title page stating the name of the document, a version indication for configuration management, and the date of its last change. Each would have a table of contents, and some might have glossaries of technical terms. When the sample documents refer to each other, they do so via the titles the separate documents would have (for example, "User's Guide for the Genealogy Program" for Appendix A). I give the correspondence with appendices via footnotes.

Sample
_____ User's Guide _____

For some projects, especially small ones, a user's reference manual can serve as a requirements document. This forces one to include details, such as what prompts to use, that some user's guides omit. Chapter 4 discusses considerations that go into specifying requirements; Section 4.4 discusses user's guides.

Section A.3 lists the system's error messages. Many of these are hard to follow, or are poorly worded. For example, "Too many persons trying to add P" means "While trying to add person P, the program ran out of room to store new persons." Ideally, the requirements review should catch these problems and require better messages.

A.1 Introduction

The GEN program manages a database of genealogical relationships. You can build a database defining relationships between several people, and then ask questions of the two forms

1. What is the relationship between person 1 and person 2?
2. Who are the relatives of person 1?

To follow this guide, you need a basic understanding of VM/CMS, including file naming conventions. Phrases of the form

!*sequence of words*!

are technical terms defined in the Glossary (Section A.4 on page 221).

To use GEN, tell CMS the name of your database file by typing the CMS command

FILEDEF DATABASE DISK fn ft fm

where "fn ft fm" is the name of your file. Then run GEN by typing

GEN

GEN reads the database file and allows you to use the commands described in Section A.2.

A.2   Commands

Once GEN has read in your database, it repeatedly prompts you for commands by printing

>

until you use the Quit or Exit commands to terminate. GEN ignores case distinctions, so you can type "QUIT," "quit," or even "QuiT."

Some commands take names of persons as arguments. You must spell names exactly as in the Add command that entered the person into the database, except for case distinctions. If GEN cannot find a name in the database, it tells you and returns to the ">" prompt.

Some commands prompt you for additional information. You can avoid some of the prompts by supplying the information on the command line. Each command description tells what information you can supply in this way.

A.2.1   Add Command

The Add command permits you to add new persons to your database. It prompts you for

Name?	The name of the person you wish to add. You may supply this on the command line instead.
Male or female?	A letter stating whether the person is male (M) or female (F).
Father?	The name of the person's father.
Mother?	The name of the person's mother.

You may leave either or both of the parents' names blank.

GEN lets you add parents either before or after their children; you need never enter information about some parents. You may not add the same person to the database twice without an intervening delete. That is, you may not answer the "Name?" prompt twice with the same name; for the purposes of this rule, GEN's reading of the input file replicates all the Add commands you have previously entered into the same database.

The !*size of the database*! may not exceed 100 people. GEN checks the information you provide in an Add command before modifying the database; Section A.3.1 lists potential exception messages.

A.2.2 Change Command

The Change command permits you to modify information recorded about a particular person. It prompts for the name of a person; you may supply this information on the command line instead.

For each piece of information you supplied in the original Add command for that person, GEN prompts you with the same prompt as the Add command, followed by the current value of the information in square brackets. To change the information, type in a new value; to leave it alone, enter a blank line.

If you change the recorded sex of a person, GEN may need to make other changes to keep the database consistent. If the person has children (which could arise if you answered the "Father" and "Mother" prompts in the wrong order when adding those children), GEN must swap the mother and father for all the children. This involves changing the sex of the other parent as well, and possibly that of several other people. For example, if P1 and P2 have child C1, and P2 and P3 have child C2, GEN must change the sex of all three of P1, P2, and P3 if you wish to change any of them. GEN prints the message

To change the sex of P, you must also change

followed by the names of all such people, and asks the !*yes-or-no question*!

Do you wish to change them all?

If you reply "no," it changes none of them and presumes you no longer wish to change the sex of the current person.

A.2.3 Delete Command

The Delete command removes information from the database. It has two subcommands, distinguished by an optional argument on the command line.

Delete with no argument removes a single person from the database. GEN prompts you for the name of the person; you may not supply this information on the command line. This may result in parents or children of the named person no longer having either ancestors or descendants; GEN lists all such persons, and asks if you want to remove them also. You may reply Y (Yes), N (No), or S (Some). In the last case, GEN lists each name individually and asks if you wish to remove that particular person.

Delete All removes all persons from the database. To confirm whether you really intended to eliminate the entire database, GEN asks the !*yes-or-no question*!

Do you want to eliminate all *nnn* entries in the database?

where *nnn* is the !*size of the database*!, and does nothing if you answer "No."

A.2.4 Exit and Quit Commands

Exit and Quit are identical commands. They cause GEN to return to CMS. If you have added any new persons to the database, GEN updates your database file before returning.[1]

A.2.5 Help Command

The Help command takes no arguments. It prints a brief (one line) summary of each command, illustrated in Figure A–1.

A.2.6 What Command

The What command allows you to ask for the relationship between two people. GEN prompts you for the names of the two people; you may enter the first name on the same line as the What command, separated from it by a space.

GEN reports relationships in the form

Name1 is the XXX of Name2 via Name3

where Name1 and Name2 are the names you entered, XXX is the name of a relationship (such as 3rd cousin twice removed), and Name3 is the name of the common ancestor that defines the relationship. For example, for first cousins once removed, the common ancestor will be a grandparent of one person and a great-grandparent of the other.

Add	Add a new person and record his or her parents.
Change	Change recorded sex or parents of a person.
Delete	Delete a person.
Delete All	Delete the entire database.
Exit	Update the database and return to CMS.
Help	Print this message
Quit	Update the database and return to CMS.
What	Find all blood relationships between two people.
Who	Find all a person's relatives of a named kind.

Figure A–1: Summary Printed by Help Command

---

[1]Editorial reflection. Neither of these gives some way to abort GEN after a serious mistake in Add, Change, or Delete. Requirements review should point out the need for an Abort command.

A.2.7 Who Command

The Who command allows you to ask for particular relatives of a person. It prompts you for

Relation?   The name of a relationship. You may supply this information on the command line.

Name?   The name of the person whose relatives you wish to find. You may supply this on the command line, provided you also supply the relation name on the command line.

GEN allows you to ask for son, daughter, child (sons and daughters), father, mother, parent (father and mother), grandfather, grandmother, grandparent (grandfathers and grandmothers), grandson, granddaughter, grandchild (grandsons and grand-daughters), uncle, aunt, nephew, niece, brother, sister, and sibling (brothers and sisters). You must spell all these names for relationships in the singular, but may use either upper or lower case.

A.3 Exception Summary

This section describes the exception messages GEN prints.

A.3.1 Add Command Exceptions

Bad value for sex.

> You didn't answer the "Male or female?" prompt with one of the letters M, m, F, or f. GEN reprompts you until you give a valid answer.

P is being defined as X, but was named as someone's Y.

> P is the name of the current person, X is "male" or "female," and Y is "mother" or "father." You are trying to define P as sex X, but GEN has already recorded that they must be of the other sex. You have previously used P as a mother or father of someone else, and have answered the "Male or female?" prompt inconsistently. GEN asks you if you wish to abort this Add command without changing the database. If you do not abort the Add, GEN assumes the sex it previously deduced is correct. To minimize the chance of this exception, add ancestors before descendants.

N1 is N2's X but is recorded elsewhere as someone's Y.

> N2 is the current person, N1 is the name you supplied for N2's father or mother, and X and Y are the words "father" and "mother" in some order. GEN asks you if you wish to abort the Add command. If not, it prompts you to retype the name that caused the exception. This exception can occur if for some prior Add command you responded to the "Father?" and "Mother?" prompts with names in the wrong order, and GEN had no prior knowledge of whether those names should represent males or females. To minimize the

chance of this exception, add ancestors before descendants.[2] You may use the Change command to change the sex recorded for a particular person.

Too many persons trying to add P.

P is a person's name, and might be any of the three names you entered (the new person, the person's mother, or the person's father). Attempting to handle this person causes GEN to exceed the limit of 100 persons.

P already entered in the database.

You answered the "Name?" prompt with the name of someone you'd already added.

A.3.2 Input File Exceptions

For every exception message about the input file, GEN prints the line number where the exception occurred. GEN ignores any line causing an exception, unless otherwise stated below. All such exceptions represent either internal defects in GEN, or damage to your database. For all such exceptions, preserve the database file that caused them, and report them to the !*GEN maintainer*!.

The input file serves to record the information you provided in prior Add commands. If the file becomes damaged, any exception that might occur with an Add command might occur while reading the input. For each Add command exception, the following reports what action GEN takes, which may differ from the action of the Add command.

Bad value for sex. Assuming this person is Male

(Add command exception). GEN accepts the line, but presumes the person is male.

P is being defined as X, but was named as someone's Y.

(Add command exception). GEN keeps the line that caused it to print this message, but ignores the sex it implies.

N1 is N2's X but is recorded elsewhere as someone's Y.

(Add command exception). GEN keeps the line that caused it to print this message, but ignores the sex it implies.

Too many persons trying to add P. Stopping with what we have.

(Add command exception).

P already entered in the database. Ignoring this line.

(Add command exception).

---

[2]Editorial reflection: This exception message should say "N1 is N2's (mother, father) but earlier information says (he, she) is (male, female)." When I first wrote this section, I ignored the case of adding person N1 as male, but then using him as N2's mother. The code of Appendix H (and the Person specification in Section E.6) cannot distinguish between these two conditions. I have left this mistake in place to show the type of problem a requirements review should catch.

Format exception: *extra information*
>   This message is a catchall for other problems with the input file format.

A.3.3   Other Command Exceptions

If GEN encounters an exception while processing a command, it abandons the command and returns to the ">" prompt.

P is not recorded in the database.
>   You have named a person not defined in the input file. Check spelling; you must type each name exactly as it is in the input file (except for case distinctions) without abbreviating it.

I don't know how to find someone's XXX.
>   XXX is a word you typed as an argument to the Who command; GEN does not support any relationship of this name. Check the list of supported relationships in Section A.2.7 on page 219.

P has no XXXs.
>   XXX is the name of a relationship supported by the Who command. Person P has no such relatives recorded in the database.

P1 is not related to P2.
>   GEN cannot find a blood relationship between P1 and P2. This can happen because they are not related, or because the input file does not track ancestors back far enough.

A.3.4   Unchecked Problems

GEN does not verify that your family tree is free of loops. This could happen if you misspell someone's name, or if someone has the same name as his or her ancestor, resulting in a situation where GEN records that a person is their own ancestor. If your database has such an exception, the What command may never terminate.

A.4   Glossary

GEN maintainer: Address for reporting internal defects or maintenance problems, or instructions about how to find such an address, goes here.

size of the database: The number of distinct names entered in response to the "Name?," "Mother?," and "Father?" prompts of Add and Change commands (including implicit Add commands from reading the input database), minus those removed via Delete commands.

yes-or-no question: A prompt, typically phrased as a question, to which you must reply either yes or no. You may abbreviate your answer to the first letter. GEN re-prompts you until you give one of these two answers.

Sample
Life-Cycle
Considerations

Part of requirements analysis is to plan for how the product may evolve during its lifetime. Chapter 4 discusses considerations that go into specifying requirements; Section 4.3.1 mentions life-cycle considerations in particular. Section 4.5 describes how to plan for delivering the system as a series of subsets.

For a larger system, Sections B.2 and B.3 might have subsections (and perhaps sub-subsections) to group together related assumptions or potential changes.

B.1 Introduction

This document describes the life-cycle considerations for the genealogy program. To follow this document, you should understand the document "User's Guide for the Genealogy Program."[1]

B.2 Fundamental Assumptions

We expect that the following assertions will be true of all versions of the genealogical system.

1. The sex of each person in the database is known.

---

[1]Appendix A.

2.   Each person has at most two parents: a mother and a father.

3.   No two distinct persons will have the same name.

4.   There will never be a need to consider "in-law" relationships (including husband or wife).

5.   One can define all relationships one might name in the Who command as a sequence of moves around the directed acyclic graph defined by the parent/child relation.[2] Each move will be one of

> move to father
> move to mother
> move to any parent
> move to all male children, in parallel
> move to all female children, in parallel
> move to all children, in parallel

B.3 Potential Changes

The following items are changes that might reasonably occur in later versions of the system.

1.   Within the constraints of Assumptions 4 and 5, we might add or remove relationships for the Who command.

2.   We might change the names of particular relationships.

3.   We might change the number of persons the system can support.

4.   We might change the format of the input file.

5.   We might add other commands.

6.   We might change the method of giving arguments for any command.

7.   We might adopt a different style of interaction, such as menu-driven input instead of command-driven, or screen-oriented instead of teletype-oriented.

8.   We might change the meaning of "nearest common ancestor."

9.   We might port the program to a different environment, with a different character set.

---

[2]Editorial reflection: This complex assumption should raise a red flag for any reviewer. It *might* be acceptable, but needs to be examined closely. It discusses a fine detail of how an implementation can work. The assumptions *must* discuss what sort of relationships the system will allow, and what room for expansion there will be. You need to avoid specifying an algorithm, while characterizing what such algorithms need to deal with. For example, these rules prevent discussing relationships like "half-sibling," "second oldest sister," "younger brother," or "heir." In fact it represents my attempt to retrofit the restrictions of the RelDef module (see Section E.8) into the fundamental assumptions. Retrofits happen in real life much more often than they should.

B.4   Subsets

The following are a series of successively larger subsets we will build.

1. The trivial subset has just the Exit, Help, and Quit commands.

2. The next subset reads the input file and prints any exception messages arising from reading the input, but has no new commands. The Person module may omit the restricted interface for the Find module.

3. The next subset adds the Who command.

4. The next subset adds the What command.

5. The next subset adds the Add command. The Quit and Exit commands must now output the modified database.

6. The next subset adds the Delete command.

7. The final subset adds the Change command for a complete system.

Sample
System
Test Plan _____

All system tests follow from the requirements, as given in the user's guide. For a large system, it might be impractical to list all the tests as I have done here. The test plan might simply outline categories of tests, the scheme for maintaining a large database, and similar global issues.

This example, and others that follow, presume that the developers decided to implement Subset 4, as described in the sample life-cycle document (Appendix B). Thus there are no tests for the Add, Change, and Delete commands. Furthermore, there are tests (Section C.3.1) for the specific database file format mentioned in the release note (Appendix I). Ideally each document should identify what subset it corresponds to, and the system test plan would reference some memo describing the format of the database file (since the release notice would not yet exist). Without proper configuration management, these details would probably become unstated assumptions.

C.1 Introduction

This document describes the plan for testing the genealogy system. To follow this document, you should understand the document "User's Guide for the Genealogy Program."[1] Throughout this document, "you" means the person or persons performing the tests.

_____

[1]Appendix A.

Sex	Name	Father	Mother
m	M2a	M1a	F1a
f	F2a	M1a	F1a
m	M2b	M1b	F1b
f	F2b	M1b	F1b
m	M3a	M2a	F2b
m	M3b	M2a	F2b
f	F3a	M2a	F2b
f	F3b	M2a	F2b
m	M3c	M2c	F2a
f	F3c	M2c	F2a
m	M4a	M3c	F3d
f	F4a	M3c	F3d

Figure C–1: Test Input File

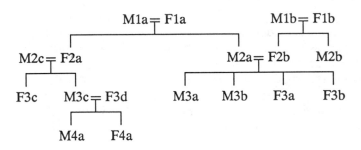

Figure C–2: Graph of Simple Family Tree

Testing requires a Show command that, given a person, would show their sex and the names of their parents. Some tests use it to verify that the program correctly represents information from a single line of the input file. Other documents do not mention this command.

C.2 Functionality Tests

Functionality tests determine whether the system works correctly for normal input.

C.2.1 Basic Functionality

Basic functionality tests use an input file that describes a simple four-generation family with no inbreeding. Names of individuals in this family are of the form SGI, where

- S is a letter, M or F, which says whether the person is male or female.

- G is a number showing what generation the person is in (1 for the eldest, 2 and 3 for the middle generation, and 4 for the youngest).

- I is a letter distinguishing persons within a generation.

Figure C–1 shows the sample test data. Figure C–2 shows a family tree for the sample test data.

Figure C–3 shows the tests of the Who command. The system may show the persons named in the answer in any order. To test for the ability to supply answers to some prompts on the command line, do the tests in groups of three. For the first command in each group, supply no information on the command line, and expect GEN to prompt for the relationship and the name. For the second command in each group, supply the relationship on the command line, and expect GEN to prompt for the name. For the third command in each group, supply the relationship and the name on the command line.

Relation	Person	Answer	Relation	Person	Answer
Father	M3a	M2a	Child	M3a	none
Mother	M3a	F2b	Parent	M1a	none
Parent	M3a	M2a, F2b	Brother	M2a	none
Child	M2a	M3a, M3b, F3a, F3b	Sister	M2a	F2a
			Sibling	M2a	F2a
Son	M2a	M3a, M3b	Brother	M3a	M3b
Daughter	M2a	F3a, F3b	Brother	F3a	M3a, M3b
Grandparent	M3a	M1a, F1a, M1b, F1b	Sister	M3a	F3a, F3b
			Sibling	M3a	M3b, F3a, F3b
Grandfather	M3a	M1a, M1b	Grandmother	M3a	F1a, F1b
Grandchild	M1a	M3a, M3b, M3c, F3a, F3b, F3c	Uncle	M3a	M2b
			Aunt	M3a	F2a

Figure C–3: Tests of Who Command

Figure C–4 shows the tests of the What command. The starred relations are ones where there is a relation by marriage but none by blood; the genealogy system records only blood relationships. To test the ability to supply answers to prompts on the command line, do the tests in groups of two. For the first command in each set, supply no information on the command line, and expect GEN to prompt for both names. For the second command in each set, supply the first name on the command line, and expect GEN to prompt for the second name.

C.2.2 Advanced Functionality

This chapter covers tests for a highly inbred family, using the English Royal family as an example. Figure C–5 shows the sample input data. Figure C–6 shows several test cases for detecting multiple relationships.

C.3   Exception Tests

Exception tests determine whether the system behaves correctly for abnormal inputs.

C.3.1 Input File Tests

This is a system test for a subset where, because there is no Add command, we have users create input files in a specific format with a text editor. Thus we can (and should) test for problems in the input file. Since the following exceptions should

Person 1	Person 2	Relationship	Person 1	Person 2	Relationship
M1a	F1a	none*	M2a	F2a	brother
F2a	M2a	sister	M2a	F1a	son
F2a	F1a	daughter	F1a	M2a	mother
M1a	M2a	father	M3a	M1b	grandson
F3a	M1b	granddaughter	M1b	M3a	grandfather
F1b	M3a	grandmother	M3a	F2a	nephew
F3a	F2a	niece	F2a	M3a	aunt
M3a	M2c	none*	M2b	M3a	uncle
M3a	M3c	first cousin	M4a	M1a	great-grandson
F4a	F1a	great-granddaughter	M1a	M4a	great-grandfather
F1a	M4a	great-grandmother	M3a	M4a	first cousin
M4a	M3a	first cousin			once removed
		once removed	M4a	M2a	great nephew
M2a	M4a	great uncle	F1b	F1a	none
M2b	M2c	none			

Figure C–4: Tests of What Command

cause exception messages but should not abort the attempt to read the input file, you may test them with a single input file.

1.   First character of a line not M or F.

2.   Only one name on a line.

Sex	Name	Father	Mother
f	Victoria	Edward, Duke of Kent	Victoria of Saxe-Coburg-Saalfeld
m	Edward VII	Albert	Victoria
m	George V	Edward VII	Alexandra of Denmark
m	George VI	George V	Mary of Teck
f	Elizabeth II	George VI	Elizabeth Bowes-Lyon
f	Alice	Albert	Victoria
f	Victoria of Hesse	Louis IV of Hesse	Alice
f	Alice of Battenberg	Prince Louis of Battenberg	Victoria of Hesse
m	Philip	Andrew of Greece	Alice of Battenberg
f	Alexandra of Denmark	Christian IX of Denmark	Louise
m	George I of Greece	Christian IX of Denmark	Louise
m	Andrew of Greece	George I of Greece	Olga of Russia
m	Frederick	George II	Caroline of Anspach
m	George III	Frederick	Augusta of Saxe-Gotha
m	Edward, Duke of Kent	George III	Charlotte
f	Mary	George II	Caroline of Anspach
m	Landgrave Frederick	Landgrave Frederick I	Mary
m	Landgrave William	Landgrave Frederick	Caroline
f	Louise	Landgrave William	Charlotte of Denmark
f	Augusta	Landgrave Frederick	Caroline
f	Mary Adelaide	Adolphus	Augusta
f	Mary of Teck	Francis, Duke of Teck	Mary Adelaide
m	Adolphus	George III	Charlotte
f	Anne	Philip	Elizabeth II
m	Peter Phillips	Mark Phillips	Anne
m	Charles	Philip	Elizabeth II
m	William	Charles	Diana Spencer
m	Henry	Charles	Diana Spencer
m	Andrew	Philip	Elizabeth II
m	Edward	Philip	Elizabeth II
m	Edward VIII	George V	Mary of Teck
m	Albert, Duke of Clarence	Edward VII	Alexandra of Denmark
m	George IV	George III	Charlotte
m	William IV	George III	Charlotte
f	Margaret Rose	George VI	Elizabeth Bowes-Lyon
m	George, Duke of Kent	George V	Mary of Teck

Figure C–5: Input File for English Royal Family

Person 1	Person 2	Relationship	Ancestors
Elizabeth	Philip	2nd cousin 1 removed	Christian IX of Denmark, Louise
		3rd cousin	Victoria, Albert
		4th cousin	Landgrave Frederick, Caroline
		4th cousin 1 removed	George III, Charlotte,
			Landgrave Frederick, Caroline
		5th cousin	George III, Charlotte
Charles	Philip	son	Philip
		2nd cousin 1 removed	Christian IX of Denmark, Louise
		2nd cousin 2 removed	Christian IX of Denmark, Louise
		3rd cousin 1 removed	Victoria, Albert
		4th cousin 1 removed	Landgrave Frederick, Caroline
		4th cousin 2 removed	Landgrave Frederick, Caroline
		5th cousin	George III, Charlotte
		5th cousin 1 removed	George III, Charlotte
Andrew of Greece	George VI	1st cousin 1 removed	Christian IX of Denmark, Louise
		3rd cousin	Landgrave Frederick, Caroline
		3rd cousin 1 removed	Landgrave Frederick, Caroline
		5th cousin	George II, Caroline of Anspach
		5th cousin 1 removed	George II, Caroline of Anspach
Victoria	Louise	3rd cousin	George II, Caroline of Anspach
Victoria	Alexandra of Denmark	3rd cousin 1 removed	George II, Caroline of Anspach
Philip	George II	$great^5$-grandson	George II
		$great^6$-grandson	George II
Philip	Landgrave Frederick	1st cousin 5 removed	George II, Caroline of Anspach
		1st cousin 6 removed	George II, Caroline of Anspach
		$great^3$-grandson	Landgrave Frederick
Charles	Mary Adelaide	$great^2$-grandson	Mary Adelaide
		1st cousin 4 removed	George III, Charlotte
			Landgrave Frederick, Caroline
		1st cousin 5 removed	George III, Charlotte
			Landgrave Frederick, Caroline

Figure C–6: Test Results for English Royal Family

3. Only two names on a line.

4. Extra text after the last name on a line.

5. Duplicate definition of a person, with the same parents as the first definition. A Who Parent command should report the correct parents.

6. Duplicate definition of a person, with different mother from first definition. A Who Parent command should report the parents from the first definition.

7. Duplicate definition of a person, with different father from first definition. A Who Parent command should report the parents from the first definition.

8. Interchange the mother and father of a person, before defining either parent. GEN should report this as an incorrect gender at the lines defining the parents. A Show command for each parent should show the mother as male and the father as female.

9. Interchange the mother and father of a person, after defining both parents. GEN should report an incorrect gender at the line containing the interchange. A Show command for each parent should show the mother as female and the father as male.

C.3.2 Capacity Exceptions

The following tests all verify the behavior of the system near the maximum number of persons. Each is a separate test case.

1. Create a test case with precisely 100 persons in the following way: A1 (male) has parents B1 and B2. A2 (female) has parents B3 and B4. A3 (male) has parents B5 and B6. A4 (female) has parents B7 and B8. C1 through C88 have parents A1 and A2. GEN should not report any exceptions.

2. To the file from the first test case, add C89 with parents A1 and A2. This should report an exception. Show C89 should report that the database has no such person.

3. To the file from the first test case, add a definition of B1 with parents A3 and A4. This should not report an exception.

Sample
Module Decomposition
and Dependencies

This appendix describes all the modules of the full system, even though the implementors decided to build a subset. The reasoning is that the implementors must be sure they have taken into account the needs of later subsets.

D.1 Introduction

This document describes the module decomposition and module dependencies for the genealogy program. To follow this document, you should understand the document "User's Guide for the Genealogy Program".[1] Statements in the document "Life-Cycle Considerations for the Genealogy Program"[2] prompted some design decisions.

There are three major software divisions in this system: modules that hide details of the host system, modules that hide details of the requirements, and modules that hide software decisions. The following sections present all the modules of the system, divided into these three groups (alphabetically within each group).

[1]Appendix A.
[2]Appendix B.

D.2   System Module

This module hides all details peculiar to the host machine.

D.2.1   Char Module

The Char module provides common functions having to do with character processing. It hides details of the character set of the host machine.

D.3   Requirements Module

This module hides all details of the requirements that the system must meet.

D.3.1   Add Module

The Add module hides the processing and output of the Add command, which adds new people to the database.

D.3.2   Change Module

The Change module hides the processing and output of the Change command, which modifies information about people in the database.

D.3.3   Delete Module

The Delete module hides the processing and output of the Delete command, which removes people from the database.

D.3.4   Command Module

The Command module hides what commands the system provides, and how it parses commands and arguments.

D.3.5   GenFile Module

The GenFile module hides details of the format of the genealogy file. Such details include how to find information about a person, how to delimit a name in the input file, and how to find a person's parents in the input.

D.3.6   What Module

The What module hides the processing and output of the What command, which shows all relationships between two persons.

D.3.7   Who Module

The Who module hides the processing and output of the Who command, which shows all people related to a given person in a particular way.

D.4   Software Decision Module

The Software Decision module hides those decisions that software designers controlled. The major kinds of decisions in this category are data structure and algorithm choices.

D.4.1   Find Module

The Find module hides the algorithm used to find the relationships between two people. It provides a facility to report all such relationships, given the two persons.

D.4.2   Name Module

The Name module hides decisions of how to represent names of persons. It provides facilities for creating new names, comparing names, and iterating over the characters of a name.

D.4.3   Person Module

The Person module hides details of how to represent an individual person. It provides facilities for representing a new person, iterating over all persons, establishing some relationships among persons, and fetching information about a person.

D.4.4   RelDef Module

The RelDef module hides the method of finding all a particular person's relatives of a particular kind. It provides facilities for defining relationships and for finding the relatives of a person given such a relationship.

D.4.5   Set Module

The Set module hides the data structure used to represent sets of persons. There may be several such sets.

D.4.6   Table Module

The Table module hides the method used to find a person given his or her name. It provides facilities for recording that a particular name maps to a particular person, and for asking what person has a given name. There need not be more than one such mapping at a time.

D.4.7   Word Module

The Word module hides the representation of single words from the command line (such as command names and relationship names).

D.5 Module Dependencies

This section lists all modules from previous sections in alphabetical order. The description of a module shows what other modules it uses. For completeness, we list even those modules that do not depend on others.

Because of Pascal language considerations, the source code for a module may need to import types from a module it does not use directly. For example, the Find module uses the Person module, which uses the Name module. The Find module may need to import the type declarations of the Name module, to allow definitions from the Person module to compile. We omit these indirect relationships.

Figure D–1 shows a topological sort of dependencies; each line shows only direct dependencies. The Main module potentially calls all other modules, since it may need to call initialization routines; we do not consider this a "use."

Module	Depends on
Main	Command, GenFile
Command	Add, Change, Char, Delete, Name, Person, Table, What, Who, Word
Add	Name, Person, Table
Change	Name, Person, Set, Table
Delete	Person, Set, Table
Who	RelDef, Person, Name, Word
What	Find, Name, Person
RelDef	Person, Set, Word
Find	Set, Person
GenFile	Name, Person, Table
Table	Name, Person
Set	Person
Person	Name
Name	Char
Word	Char
Char	nothing

Figure D–1: Topological Sort of Module Dependencies

D.5.1 Add Module

The Add module depends on the Name module to represent names from the command line, on the Table module to map names to persons, and on the Person module to create representations of new persons and record relationships.

D.5.2 Change Module

The Change module depends on the Name module to represent names from the command line; on the Person module to fetch and store information about a person, and create representations of new persons; on the Set module to represent sets of persons involved in changing the sex recorded for a person; and on the Table module to map names to persons.

D.5.3 Char Module

The Char module depends on nothing else.

D.5.4 Delete Module

The Delete module depends on the Person module to manipulate information about persons, on the Set module to represent sets of persons who might have neither ancestors nor descendants after the deletion, and on the Table module to remove names of deleted persons.

D.5.5 Command Module

The Command module depends on the Name module to represent names typed by the user, on the Table and Person modules to map names to persons, on the Char module to convert characters to upper case, on the Word module to represent portions of parsed commands, and on the Add, Change, Delete, What, and Who modules to implement the commands of the same name.

D.5.6 Find Module

The Find module depends on the Person module to follow relationships among people, and on the Set module to build sets of related persons.

D.5.7 GenFile Module

The GenFile module depends on the Name module to represent names found in the input file, on the Table module to map names to persons, and on the Person module to create representations of new persons and record relationships.

D.5.8 Main Module

The Main module depends on the Command module to interpret commands, and on the GenFile module to read and write the database.

D.5.9 Name Module

The Name module depends on the Char module to convert characters from lower case to upper case.

D.5.10 Person Module

The Person module depends on the types of the Name module to provide a representation of a person's name.

D.5.11 RelDef Module

The RelDef module depends on the Word module to name relationships among persons, on the Person module to follow relationships among persons, and on the Set module to represent sets of persons.

D.5.12 Set Module

The Set module depends on the Person module to represent elements of the set.

D.5.13 Table Module

The Table module depends on the Name module to compare names. It makes use of the Person module, but only assignment and parameter passing capabilities.

D.5.14 What Module

The What module depends on the Find module to determine the relationship between two people, on the Person module to represent people, and on the Name module to print out people's names.

D.5.15 Who Module

The Who module depends on the RelDef module to find the relatives of a person, on the Word module to name relationships, on the Person module to represent people, and on the Name module to print out people's names.

D.5.16 Word Module

The Word module depends on the Char module to convert characters from lower case to upper case.

Sample
Module
Specifications

This appendix shows specifications of some of the modules from Appendix D. In a real system, you would likely use a module development folder for each module, rather than collecting all the implementation descriptions into a single document.

Find and Person (Sections E.3 and E.6) use first-order logic. Name and Rel-Def (Sections E.5 and E.8) use trace specifications. Word could use a specification similar to Name (since each implements some type of string), so I have omitted it. Set (Section E.9) uses an algebraic specification.

The remaining module specifications show compromises of various kinds. Command, Who, and What use English to describe what is going on. GenFile uses equations, but had to reveal the module's secret (format of the input file) to do so.

E.1 Introduction

This document contains specifications of the individual modules of the genealogy program. To read this document, you should be familiar with the overall system decomposition as described in "Module Decomposition and Dependencies for the Genealogy System".[1]

_____

[1]Appendix D.

Each chapter describes one module. The chapters are sorted alphabetically by module name. Within each module description, interface procedure definitions are sorted by procedure name.

E.2 Command Module

The Command module hides what commands the system provides, and how it parses commands and arguments.

HandleCommand

Read and execute a single command from the terminal.
Parameters: none
Results: boolean
Value: **false** iff the command was a "Quit" or "Exit."
Effects: Reads and executes one command from the terminal.

E.3 Find Module

The Find module hides the algorithm used to find the relationship between two people. It provides a facility to report all such relationships, given the two persons.

FindRelation

Report all relationships between two people.
Parameters: person p1,p2; procedure R(person p; integer d1,d2)
Results: none
Effect: Call R' for each person p and integers M, N such that p is a "nearest common ancestor" of p1 and p2, and p is M generations from p1 and N from p2. More precisely,

$$\text{IsAncestor}(p,p1,M) \wedge \text{IsAncestor}(p,p2,N) \wedge$$
$$\exists c \in \text{person} \mid \text{IsParent}(p,c) \wedge$$
$$((\text{IsAncestor}(c,p1,M-1) \wedge (\neg \exists K \mid \text{IsAncestor}(c,p2,K)))\vee$$
$$(\text{IsAncestor}(c,p2,N-1) \wedge (\neg \exists K \mid \text{IsAncestor}(c,p1,K))))$$

where IsAncestor(a,b,K) means that a is an ancestor of b separated by K generations. More precisely,

$$\exists q_1, q_2, \cdots q_K \mid q_1 = b \wedge q_K = a \wedge \forall i \in [1..K-1] \text{ IsParent}(q_{i+1}, q_i)$$

where IsParent(a,b) means a = Father(b) or a = Mother(b)

E.4 GenFile Module

The GenFile module hides details of the format of the genealogy file. Such details include how to find information about a person, how to delimit a name in the input file, and how to find a person's parents in the input.

GetInput

Read an input file.
Parameters: file f
Results: none
Effects: Reads the contents of the input file and builds an internal representation.

Once GetInput reads all lines of the file, and provided there are no exceptions, for each line of the form

$$\text{xName}_1 * \text{Name}_2 * \text{Name}_3 *$$

such that $\text{Name}_1 \neq \lambda$ we have

$$\forall i \in [1..3]\ \text{Name}_i \neq \lambda \rightarrow \exists p_i \mid \text{NamePerson}(p_i) = \text{Name}_i \land$$
$$\text{Lookup}(\text{Name}_i) = (\text{true}, p_i)$$
$$\text{Name}_2 \neq \lambda \Rightarrow p_2 = \text{Father}(p_1)$$
$$\text{Name}_3 \neq \lambda \Rightarrow p_3 = \text{Mother}(p_1)$$
$$((x={}'M' \lor x={}'m') \Rightarrow \text{IsMale}(p_1)) \land ((x={}'F' \lor x={}'f') \Rightarrow \neg\text{IsMale}(p_1))$$

PutOutput

Write an output file.
Parameters: file f
Results: none
Effects: Writes the internal representation to an output file so that a subsequent
   input from the file would give the same internal representation.

For each person P_1 reported by the AllPerson procedure of the Person module, the output file contains a line of the form

$$\text{xName}_1 * \text{Name}_2 * \text{Name}_3 *$$

where

if $\text{IsMale}(P_1)$ then $x={}'M'$ else $x={}'F'$
$\text{Name}_1 = \text{NamePerson}(P_1)$
$\text{Name}_2 = (\text{if HasFather}(P_1)\ \text{then NamePerson}(\text{Father}(P_1))\ \text{else}\ \lambda)$
$\text{Name}_3 = (\text{if HasMother}(P_1)\ \text{then NamePerson}(\text{Mother}(P_1))\ \text{else}\ \lambda)$

From this, and the specification of GetInput, we can deduce that if Name_2 and Name_3 are both empty, and P_1 has at least one child, then you may omit the entire line for P_1.

E.5   Name Module

The Name module hides decisions of how to represent names of persons. It provides facilities for creating new names, comparing names, and iterating over the characters of a name.

AllChars

Do something with each character of a name.
Parameters: Procedure EachChar(character c)
Results: none
Effect: see below

MakeName

Create a name, given individual characters.
Parameters: Procedure GetChar returns (boolean b, character c)
Results: name
Value: see below

The following trace specification gives the meaning of MakeName and AllChars. GetChar is a generator of characters; you can keep calling it and getting new characters as long as it keeps returning **true**. The sequence of characters is whatever GetChar returns via the character result, not including the value of this result when GetChar returns **false**. GetChar must satisfy the following conditions.

$$L(GetChar)$$
$$T=T1.GetChar \wedge L(T) \Rightarrow$$
$$\quad V(T)=(\textbf{true},s) \Rightarrow (s \neq undefined) \wedge L(T.GetChar)$$
$$\quad V(T)=(\textbf{false},s) \Rightarrow s = undefined$$

MakeName calls GetChar repeatedly, and does something with the characters it returns so that AllChars can do something with them. Thus there exists some i such that calling MakeName results in a trace of the form $T_i.GetChar$, where

$$T_0 = \epsilon$$
$$\forall j > 1 \; T_j = T_{j-1}.GetChar$$

Thus i is the least integer such that $V(T_i.GetChar) = (\textbf{false},s)$, or alternatively the largest integer such that $T_i.GetChar$ is legal.

AllChar's parameter EachChar is any consumer of characters, with specification

$$L(T) \Rightarrow L(T.EachChar(c))$$

The effect of AllChars(MakeName(GetChar),EachChar) is $T_i.GetChar.E_i$, where T_i is the same as before, and

$$E_0 = \epsilon$$
$$\forall k \in [1..i] \; \exists C_k \mid V(T_k)=(\textbf{true},C_k) \wedge E_k = E_{k-1}.EachChar(C_k)$$

CmpName

Compare two names.
Parameters: names n1,n2
Results: enumeration (CmpLess, CmpEqual, CmpGreater)
Value: see below

In the definitions for CmpName below,

$\qquad$ Less(c1,c2) $\equiv$ UpperCase(c1) $<$ UpperCase(c2)

$\qquad$ Equ(c1,c2) $\equiv$ UpperCase(c1) $=$ UpperCase(c2)

From the definition of MakeName and AllChars, and since MakeName is the only way to create a new name,

$\qquad \exists M, N, c_{1,1}, c_{1,2}, \cdots c_{1,M}, c_{2,1}, c_{2,2}, ..., c_{2,N} \mid \forall$ procedures XX

$\qquad\qquad$ AllChars(n1,XX) $\equiv$ XX$(c_{1,1})$.XX$(c_{1,2})$ $\cdots$ XX$(c_{1,M})$

$\qquad\qquad$ AllChars(n2,XX) $\equiv$ XX$(c_{2,1})$.XX$(c_{2,2})$ $\cdots$ XX$(c_{2,N})$

CmpName returns CmpEqual if

$\qquad$ M=N $\wedge \forall i \in [1..M]$ Equ$(c_{1,i}, c_{2,i})$

It returns CmpLess if

$\qquad (M < N \wedge \forall i \in [1..M]$ Equ$(c_{1,i}, c_{2,i}))$

$\qquad \vee (\exists 0 \leq j \leq \min(M,N) \mid (\forall i \in [1..j-1]$ Equ$(c_{1,i}, c_{2,i})) \wedge$ Less$(c_{1,j}, c_{2,j})$

It returns CmpGreater if

$\qquad (M > N \wedge \forall i \in [1..N]$ Equ$(c_{1,i}, c_{2,i}))$

$\qquad \vee (\exists 0 \leq j \leq \min(M,N) \mid (\forall i \in [1..j-1]$ Equ$(c_{1,i}, c_{2,i})) \wedge$ Less$(c_{2,j}, c_{1,j})$

E.6   Person Module

The Person module hides the representation of individual persons. It provides facilities for representing a new person, establishing some relationships among persons, and fetching information about a person.

AllPerson

Iterate through all persons ever created by NewPerson.
Parameters: Routine R
$\qquad$ Parameters: person
$\qquad$ Results: none
Results: none
Effect: Call R for each person returned by NewPerson, in some order.

Child

Return I'th child of a person.
Parameters: person p, integer i
Results: persons
Value: determined by NewPerson, SetMother, SetFather
Exceptions:
$\qquad$ if i $\notin$ [1..NumChildren(p)] then ErrNumChild

Father

Report the father of a person.
Parameters: person p
Results: persons
Value: determined by NewPerson, SetFather
Exceptions:
    if ¬HasFather(p) then ErrNoFather

HasFather

Determine whether some client has called SetFather.
Parameters: person p
Results: true, false
Value: determined by NewPerson, SetFather

HasMother

Determine whether some client has called SetMother.
Parameters: person p
Results: true, false
Value: determined by NewPerson, SetMother

IndexPerson

Return a unique number corresponding to a person.
Parameters: person p
Results: 1..NumPerson
Value: determined by NewPerson

MaxPerson

Maximum number of persons clients can create via NumPerson.
Parameters: none
Results: positive integers
Value: unaffected by existing interface procedures

Mother

Report the mother of a person.
Parameters: person p
Results: persons
Value: determined by NewPerson, SetMother
Exceptions:
    if ¬HasMother(p) then ErrNoMother

NewPerson

Create a new person representation.
Parameters: name n, boolean b
Results: person p, such that
   NamePerson(p) = n
   NumChildren(p) = 0
   IsMale(p) = b
   ¬(HasMother(p) or HasFather(p))
   IndexPerson(p) = NumPerson
   NumPerson = 'NumPerson' + 1
   $\forall i \in [1..2]$ NumWaysRelated(p,i) = 0
    (see Section E.7 for NumWaysRelated)
Exceptions:
   if 'NumPerson' = MaxPerson then ErrTooMany

This definition overconstrains IndexPerson. All we need is for IndexPerson to return a different number between 1 and MaxPerson for each person.

NumChildren

Return number of children recorded for a person.
Parameters: person p
Results: nonnegative integers
Value: determined by NewPerson, SetMother, SetFather

NumPerson

Current number of persons represented.
Parameters: none
Results: 0..MaxPerson
Initial value: 0
Value: Determined by NewPerson

SetFather

Record the father of a person.
Parameters: person p,f
Results: none
Effect:
   HasFather(p) = true $\land$ Father(p) = f
   NumChildren(f) = 'NumChildren(f)' + 1
   $\exists i \mid 0 \le i \le$ NumChildren(f)$\land$ Child(f,i)=p
   $\forall i \in [1..$'NumChildren(f)'$]$ $\exists j \in [1..$NumChildren(f)$] \mid$ 'Child(f,i)'=Child(f,j)
Exceptions:
   if 'HasFather(p)' then ErrHasFather

SetMother

Record the mother of a person.
Parameters: person p,m
Results: none
Effect:
   HasMother(p) = true
   Mother(p) = m
   NumChildren(m) = 'NumChildren(m)' + 1
   $\exists i \mid 0 \leq i \leq$ NumChildren(m)$\wedge$ Child(m,i)=p
   $\forall i \in$ [1..'NumChildren(m)'] $\exists j \in$ [1..NumChildren(m)] |
      'Child(m,i)' = Child(m,j)
Exceptions:
   if 'HasMother(p)' then ErrHasMother

E.7   Person Module, Find Interface

The person module also exports interface procedures for the sole use of the Find module. Find expects to record the distance (number of generations) between many persons (represented by parameter p to these procedures) and two particular persons P_1 and P_2, which are parameters to Find. Each time someone calls Find with new persons P_1 and P_2, Find calls InitWaysRelated for all persons, then calls AddRelation many times, then calls NumWaysRelated and Distance for certain particular persons.

AddRelation (R)

Record a new path of length Depth between person p and person P_i.
Parameters: person p, integer Depth, integer i (in [1..2])
Results: none
Effect:
   if $\exists j \in$ [1..'NumWaysRelated(p,i)'] | Distance(p,j,i) = Depth, then no effect
   otherwise
      NumWaysRelated(p,i) = 'NumWaysRelated(p,i)' + 1
      $\forall j \in$ [1..'NumWaysRelated(p,i)'] $\exists k \in$ [1..NumWaysRelated(p,i)] |
         Distance(p,k,i) = 'Distance(p,j,i)'
      $\exists j \in$ [1..NumWaysRelated(p,i)] | Distance(p,j,i) = Depth
Exceptions:
   if i $\notin$ [1..2] then ErrWhichPerson
   if 'NumWaysRelated' = MaxWaysRelated then ErrWaysRelated
Restriction: called only from Find

The specification of AddRelation is complex because it allows AddRelation to change the indices of distances returned by Distance. Thus it might record distances in a linked list in LIFO order.

Distance (R)

Report jth distance between person p and person P$_i$.
Parameters: person p, integer i, j
Results: integers
Value: determined by InitWaysRelated and AddRelation
Exceptions:
    if i $\notin$ [1..NumWaysRelated(p,j)] then ErrRelation
    if j $\notin$ [1..2] then ErrWhichPerson
Restriction: called only from Find

InitWaysRelated (R)

Set up for calling AddRelation.
Parameters: person p
Results: none
Effect:
    $\forall$ i $\in$ [1..2] NumWaysRelated(p,i) = 0
Restriction: called only from Find

MaxWaysRelated (R)

Reports the maximum number of distinct path lengths recordable via AddRelation
between person p and person P1 or P2.
Parameters: none
Results: nonnegative integers
Restriction: called only from Find

Since no procedures affect the value of MaxWaysRelated, it is a constant.

NumWaysRelated (R)

Reports the number of distinct path lengths between person p and person P$_i$, as
recorded via AddRelation.
Parameters: person p, integer i (in [1..2])
Results: nonnegative integers
Value: determined by InitWaysRelated and AddRelation
Exceptions:
    if i $\notin$ [1..2] then ErrWhichPerson
Restriction: called only from Find

E.8   RelDef Module

The RelDef module hides the method of finding all a particular person's relatives of
a particular kind. It provides facilities for defining relationships, and for finding the
relatives of a person given such a relationship.

We use a trace specification. We require auxiliary enumeration types

Direction: Up, Down
Restriction: Male, Female, None

The specification has two parameters, MaxPathLength and MaxNumRelations, and uses the NumPerson interface procedure from the Person module.

syntax
StartRelation: word $\rightarrow$
AddPath: direction $\times$ restriction $\rightarrow$
EndRelation: $\rightarrow$
Relatives: person $\times$ word $\times$ procedure $\rightarrow$

The procedure argument to Relatives takes a single person as an argument.

legality
$\quad$(**count**(T,StartRelation)= **count**(T,EndRelation) < MaxNumRelations$\wedge$
$\quad(\neg\,\exists A,B\mid T{=}A.StartRelation(w).B)\wedge L(T))\Rightarrow$
$\qquad\forall M\in[0..MaxPathLength]$
$\qquad\quad L(T.StartRelation(w).AddPath_{i=1}^{M}(d_i,r_i).EndRelation)$

equivalences
$\quad(\exists T1\mid T{=}T1.Relatives(p,w,C)\wedge L(T1)\wedge$
$\quad(\ \exists X,Y\mid\ \exists\,I\geq 0,\ A_i,\ i\in[1..I]\mid$
$\qquad T1 = X.StartRelation(w).A_I.EndRelation.Y\wedge$
$\qquad A_0 = \epsilon\wedge(i{>}0\Rightarrow\exists d_i,r_i\mid A_i = A_{i-1}.AddPath(d_i,r_i))\,)\,)$
$\quad\Rightarrow\exists K\in[0..NumPerson]\mid\ \forall k\in[1..K]\exists D_k,\,p_k\mid$
$\qquad T\equiv T1.D_K\wedge D_0 = \epsilon\wedge D_k = D_{k-1}.C(p_k)\wedge$
$\qquad\forall m,n\in[1..K],\,p_m = p_n\Rightarrow m = n\wedge$
$\qquad\forall j\in[0..I]\exists q_j\mid q_0 = p\wedge q_I = p_k\wedge 0{<}j{\leq}I\Rightarrow($
$\qquad\quad(r_j = Male\Rightarrow IsMale(q_j))\wedge(r_j = Female\Rightarrow\neg IsMale(q_j))\wedge$
$\qquad\qquad d_j = Up\ \Rightarrow\ (q_j = Mother(q_{j-1})\vee q_j = Father(q_{j-1}))\wedge$
$\qquad\qquad d_j = Down\ \Rightarrow\ (q_{j-1} = Mother(q_j)\vee q_{j-1} = Father(q_j))\,)$

The legality assertion says that defining a new relation (via a constrained sequence of calls on StartRelation, AddPath, and EndRelation) is legal whenever we aren't in the midst of defining an old relation, and we have fewer than MaxNumRelations relations. The equivalence rule says that a call to Relatives with procedural parameter C is equivalent to calling C for each person you reach by starting with person p and following the path directives associated with word w.

Strictly speaking, the limit on K could have read "$\exists K\geq 0$" since K is an upper bound on the length of the sequence of p_j's, and the assertion says that no two p's in such sequences are equal. Thus we do not need to use NumPerson.

E.9 Set Module

The Set module hides the data structure used to represent sets of persons. There may be several such sets. We define sets with an algebraic specification.

E.9.1 Syntax

The following shows the formal signatures of the procedures.

IsEmpty: set $\rightarrow$ boolean
MakeNull: $\rightarrow$ set
Intersect: set $\times$ set $\rightarrow$ set
Union: set $\times$ set $\rightarrow$ set
AddMember: set $\times$ person $\rightarrow$ set
IsMember: set $\times$ person $\rightarrow$ boolean
SetMinus: set $\times$ set $\rightarrow$ set

E.9.2 Auxiliary Functions

We will need an auxiliary function, DelMember, to define the meaning of the Set-Minus operation.

DelMember: set $\times$ person $\rightarrow$ set; hidden

DelMember(MakeNull,p1) = MakeNull
DelMember(AddMember(s1,p1),p2) =
   if p1=p2 then DelMember(s1,p2)
            else AddMember(DelMember(s1,p2),p1)

E.9.3 Equations

IsEmpty(MakeNull) = true
IsEmpty(AddMember(s,p)) = false
IsMember(MakeNull,p) = false
IsMember(AddMember(s,p1),p2) =
   if p1=p2 then true else IsMember(s,p2)
Union(s,MakeNull) = s
Union(s1,AddMember(s2,p)) = AddMember(Union(s1,s2),p)
Intersect(s1,MakeNull) = MakeNull
Intersect(s1,AddMember(s2,p1)) =
   if IsMember(s1,p1)
      then AddMember(Intersect(s1,s2),p1)
      else Intersect(s1,s2)
SetMinus(s1,MakeNull) = s1
SetMinus(s1,AddMember(s2,p1)) = SetMinus(DelMember(s1,p1),s2)

E.10 What Module

The What module hides the processing and output of the What command, which shows all relationships between two persons.

DoWhatCommand

Implement the What command.
Parameters: persons p1,p2

Effects: For each relationship between p1 and p2 (as defined by FindRelation), print the name of the relationship according to the following table. P, D1, and D2 are the three parameters passed by FindRelation to the routine it calls.

min (D1,D2)	max (D1,D2)	sign (D1-D2)	P1 is the — of P2
0	0	0	same person
0	1	-	father/mother
0	1	+	son/daughter
0	$n+2$	-	$great^n$ grandfather/grandmother
0	$n+2$	+	$great^n$ grandson/granddaughter
1	1	0	sibling (brother, sister)
1	$n+2$	-	$great^n$ uncle/aunt
1	$n+2$	+	$great^n$ nephew/niece
$n+1$	$n+1$	0	n^{th} cousin
$n+1$	$m+n+1$	any	n^{th} cousin m times removed

E.11 Who Module

The Who module hides the processing and output of the Who command, which shows all people related to a given person in a particular way.

DoWhoCommand

Implement the Who command.
Parameters: word w, person p
Effect: for all persons c passed by Relatives(w,p,X) to X, print NamePerson(c).

Sample
Integration
Test Plan

This appendix shows a sample plan for integrating the genealogy system. It follows a bottom-up incremental strategy, except for partial top-down testing of the GenFile module (step 4) and the Command module (step 6).

I have included descriptions of test drivers here simply because integration test planning must include thinking about what test drivers are necessary. It is equally (or perhaps, more) valid to describe the driver for a module in the unit test plan for the module, if the integration test plan says something about what modules need drivers and stubs, and how complex a driver each module needs. Without the driver descriptions, you can write the integration test plan immediately after approval of the module dependency document. With them, you may need to wait until after approval of the specifications, or at least the list of interface procedures.

In this simple system, you test each module only once, so you need only one driver per module (though you may delay adding the Show facility to the Input driver). In a more complex system, there might be several versions of a driver if you integrate it with lower-level modules several ways.

F.1 Introduction

This document describes the plan for integrating the genealogy system. To follow this document, you should understand the document "Module Decomposition and

Dependencies for the Genealogy System."[1] Descriptions of individual test drivers require an understanding of the specification of the corresponding module. Throughout this document, "you" means the person or persons performing the tests.

Testing requires a Show command that, given a person, would show his or her sex and parents' names. Some tests use it to verify that the program correctly represents information from a single line of the input file. Other documents do not mention this command.

F.2   Unit Testing

You will not do unit testing for all modules; you will test some only during integration. This section describes the general form of unit tests for those modules that do have unit tests.

1.   Char depends on nothing else; test it with the driver of Section F.4.1.

2.   Set depends on Person only via the IndexPerson function. Test it with the driver of Section F.4.8 and a stub Person module representing persons as integers (Section F.5.1), with IndexPerson being an identity function.

These tests may proceed in parallel.

F.3   Integration Testing

Module dependencies guide integration order. Figure D–1 on page 238 summarizes the *uses* relation between modules.[2]

Do integration tests in the order shown here, except for the first two and last two stages. The Name and Word module integration tests may occur in either order. The Who and What module integration tests may occur in either order.

1.   Name depends only on Char. Integrate it with Char and test it with the driver of Section F.4.5.

2.   Word depends only on Char. Integrate it with Char and test it with the driver of Section F.4.12.

3.   Table depends on Person only to have something to store in the table. Integrate it with the stub Person module described in Section F.5.1, which represents persons as integers, and with the unit-tested Name module. This requires the test driver of Section F.4.9.

4.   Integrate GenFile with the tested Table, Name, and Char modules and the driver of Section F.4.4. Use the stub Person module of Section F.5.1.

---

[1] Appendix D.

[2] You would normally reproduce this figure here, so that the test plan could stand alone.

5.   Partially test the full Person module by replacing the stub Person module of the previous example with the full Person module. This requires extending the driver from the previous example to add a Show-like command. This exercise does not test the Find restricted interface.

6.   Integrate the Command module with the tested Char, GenFile, Name, Person, Table, and Word modules and stubs for What and Who (Sections F.5.2 and F.5.3). This tests that parsing of the What and Who commands works, and provides a full test of the Show and Quit commands. The test driver for this case is the main module.

7.   Add the Who and RelDef modules and test them with the Who command. All the Who command tests from system testing are suitable.

8.   Add the What and Find modules and test them with the What command. All the What command tests from system testing are suitable.

F.4   Test Drivers

This section describes the drivers used during unit testing and integration testing. It requires an understanding of the integration testing section (Section F.3).

F.4.1   Char Module

The driver for the Char module reads in a line from the terminal, calls UpperCase for each character, and prints the result.

F.4.2   Command Module

The Command module requires no drivers.

F.4.3   Find Module

The Find module requires no special drivers; the Command and What modules serve as drivers.

F.4.4   GenFile Module

The driver for the GenFile module is simply a cut-down version of the main program that avoids calling the Command module after calling the input routine (there is no output routine in this version of the system). It includes the subroutine from the Command module that implements the Show command, and uses the AllPerson procedure of the Person module to invoke the Show procedure for all persons in the database.

F.4.5   Name Module

The driver for the Name module is a loop that reads two names using MakeName, compares them with CmpName, then prints out the result of the comparison, and the two names using AllChars.

F.4.6 Person Module

The Person module requires no driver.

F.4.7 RelDef Module

The RelDef module requires no driver; test it with the Command and Who modules.

F.4.8 Set Module

Test the Set module with a driver that implements the following commands.

The driver maintains a "current set," initially empty. At the end of each command it prints this set using AllMembers. It represents set elements as integers; a dummy Person module provides IndexPerson and IthPerson procedures that are identity mappings.

S (for Set) prompts for a list of numbers and builds a current set.

A (for AddMember) prompts for a single number and adds it to the current set.

N (for Null) makes the current set empty.

E (for Empty) reports whether the current set is empty.

U (for Union) prompts for a list of numbers, constructs a temporary set, and changes the current set to the union of the current set and the temporary set.

I (for Intersect) prompts for a list of numbers, constructs a temporary set, and changes the current set to the intersection of the current set and the temporary set.

D (for Difference) prompts for a list of numbers, constructs a temporary set, and changes the current set to the difference of the current set and the temporary set. That is, the D command removes members of the temporary set from the current set.

F.4.9 Table Module

The test driver for the Table module implements the following commands. It represents persons as integers using the dummy module that provides identity functions for IndexPerson and IthPerson.

E (for Enter) prompts for a name and an integer, and calls the Enter function.

L (for Lookup) prompts for a name and calls the Lookup function. It reports whether Lookup returned true or false; if true, it prints the integer result.

A (for AllEntries) prints all pairs of name and corresponding integer in the table.

F.4.10 What Module

The What module requires no drivers; test it with the Command module.

F.4.11 Who Module

The Who module requires no drivers; test it with the Command module.

F.4.12 Word Module

Testing of the Word module is similar to the Name module, since both involve reading, representing, and writing strings of characters. See Section F.4.5.

F.5 Stubs

Only a few modules require stubs.

F.5.1 Person Module

Testing of the Set and Table modules requires a stub for the Person module. The stub may represent persons as integers. These two tests use only the IndexPerson and IthPerson procedures, which may be identity functions.

For testing the GenFile module, you need to add stubs for all the other interface procedures it calls. Value-returning procedures should return constants. For example, module initialization for the stub might create a single name, and NamePerson would always return this particular name.

F.5.2 What Module

Testing the Command module requires a stub for DoWhatCommand that prints the names of the two person arguments.

F.5.3 Who Command

Testing the Command module requires a stub for DoWhoCommand that prints the name of its person argument and the word naming the relationship.

Sample
Module Implementation
_____ Summary _____

This appendix describes the implementations of individual modules. In a real system, you would likely use a module development folder for each module, rather than collecting all the implementation descriptions into a single document. As with the sample specifications, I include only a few representative modules.

G.1 Introduction

This document describes design details of the individual modules of the genealogy program. To read this document, you should be familiar with the overall system decomposition as described in "Module Decomposition and Dependencies for the Genealogy System"[1] and with the module specifications as described in "Module Specifications for the Genealogy System."[2]

The sections each describe one module; they are sorted by module name.

G.2 Find Module

The Find module hides the algorithm used to find the relationship between two people. Figure G–1 gives pseudo-code for the algorithm. Figure G–2 shows a sketch of the AddGeneration internal procedure.

[1]Appendix D.
[2]Appendix E.

```
forall persons P do InitWaysRelated(p);
P1Ancestor := P1Add := { P1 };
P2Ancestor := P2Add := { P2 };
Depth := 0;
AddRelation(P1,0,1); AddRelation(P2,0,2);
repeat
  Depth := Depth + 1;
  P1Add := AddGeneration(P1Add,Depth,1);
  P2Add := AddGeneration(P2Add,Depth,2);
  P1Ancestor := P1Ancestor union P1Add;
  P2Ancestor := P2Ancestor union P2Add
until IsEmpty(P1Add) and IsEmpty(P2Add);

CommonAncestor := P1Ancestor intersect P2Ancestor;
OtherAncestor := (P1Ancestor union P2Ancestor) minus CommonAncestor;
RootAncestor := nullset;
foreach p in CommonAncestor
  foreach c in children(p)
    if IsMember(c,OtherAncestor) then
      RootAncestor := RootAncestor union { p }
foreach p in RootAncestor
  for i in [1..NumWaysRelated(p,1)]
    for j in [1..NumWaysRelated(p,2)]
      R(p,Distance(p,i,1),Distance(p,j,2))
```

Figure G–1: Sketch of Find Algorithm

G.3 GenFile Module

The GenFile module hides details of the format of the genealogy file. Such details include how to find information about a person, how to delimit a name in the input file, and how to find a person's parents in the input. Figure G–3 gives a pseudo-code sketch of the workings of the GenFile module. Figure G–4 shows the internal procedure FindParent.

G.4 Name Module

The Name module hides decisions of how to represent names of persons. It provides facilities for creating new names, comparing names, and iterating over the characters of a name.

AddGeneration
Parameters: set S1, integer Depth, I

Returns a set consisting of the parents of each person in S1. For each such parent P, call AddRelation(P,Depth,I)to record that P is at distance Depth from person Pi.

Figure G–2: Sketch of AddGeneration Procedure

```
for each input line
    read sex
    read name1
    read name2
    read name3
    check for end-of-line
    if name1 already in table
        then
            if already defined (that is, has parents)
                then report duplicate definition
            endif
        else make new person; enter in table
    endif
    father := FindParent(name2,male);set father
    mother := FindParent(name3,female);set mother
end for
```

Figure G–3: Sketch of Input Routine

It represents a name as a pointer to a linked list of chunks, each chunk capable of holding a fixed number (currently 10) of characters. This allows for arbitrary-length names while reducing the cost of short names. The specifications require that MakeName must store characters exactly as it receives them, but CmpName must compare them ignoring case. Thus CmpName must convert characters to upper case before comparing them.

FindParent(name n, sex s): person p

if n is in the table
    then check if recorded sex is the same as s
    else make new person

Figure G–4: Sketch of FindParent Procedure

G.5 RelDef Module

The RelDef module hides the method of finding all a particular person's relatives of a particular kind. It provides facilities for defining relationships, and for finding the relatives of a person given such a relationship.

The StartRelation/AddPath/EndRelation procedures build up a data structure used to interpret calls on Relatives. The structure is an array of entries, stored in the order in which clients passed the entries to StartRelation. Each entry contains the name of the relationship (the word passed to StartRelation) and a linked list of directives (supplied by AddPath) describing how to traverse the ancestor tree to discover all persons having the given relationship to the person passed to Relatives. The module stores the path descriptors in the same order as the calls to AddPath.

The Relatives function has calling sequence

function Relatives(p:person;RelName:Word;procedure R(r:person)):boolean;

It goes through three stages. First, it finds the table entry corresponding to Rel-Word (if any). Second, it builds a set of relatives by interpreting the path directives associated with the table entry according to the algorithm of Figure G–5. This sketch assumes that clients represent all relationships as a set of zero or more Ups, followed by zero or more Downs.[3] UpSet makes sure that the Downs do not get us back to someone we skipped over during the Ups, so that we don't (for example) report a father as an uncle. Third, it calls the function R for each member of the CurrentSet that results from the last step of the second stage.

---

[3]Editorial reflection: This algorithm violates the assumption in the life-cycle document (Assumption 5, Section B.2) and in the specification (Section E.8) that Ups and Downs can go in any order. Testing will probably not discover this problem. In practice it might not matter much, since we would define all the relationships we typically use in western societies via a sequence of Ups to the nearest common ancestor, followed by Downs. Downs followed by Ups could lead us to spouses, in-laws, and so on. This kind of flaw creeps in when implementors look at the particular data they will have to deal with, rather than the full set of possibilities the module must support.

```
CurrentSet := {P}; UpSet := {};
foreach directive in linked list
    NextSet := NulSet;
    case direction of
Up:     foreach x in CurrentSet do
            if Inclusion ≠ Female then NextSet := NextSet union { Father(x) }
            if Inclusion ≠ Male then NextSet := NextSet union { Mother(x) }
        UpSet := UpSet union CurrentSet;
Down: foreach x in CurrentSet do
            foreach c in Children(x) do
                if c is of sex Inclusion requires then NextSet := NextSet union {c}
        NextSet := NextSet minus UpSet
    end case;
    CurrentSet := NextSet
```

Figure G–5: Sketch of Relatives Function

G.6   Set Module

The Set module hides the data structure used to represent sets of persons. There may be several such sets.

The module represents sets as bitvectors (boolean arrays), where an element is present if the corresponding element of the vector is on (true). IndexPerson and IthPerson convert between a person and an index into the bitvector. Algorithms for all functions follow directly from this representational choice.

For efficiency, all procedures take sets as **var** parameters, even those they will not modify. They return results via **var** parameters; some procedures modify one parameter rather than return a new result. I based this choice on how the Find module uses the procedures. The signatures and meanings of the procedures are

```
procedure MakeNull(var s:PersonSet);
    s := NullSet
procedure Intersect(var Result,s1,s2:PersonSet);
    Result := s1 intersect s2
procedure AddMember(var s:PersonSet; p:Person);
    s := s union { p }
procedure AssignSet(var Result,Old:PersonSet);
    Result := Old
```

```
procedure AllMembers(var s:PersonSet; procedure R(p:Person));
    forall p in s do R(p)
procedure Union(var Result,Other:PersonSet);
    Result := Result union Other
procedure SetMinus(var Result,Other:PersonSet);
    Result := Result minus Other
```

G.7 Who Module

The Who module hides the processing and output of the Who command, which shows all people related to a given person in a particular way.

Initialization of the Who module involves calling StartRelation, AddPath, and EndRelation to define all the relationships that clients of the Who command might ask about. Table G–6 shows relationships. "U" and "D" mean that one takes a step up or down in the ancestor tree; "M," "F," and "B" mean that one follows male, female, or both lines. DoWhoCommand calls the Relatives procedure of the RelDef module to report relatives.

G.8 Word Module

The Word module hides the representation of single words from the command line (such as command names and relationship names).

The module represents words as packed arrays of 14 characters, enough to represent the longest word from any legal command ("granddaughter"). MakeWord takes advantage of the Pascal/VS language feature that allows passing a literal as a packed-array-of-char parameter; it expects the literal to have characters in upper case. NewWord converts characters to upper case as it stores them.

Relationship	Path	Relationship	Path	Relationship	Path
Aunt	UB UB DF	Brother	UB DM	Child	DB
Daughter	DF	Father	UM	Grandchild	DB DB
Granddaughter	DB DF	Grandfather	UB UM	Grandmother	UB UF
Grandparent	UB UB	Grandson	DB DM	Mother	UF
Nephew	UB DB DM	Niece	UB DB DF	Parent	UB
Sibling	UB DB	Sister	UB DF	Son	DM
Uncle	UB UB DM				

Figure G–6: Relationships for Who Command

Sample
Listing

This appendix shows a sample listing for the GenFile module. Section H.1 explains several aspects of the listing. Section H.2 contains the listing. The listing has a few problems; Section H.3 gives a sample code walkthrough report for this module.

H.1 Explanation of the Listing

I wrote the module in IBM Pascal/VS, a variant that allows separate compilation [IBM 1981]. The **segment** declaration on line 1 says that this is a separately compiled segment, rather than a main program. Lines 21–31 direct the compiler to fetch text from a library to define constants (lines 21–23), types (lines 25–27), and procedures (lines 28–30) that this module imports from other modules. Using an inclusion library like this ensures that all separately compiled modules use the same definitions; when any of these definitions change, one need only change the single copy in the library, and recompile the modules that use the library. Line 31 includes the definitions of procedures that the GenFile module exports, to ensure consistency between the definition of the exported procedures in this module, and their use in other modules. The compiler treats external declarations from these files similarly to forward declarations; thus the real definitions of the procedures do not have parameter declarations. Consequently, the implementor listed the parameter declarations for interface procedure GetInput in a comment on line 222.

Lines 2–19 contain the *module-level comment* discussed in Section 7.4.2. Line 3 describes the secret of the module. Line 5 names the modules this one depends on;

this should be consistent with the information from the Module Dependencies document (Section D.5.7 on page 239). Lines 5–13 describe the essential design details needed to understand the remainder of the module: the format of the file, and the restrictions on its contents. Lines 14–18 are the *change log*, in reverse chronological order. Line 18 states when the first version of the module became available, presumably for testing. Line 16 states that testing is complete, and that I commented out some debugging code (lines 107 and 202).

Each procedure begins with a brief comment summarizing what it does, what its parameters are for, and what global variables it accesses. For example, lines 53–57 describe the EachLine procedure. This is local to the GenFile module, not accessible to procedures from other modules; the coder might easily have decided to nest it within procedure GetInput. It imports global variable LineCount from the surrounding context; some languages such as Euclid and Turing have programming constructs that permit the compiler to ensure that the body of a procedure uses only those global variables declared as imported.

The comments are sparse; they provide just enough information for someone familiar with the other design documents to follow what is happening. Some procedures are so small that they need almost no comments; WParent, on lines 34–38 is an example.

Procedures WName (lines 39–51) and GetName (lines 84–112) show two uses of iterators. In each case the GenFile module passes a procedural parameter to a procedure from the Name module; the Name procedure calls the parameter repeatedly, either to consume or produce characters for a name. In most language implementations, the overhead of calling a procedure is high, especially for small procedures like this. Modern languages have ways to tell the compiler to expand the call inline; you can get similar effects in some environments by using macros.

Procedures such as ErrTooMany (line 113), ErrAlready (line 122), and SexChange (line 132) are examples of exception-handling procedures. Each prints an exception message and takes some recovery action. ErrTooMany does a global abort (line 120); instead of returning to its caller, it sets a flag and branches to the end of EachLine. Setting the flag tells EachLine's caller not to call again. ErrAlready does a local abort (line 130); it branches to the end of EachLine without setting a flag, thus ignoring the current input line without preventing later calls. SexChange does no special recovery, thus allowing its caller to proceed normally.

All the procedure bodies have a comment with the procedure's name just past the final **end**. This helps someone reading the listing determine what procedure to associate the body with; this is especially important if the procedure spreads across more than one page of a listing, or more than one screen of a text editor. This can be a good idea for any **begin/end** block where the bracketing keywords are far apart, such as the block between lines 193 and 218.

H.2 The Listing

```
 1 segment GenFile;
 2 {
 3 Module to hide the format of the database file for the
 4 genealogy system.
 5 Depends on modules Name, Person, and Table.

 6 Genealogy files are a sequence of lines of form
 7        xName1*Name2*Name3*
 8 Each line defines one person in the family tree.  Name1
 9 is the person's name;  Name2 and Name3 are the names of
10 their father and mother, respectively. x is a letter M
11 or F (either upper or lower case) saying whether the
12 person is male or female.  No two lines may have the
13 same Name1.  The lines may be in any order.

14 Last maintainer: David Lamb, January 1986
15 Change log:
16 860127 dalamb  Initial testing complete.  Comment out
17                some debugging code.
18 860115 dalamb  Created.
19 }

20 const
21 %INCLUDE cname
22 %INCLUDE ctable
23 %INCLUDE cperson

24 type
25 %INCLUDE tname
26 %INCLUDE ctable
27 %INCLUDE tperson

28 %INCLUDE pname
29 %INCLUDE ptable
30 %INCLUDE pperson
31 %INCLUDE pgenfile

32 static
33 LineCount : integer; { index of current line in file }

34 procedure WParent(b:boolean);
35    { Top-level local procedure, no imports }
36    begin
37    if b then write('father') else write('mother')
38    end { WParent };
```

```
39  procedure WName(n:Name);
40     { Top-level local procedure, imports nothing.
41        Write out the characters of a name. }

42     procedure WChar(ch:char);
43        { Within WName, imports nothing.
44           Write out an individual character.  Intended to
45           be passed to AllChars from the Name module. }
46        begin
47        write(ch)
48        end { WChar };

49     begin { WName }
50     AllChars(n,WChar);
51     end { WName };

52  procedure EachLine(var InFile:text; var Quit:boolean);
53     { Top-level local procedure, imports LineCount.
54        Read the next line from the input file and process
55        it.  InFile is the file to use.  Leaves Quit alone
56        normally, sets it to true if further calls to
57        EachLine cannot succeed. }

58     var Male:boolean;     { sex of current person }
59        names: array[1..3]
60                 of Name; { names from current line }
61        ch:char;  { current character }
62        ThisP,    { person being defined (name1) }
63        FatherP,  { father of current person (name2) }
64        MotherP   { mother of current person (name3) }
65           : person;
66     label EndInputLine;  { for abnormal termination }

67     procedure ShowLine;
68        { Within EachLine, imports Male, names.
69           Debugging routine.  Display the data read in
70           from the current line }
71        begin
72        if Male then write('Male ') else write('Female ');
73        WName(names[1]);
74        write(' Father '); WName(names[2]);
75        write(' Mother '); WName(names[3]);
76        writeln;
77        end { ShowLine };
```

```
78    procedure Identify;
79        { Within EachLine, imports LineCount.
80          Identify the current line for exception messages }
81        begin
82        write('GetInput, Line ',LineCount:1,': ')
83        end { Identify };


84    procedure GetName(Which:integer);
85        { Within EachLine, imports and changes names, InFile.
86          Read the Which'th name on the input line.  Each
87          name ends with an asterisk }

88        procedure NameException;
89            { Within GetName, imports Which.
90              Report incorrect line format: name does not
91              end with an asterisk.  Abort by going to end
92              of EachLine. }
93            begin
94            Identify;
95            writeln('Format exception: Name ',Which:1,', no ',
96                 'asterisk (*).  Ignoring this line.');
97            goto EndInputLine
98            end { NameException };

99        function NextChar(var ch:char):boolean;
100           { Within GetName, imports and reads InFile.
101             Sets ch to the next character from the input.
102             Returns true iff the character is not an *.
103             To be called from MakeName, which expects it
104             to return false at the end of the name }
105           begin
106           if eoln(InFile) then NameException;
107           read(InFile,ch); { write(ch); } { debug }
108           NextChar := (ch <> '*')
109           end { NextChar };


110       begin { body of GetName }
111       Names[Which] := MakeName(NextChar)
112       end;  { GetName }
```

```
113     procedure ErrTooMany(n:Name);
114         { Within EachLine, imports Quit and EndInputLine.
115           Report attempt to overflow the person database }
116         begin
117         Identify;
118         write('Too many persons trying to add '); WName(n);
119         writeln('.  Stopping with what we have.');
120         Quit := true; goto EndInputLine
121         end { ErrTooMany} ;

122     procedure ErrAlready;
123         { Within EachLine, imports names.
124           Report attempt to redefine a name. }
125         begin
126         Identify;
127         WName(names[1]);
128         writeln(' already entered in the database.  ',
129                 'Ignoring this line.');
130         goto EndInputLine
131         end { ErrAlready };

132     procedure SexChange;
133         { Within EachLine, imports Male, names.
134           Report a confict between new and old information
135           about the sex of the current person }
136         begin
137         Identify;
138         WName(names[1]); write(' is being defined as ');
139         if Male then write(' male ') else write(' female ');
140         write('but was named as someone''s ');
141         WParent(not Male);  writeln('.');
142         end { SexChange };

143     procedure SexException;
144         { Within EachLine, imports and modifies Male.
145           Report incorrect line format: first character
146           doesn't identify the person's sex }
147         begin
148         Identify;
149         writeln('Bad value for sex.'
150                 '  Assuming this person is Male.');
151         Male := true
152         end { SexException };
```

```
153      procedure EOLexception;
154          { Within EachLine, no imports.
155            Report incorrect line format: junk past the end
156            of the last name }
157          begin
158          Identify;
159          writeln('Format exception: ',
160                      'Extra data past the third name is ignored.')
161          end { EOLexception };

162      function EnsurePerson(n:Name; Male:boolean):Person;
163          { Within EachLine, imports names.
164            Find the person record for name n, or create one
165            if none exists, and return it.  The person should
166            be male if Male is true, female otherwise. }

167          var p:Person;

168          procedure ParentSex;
169              { Within EnsurePerson, imports n, Male, names.
170                Report that a particular parent's recorded sex
171                differs from the one required by the parent's
172                place on the input line. }
173              begin { body of ParentSex }
174              Identify;  WName(n); write(' is ');
175              WName(names[1]); write('''s '); WParent(Male);
176              write(' but is recorded elsewhere as someone''s ');
177              WParent(not Male); writeln;
178              end   { ParentSex };

179          begin { body of EnsurePerson }
180          if Lookup(n,p)
181              then begin
182                  if IsMale(p) <> Male then ParentSex
183                  end
184              else begin
185                  if NumPerson = MaxPerson then ErrTooMany(n);
186                  p := NewPerson(n,Male);
187                  Enter(n,p)
188                  end;
189          EnsurePerson := p
190          end { EnsurePerson };
```

```
191     begin { body of EachLine }
192     LineCount := LineCount + 1;
193     if not eoln(InFile) then begin
194         read(Infile,ch);
195         if ch in ['m','M']
196             then Male := true
197         else if ch in ['f','F']
198             then Male := false
199         else SexException;
200         GetName(1); GetName(2); GetName(3);
201         if not eoln(InFile) then EOLexception;
202         { ShowLine; } { debug }
203         if Lookup(names[1],ThisP)
204             then begin
205                 if HasMother(ThisP) or HasFather(ThisP)
206                     then ErrAlready;
207                 if IsMale(ThisP) <> Male then SexChange
208                 end
209             else begin
210                 if NumPerson = MaxPerson then
211                     ErrTooMany(names[1]);
212                 ThisP := NewPerson(names[1],Male);
213                 Enter(names[1],ThisP)
214                 end;
215         FatherP := EnsurePerson(names[2],true);
216         MotherP := EnsurePerson(names[3],false);
217         SetFather(ThisP,FatherP); SetMother(ThisP,MotherP);
218         end { if not eoln(InFile) };
219 EndInputLine:
220     readln(InFile)
221     end { EachLine };




222 procedure GetInput; {(var InFile:text); external; }
223     { An interface procedure.
224         Fetch input from a given file.  The file must
225         already be opened before GetInput is called. }

226     var Stop:boolean;

227     begin
228     LineCount := 0; Stop := false;
229     while (not eof(InFile)) and (not Stop) do
230         EachLine(InFile,Stop);
231     end { GetInput };
232 .
```

H.3 Code Walkthrough Report

Module: GenFile
Time of Meeting: 15:00 30 Jan 86
Present: J. Smith (chair)
                    D. Lamb (implementor)
                    F. Jones, J. Brown
Duration: 45 minutes

H.3.1 Observations

1. Exception messages conform to the User's Guide. There are two forms of the Format Exception message.

2. Module conforms to the Module Decomposition and Dependencies documents.

3. The walkthrough took place after testing (listing line 16) instead of before, contrary to policy.

4. The body of EachLine follows the implementation sketch (Figure G–3 on page 261).

5. The module implementation note calls internal procedure EnsurePerson (listing line 162) FindParent (Figure G–4 on page 262).

6. There is no provision in the code for handling missing names. The MakeName procedure gives no way to detect this, but the GetName procedure (listing lines 84–112) has enough information to figure this out itself.

7. Calling NameException from within NextChar (listing line 106) does a nonlocal **goto** which forces an exit from the MakeName interface procedure from the Name module. The MakeName specification does not say that it expects this possibility, so this abnormal exit may leave the Name module in an unexpected state.

8. The module reports exceptions by direct writes to the terminal. This conforms with current system requirements, but may require extensive changes if we attempt changing to full-screen interaction (Possible Change 7 on page 224). It appears that the module decomposition does not provide for this class of change, and programmers were unaware of the possibility.

H.3.2 Action Items

The implementor shall:

1. Reread the company practices document and conform to policy in future.

2. Rename EnsurePerson to FindParent to correspond to module implementation sketch.

3. Modify GetName to avoid the nonlocal **goto** which exits NextChar (and thus MakeName).

4.   Temporarily patch GetName to detect zero-length names and report this to callers.

5.   Modify callers of GetName to handle missing names.

The chairperson shall:

6.   Record the details of the Format Exception messages for inclusion in a release notice.

7.   Request configuration manager to permit time to study the effect of changing the Name module specification, either to add a NameLength interface procedure for determining the length of a name, or to have MakeName report an exception for zero-length names.

8.   Request the system designers consider the implications of Observation 8 for expected system evolution.

Sample
Release Notice

I.1 Introduction

This note documents release 1.0 of the genealogy program, GEN, which implements subset 4 of the life-cycle plan.[1] Readers should be familiar with the User's Guide[2]. Users of this subset should be familiar with creating text files under CMS.

I.2 Restrictions

This subset does not implement the Add command (Section A.2.1 of the User's Guide), the Delete command (Section A.2.3), or the Change command (Section A.2.2). Users must create and modify database files manually; Section I.3 describes the file format.

I.3 Input Files

GEN reads an input file containing lines of the form
    xName1*Name2*Name3*

---

[1]See Section B.4.

[2]Appendix A

Each line defines one person in the family tree. Name1 is the person's name; Name2 and Name3 are the names of the person's father and mother, respectively. x is a letter M or F (in either upper or lower case) saying whether the person is male or female. You must define each person only once. You may omit either or both parents. You do not need to define every parent. Your database can have at most 100 people, including people who only appear as parents.

These rules correspond exactly to the rules for the Add command. GEN checks for violations of these restrictions.

I.4 Exception Messages

The "Format exception" message mentioned in Section A.3.2 has the following two special cases.

Format exception: Extra data past the third name is ignored.
>   The third asterisk (at the end of the third name) was not immediately followed by end-of-line.

Format exception: Name N, no asterisk (*). Ignoring this line.
>   N is a number (1, 2, or 3). While trying to read the Nth name on a line, GEN found the end of the input line. You probably left out an asterisk.

Glossary

This section defines the nonobvious technical terms I have used in this book. Words in italics are other technical terms whose definitions you should refer to.

alpha testing: *System testing* performed by the development organization.

baseline: An immutable ("frozen") *configuration*.

beta testing: *System testing* performed by a select group of customers prior to official release.

client: With respect to a particular *module*, any module that *uses* it.

configuration: The collection of objects (source files, documents, tools, and so forth) making up a particular version of a system.

constraint: Any *implementation detail* imposed on the designers by the customers.

enhancement: The process of changing a delivered system in unpredictable or unpredicted ways, especially in response to unanticipated changes of requirements. See also *maintenance*.

goal: Any desired but unmeasurable property of a system. See also *constraint* and *requirements*.

implementation detail: Any property of a system not directly visible to users. Often used in the more restrictive sense of invisible properties customers do not care about. See also *constraint*.

information hiding: The principle that you should divide a system into *modules* so that each module hides some *secret*, so that you can change design decisions without affecting more than one module.

maintenance: The process of changing a delivered system in predicted or predictable ways, including fixing defects (corrective), improving system quality in small ways (perfective), and adapting to predicted changes in requirements (adaptive). See also *enhancement*.

milestone: Any significant event in the development process such that you can clearly tell whether or not it has occurred.

mode: A collection of system states such that observable system behavior differs from mode to mode and the transitions between modes occur on observable events.

module: A collection of related programming language objects (types, procedures, and so forth) given as a work assignment to a single person. *Information hiding* is this book's main criterion for dividing a system into modules.

requirements: A system's *specification*.

requirements document: A document defining a system's *requirements*, plus related matters such as fixed interfaces, *constraints*, *goals*, and life-cycle considerations.

secret: The design decision or decisions hidden by a *module*.

signature: The "calling sequence" of a procedure: the parameter types, parameter passing modes, and result type.

specification: A precise statement of the desired observable behavior of a *module* or system. See also *requirements*.

system model: A record of the relationships between the source, derived, and exported objects making up a particular *configuration*.

system testing: The process of verifying that a complete system satisfies its *requirements*.

test suite: An organized collection of test cases.

user interface: The observable behavior of a system. See also *requirements*.

uses: A relationship between *modules*. X uses Y if and only if the system must contain a correct version of Y in order for X to be correct.

walkthrough: The process of reviewing the implementation of a *module*.

_____ Bibliography _____

Babich, Wayne A., *Software Configuration Management: Coordination for Team Productivity*. Reading, MA: Addison-Wesley, 1986.

Bartussek, A. W. and D. L. Parnas, "Using Traces to Write Abstract Specifications for Software Modules," UNC 77–012, University of North Carolina at Chapel Hill, 1977.

Bastani, F. B., "Experiences with a Feedback Version Development Methodology," *IEEE Transactions on Software Engineering* 11(8):718–723, August 1985.

Bell, T. E. and T. A. Thayer, "Software Requirements: Are They Really a Problem?," in *Proceedings of the Second International Conference on Software Engineering*, pages 61–68, 1976.

Berg, H. K., W. E. Boebert, W. R. Franta, and T. G. Moher, *Formal Methods of Program Verification and Specification*. Englewood Cliffs, NJ: Prentice-Hall, 1982.

Britton, K. H., R. A. Parker, and D. L. Parnas, "A Procedure for Designing Abstract Interfaces for Device Interface Modules," in *Proceedings of the Fifth International Conference on Software Engineering*, 1981.

Brooks, Frederick P., *The Mythical Man-Month: Essays on Software Engineering*. Reading, MA: Addison-Wesley, 1975.

Browning, Christine, *Guide to Effective Software Technical Writing*. Englewood Cliffs, NJ: Prentice-Hall, 1984.

Cameron, John R., "An Overview of JSD," *IEEE Transactions on Software Engineering* **12**(2):222–240, February 1986.

Curtis, Bill, "Fifteen Years of Psychology in Software Engineering: Individual Differences and Cognitive Science," in *Seventh International Conference on Software Engineering*, March 1984.

Dijkstra, E. W., *A Discipline of Programming*. Englewood Cliffs, NJ: Prentice-Hall, 1976.

Glass, Robert L., *The Universal Elixir and Other Computing Projects Which Failed*. Seattle: Computing Trends, 1977.

———, *Tales of Computing Folk: Hot Dogs and Mixed Nuts*. Seattle: Computing Trends, 1978.

———, *The Power of Peonage*. Seattle: Computing Trends, 1979.

———, *Software Soliloquies*. Seattle: Computing Trends, 1981.

——— and Ronald A. Noiseux, *Software Maintenance Guidebook*. Englewood Cliffs, NJ: Prentice-Hall, 1981.

Goldschlager, Les and Andrew Lister, *Computer Science: A Modern Introduction*. Englewood Cliffs, NJ: Prentice-Hall, 1982.

Gries, David, *The Science of Programming*. New York: Springer-Verlag, 1981.

Guttag, J. V., J. J. Horning, and J. M. Wing, "Larch in Five Easy Pieces," Technical Report 5, Digital Equipment Corporation Systems Research Center, July 1985.

Henninger, Kathryn, "Specifying Software Requirements for Complex Systems," *IEEE Transactions on Software Engineering* **6**(1):2–23, January 1980.

Hester, S. D., D. L. Parnas, and D. F. Utter, "Using Documentation as a Software Design Medium," *Bell System Technical Journal* **60**(8):1941–1977, October 1981.

Hoffman, Daniel and Richard Snodgrass, "Trace Specifications: Methodology and Models," DCS-53-IR, Department of Computer Science, University of Victoria, March 1986.

IBM, "Pascal/VS Language Reference Manual," SH20-6168-1, April 1981.

Jones, T. Capers, *Programming Productivity*. New York: McGraw-Hill, 1986.

Kernighan, Brian and P. J. Plauger, *Software Tools in Pascal*. Reading, MA: Addison-Wesley, 1981.

Lustman, Francois P., *Managing Computer Projects*. Reston, VA: Reston Publishing Company, 1985.

McLean, John, "A Formal Method for the Abstract Specification of Software," *Journal of the ACM* **21**(3):600–672, July 1984.

Parnas, David L., "On the Criteria to be Used in Decomposing Systems into Modules," *Communications of the ACM* **15**(2), December 1972.

——, "On a Buzzword: Hierarchical Structure," in *Proceedings of IFIP Congress 74*, Amsterdam: North Holland, 1974.

——, "The Use of Precise Specifications in the Development of Software," in *Proceedings of the IFIP Congress*, Amsterdam: North Holland, 1977.

——, "Use of Abstract Interfaces in the Development of Software for Embedded Computer Systems," NRL 8047, Naval Research Laboratory, June 1977.

——, "Software Aspects of Strategic Defense Systems," *Communications of the ACM* **28**(12):1326–1335, December 1986.

—— and Paul C. Clements, "A Rational Design Process: How and Why to Fake It," *IEEE Transactions on Software Engineering* **12**(2):251–257, February 1986.

Reid, Brian K., *Scribe: A Document Specification Language and Its Compiler*, Ph.D. dissertation, CMU-CS-81-100, Carnegie-Mellon University, October 1980.

—— and Janet H. Walker, "Scribe User Manual, Second Edition," Computer Science Department, Carnegie-Mellon University, July 1979.

Strunk, W., Jr. and E. B. White, *The Elements of Style*. MacMillan, 1972.

Swanson, E. Burton, "The Dimensions of Maintenance," in *Proceedings of the Second International Conference on Software Engineering*, pages 492–497, 1976.

Sweet, Frank, "Milestone Management," *Datamation* **32**(20):107–114, October 15, 1986.

Tennent, R. D., *Principles of Programming Languages*. Englewood Cliffs, NJ: Prentice-Hall, 1981.

Weinberg, Gerald M., *The Psychology of Computer Programming*. New York: Van Nostrand Reinhold, 1971.

Wulf, W. A., R. Levin, and S. P. Harbison, *Hydra/C.mmp: An Experimental Computer System*. New York: McGraw-Hill, 1981.

——, M. Shaw, P. N. Hilfinger, and L. Flon, *Fundamental Structures of Computer Science*. Reading, MA: Addison-Wesley, 1981.

Yeager, Chuck and Leo Janos, *Yeager*. Toronto: Bantam Books, 1985.

Index